WHAT THE BIBLE SAYS ABOUT PREACHING

WHAT THE BIBLE SAYS ABOUT PREACHING

ALGER FITCH

Originally published by
College Press Publishing Co.
1989

Printed and Bound in the
United States of America

Table of Contents

PART FIVE: THE METHOD
(The Here's How of Preaching)

PART SIX: THE MEETINGS
(The Here's Where and When of Preaching)

PART SEVEN: THE MODELS
(The Here's an Example of Preaching)

PREFACE

There is more to preaching than meets the ear. Behind the sermon of any particular hour, lies a life of many years. There is far more than the preceding weekly prayer, research, study and reflection. There was the time of conversion to Christ. There was the development toward decision for ministry through the church. And there were the long years of diligent study and personal development to make that service in preaching an acceptable sacrifice of praise to God.

Long before any pair of lips expresses the Gospel story to the listening ears of some Tom, Dick and Harriet, there were the redeeming actions of heaven's Father, Son and the Holy Spirit in history, so that there could be this Good-News to tell. There were the faithful ministries of Apostles and Prophets that gave us the story. There were the supportive services of Christian scribes and scholars that have preserved the written New Testament records.

Library shelves bend under the weight of books striving to

comprehend the mystery of God's love toward the humans He created. Volumes of manuscripts struggle to grasp the rich meaning of each action and word of the Incarnate Jesus from His birth to His death, resurrection, ascension, coronation and promised return. Now, after almost two thousand years of grateful voices heralding in many languages what our God has done for us in Christ, another tongue prepares to continue the telling of that eternal story.

As the man enters the pulpit on a given day, he joins the august procession of preachers, who, with a sparkle in their eye and love in their heart, pass on the transforming story that can change any responsive life. The religion we call Christianity was launched by preaching. Its converts were nourished by preaching. Its future is assured, as long as the church follows the assignment of its Founder: "Go into all the world and preach the good news to all creation" (Mark 16:15).[1]

This book, *What the Bible Says about Preaching*, is dedicated both to all who long to "do the work of an evangelist" (II Timothy 4:4) and to every listener that joins Cornelius in the words: "Now we are all here in the presence of God to listen to everything the Lord has commanded you to tell us" (Acts 10:33). It is based on a conviction that Paul's words to Timothy are worthy of every "Timothy": "All Scripture is God-breathed and is useful for teaching, rebuking, correcting and training in righteousness, so that the man of God may be thoroughly equipped for every good work" (II Timothy 3:16-17). In the "good work" of preaching, your Bible can prove to be an adequate source for your message and also an excellent textbook in the art of sermon preparation and delivery.

Taking the Scripture at its word, that it can equip its readers "for every good work," we will learn about preaching from what

---

1. All the Scripture quotations, unless otherwise noted, will be from the *New International Version* (Grand Rapids, Michigan: Zondervan Bible Publishers, 1978).

the Bible says. God's Book gives us meanings (Introduction) and points to moorings (Part One). It calls and prepares messengers (Part Two) and determines the messages (Part Three). The Bible explains motives for preaching (Part Four), exposes methods in preaching (Part Five) and describes meetings where preaching occurred (Part Six). The Sacred Writings preserve for the church models of preaching at its best (Part Seven) and inspire spokesmen to its mastery (Conclusion).

INTRODUCTION: THE MEANINGS

Calling the preacher names can be an educational exercise, if the names you call him come from the Bible. God's spokesman will better understand his precise mission when the Bible's terminology helps hone his understanding of what he is to do and how he is to do it. No Holy Spirit chosen nouns, such as "herald," "evangelist" or "teacher" are to be considered insignificant word-choices. No verbs of Scripture, such as "preach," "testify" or "plead" are without intention. Even to peruse the Sacred Records for the adjectives, adverbs and prepositional phrases that inspired writers used to describe proclaimers and their proclamations is to find norms by which to test the modern heirs of the world's highest task.

DEFINITIONS

From the first speech in the Old Testament by Lamech to his

wives (Genesis 4:23-24) to the last speech in the New Testament by Jesus to His church (Revelation 22:12-16), let us search for the definition God's book gives to the work a preacher does.

An early discovery is that "preaching" is a term that in our time has become a baptized member of the Christian church. It has risen to walk in a newness of life and has been attired in a fresh meaning that it could never have had in Old Covenant times.

Yes, Ezra did mount "a high wooden platform" (Nehemiah 8:4) or "pulpit" (K.J.V.) to read from the Law, but there was, as yet, no gospel to preach. And yes, Noah was remembered as a "preacher of righteousness" (II Peter 2:5), but his message was a fearsome warning that called for repentance. Its burden, to the hostile world of his day, was judgment, not the glad-tidings of grace. And, yes, Jonah was sent of the Lord: "Go to the great city of Nineveh and preach against it" (Jonah 1:2), yet the words "against it" hang heavy with condemnation and potential destruction rather than encouragement and hope. He brought God's demand of unconditional surrender into territory outside Israel's borders.

Old Testament prophets, with direct revelation from God, summoned the covenant-breakers of Israel to repentance. Unfaithfulness to God was assailed in their pronouncements. Old Covenant priests taught the faithfulness of their God, who both had saved His people Israel, made treaty with them and was expecting loyalty from them. Before the rise of the synagogue, the closest thing to a sermon would be those times in the temple, when some large portion of the Jewish Scriptures, fitting to the occasion, would be read without comment in the hearing of the people. The Hebrew words translated "preach" include "*natap*" in the Prophets Ezekiel, Amos and Micah or "*qohelet*" in Ecclesiastes. The root of the first word is "*ntp*," meaning "drip," as in the falling of rain (cp. Job 29:22-23) or in the spraying of saliva from the mouth of a passionate speaker. The second word has the root "*qhl*," implying an assembly. This is either suggesting one who calls together a congregation of people or one who assembles together wise sayings to pass on to the congregation. In some instances the Hebrew word is "*basar*," as in the Isaiah 61:1 passage Jesus applied to Himself when He preached in Nazareth. At other times, the term is "*gara*," as in Jonah's orders to proclaim God's message to Nineveh (Jonah 3:2).

Our burgeoning source of information, as to the Christian preacher's task, is the New Testament. There, instead of finding a single word for preaching, there are at least seven terms. The King James Version confuses us by giving the single meaning "preach" to ten different Greek words. Later revisions bring the number down by three. Fortunately, each Greek word reflects a truth about the work the church's spokesman has to do that will serve as a guiding star to his ministry of the Word.

PREACHING AS CONVERSING

In some Bibles the English word "preach" is used to translate such untechnical terms as λαλέω (speak, tell), λέγω (say), λόγος (word) and ῥῆμα (word). When a person says something, speaks a word or tells a message, more than strange sounds hit the ear. Some truth or content is conveyed. From the speaker comes a message for a listener.

In this sense it has been suggested that preaching is "gossiping the gospel," or the sharing of the story of God's love with another. No implication is found here of a well-organized speech with introduction, body and conclusion, spiced with good illustrations and delivered with oratorical technique. Rather the person of Christ is introduced by one human, who knows Him, to another individual, who has previously not met Him. This concept gives new meaning to old definitions of preaching, such as "truth through personality," or "the church confessing its faith." Personal encounter is a high understanding of the preaching concept. It is sharing Christ. It is talking the gospel. Bernard Manning called preaching, "a manifestation of the Incarnate Word, from the Written word, by the spoken word."[1] It is well to remember that the Latin *verbum*, which we translate as the noun "Word," is transliterated "verb," implying an action. In our context, the action is communicating the gospel.

In the sense of sharing one's faith, the "men and women . . . who had been scattered preached the word wherever they went" (Acts 8:3-4). In this conversational way, "Paul spoke to the people" at Troas, as he "kept on talking until daylight" (Acts 20:11). In this informal style, Jesus was observed "talking" with the woman at the well about the water of life (John 4:27).

PREACHING AS HERALDING

Our English word "preach" comes from the Latin *praedicare*, which signifies public proclamation or declaration. That is the root meaning in the Greek New Testament words κηρύσσω (the verb meaning to herald, proclaim, announce and preach) κήρυξ (the noun describing a herald, an envoy, a crier, a public messenger and a preacher) and κηρύγμα (the noun depicting the message proclaimed, such as the announcement of a victory). The Bible's Book of Revelation is filled with examples of heralding done by angels (cp. Revelation 12:10-12; 14:6-7; 19:5-8).

The idea of a herald who announces a message by the authority of his King, has rich significance to anyone who thinks of himself as a preacher. A herald is not one sent to give a personal discourse on some religious theme. He is not a person who is free to express his personal views concerning any number of themes on which he holds strong opinions. He has not been com-

---

1. Quoted in W.E. Sangster, *The Craft of the Sermon* (London: Epworth Press, 1954), p. 4.

missioned to recite anecdotes, personal experiences or the latest jokes he has heard at the office. A herald is not even intended to lead discussions by the public about topics of general interest.

The term "herald" speaks loud and clear of a man whose one job is to publish abroad the message given him by his superior. The facts are not to be considered subjects for debate. The orders are not intended to become topics for questioning by a rebellious populace. By authority of the king, the assigned facts, promises, commands and warnings are the ones to be announced in the hearing of all. And this is to be done without any modification, alteration or hesitation.

There is a legitimate tone of dogmatism in any message that begins, "Thus saith the Lord." As the old town crier heralded the official announcements of his king, let the modern proclaimer of the King of kings make known far and wide the news from King Jesus. This common New Testament verb, "to herald or proclaim," implies that there is significant news from heaven intended for the ears of men. The noun "preacher," found but three times from Matthew to Revelation (I Timothy 2:7; II Timothy 1:11; II Peter 2:5), refers to an announcer of news given to him and does not deal with some brilliant mind that has manufactured a message of its own.

We need to give careful attention to a word God has used over sixty times in the New Testament and some thirty times as the Septuagint (LXX) translation of Hebrew Old Testament equivalents.[2] In extra-biblical literature the same connotation, of speaking on behalf of another in authority, stands. To reject the herald was to reject the king whose message was being carried. No herald was responsible to engage in negotiating compromises. Rather, he was to deliver the message exactly as he had been instructed. Upon the faithful delivery of the message, the herald's

---

2. The Hebrew *basar*, for example in I Samuel 4:17; II Samuel 1:20 and I Chronicles 16:24.

responsibility was completed. The response of the recipients might bring him joy or sorrow, but the positive response of the hearer was not part of the herald's responsibility.

Gerhard Friedrich, in the *Theological Dictionary of the New Testament*, edited by Gerhard Kittel, reminds his readers that in the New Testament κηρύσσω is not "the delivery in well-chosen words with a pleasant voice. It is the declaration of an event."[3] In other words, moralizing is not New Testament preaching. Rather, it is announcing the happening in history called the incarnation which climaxed in 30 A.D. with the death, resurrection and ascension of Jesus and left behind a church with the message of salvation.

C.H. Dodd, after analyzing the written Gospels and the sermons of Acts, noted common elements in all apostolic proclamation. His work, entitled *Apostolic Preaching and Its Development,*[4] listed the following six strands in the Biblical material: (1) The age of fulfillment had arrived, (2) This was through Jesus' ministry, death and resurrection, (3) In Christ's resurrection, He was exalted to God's right hand as head of the new Israel, (4) The Holy Spirit in the church is evidence of Christ's present power and glory, (5) The messianic age is to consummate shortly in Christ's return, and (6) there is a message of repentance, forgiveness, the Holy Spirit and eternal life for those who enter this elect community.

Let each gospel proclaimer remember that preaching is not the science of homiletics, it is the heralding of a king. Paul was "appointed a herald" (I Timothy 2:7; II Timothy 1:11). So were preachers from Century One to Century Twenty-one. Pray that they do not suffer from amnesia and forget who they are. Let them become articulate and speak out clearly their message, which is the "good news" (Mark 16:15). Let them resist all temp-

---

3. (Grand Rapids: Eerdmans, 1965), Vol III, p. 703.
4. (New York: Harper and Row, 1964).

tations to *ad lib* rather than follow the script given.

PREACHING AS EVANGELIZING

The herald's message from the king comes into clearer focus by a second Biblical term, εὐαγγελίζω, that means to proclaim or preach good news. Εὐαγγελίζω, a verb, means to announce good news; εὐαγγέλιον, a noun, is the announcement of good news; and εὐαγγελίστης, a noun, is the announcer of good news.

The eye is quick to note in the heart of the English word, evangelist, is the word, angel, as in the Greek term, εὐαγγελίστης is ἄγγελος. As ἀγγέλλω means to announce, the ἄγγελος is the announcer or the messenger. Add the prefix εὐ, that means "well" or "good," to ἄγγελος, that means "messenger," and you grasp that the person described is a messenger of some good tidings or the bearer of news about some victory. In New Testament usage, the specific good news is that about Christ. Where κηρύσσω stressed the manner of delivery (i.e. that it was an authorized, public message), εὐαγγελίζω emphasizes the content of the message.

In the same family of Greek words of the New Testament as εὐαγγελίζω are διαγγέλλω and καταγγέλλω. The former has the meaning of declaring abroad or giving notice. The latter connotes publicizing, promoting or talking about a person, place or thing. The first is exemplified in Jesus telling a man "to go and proclaim the kingdom of God" (Luke 9:60), in Paul entering the temple "to give notice" (Acts 21:26) and in Jehovah raising up Pharaoh that His name "might be proclaimed in all the earth" (Romans 9:17). The second is illustrated by the work of Paul and Barnabas who "proclaimed the word of God" (Acts 13:15) and worshipers at communion who "proclaim the Lord's death" at every participation in the Lord's supper (I Corinthians 11:26).

While a preacher finds look-alikes in the family εὐαγγελίζω, διαγγέλλω and καταγγέλλω (evangelize, declare abroad and publish), the sharpest likeness is evangelize. That word is the exact image of the work and not just a point here and there of similarity.

The evangel (the good news) of the evangelist (the bearer of the good news) is the gospel of Jesus. While every redeemed person was to evangelize and share the saving gospel with others, there was also an office or function (πρᾶξις) in the church performed by those called evangelists (Acts 21:8; Ephesians 4:11; II Timothy 4:5). The job description built into the word evangelist makes preaching the gospel the assignment. It talks of the work to be done, but nothing about the length of stay in a given community. The modern connotation, that an evangelist is of necessity a traveling preacher as opposed to a located one, was not inherent in the Biblical usage. This is demonstrated by the long stay in Caesarea by "Philip the evangelist" (Acts 21:8).

For "the work of an evangelist" (II Timothy 4:5) to be discharged, there must be a preacher, an audience and the gospel message. In that moment, when one man presses upon other men the Savior's message of redemption, the Biblical concept of preaching occurs. Heralds in the secular world may be detached from their message, but gospel heralds, by the very nature of the Christian message, cannot be. Where the former is only a mouthpiece, the latter has been rescued himself by the very message he now passes on. In relating the message, the gospeler is giving of himself, as he tells of the self-giving of God for all sinners — he who speaks and they who hear. The all-consuming flame of gratitude for his own forgiveness, that burns the teller, cannot be quenched until it reaches out to ignite the listener in the all-consuming love of God. The preacher has become the outreached hand of God, seeking to touch another life and fill it with redemption.

Be an angel. That is, be a messenger, an evangelist. Bring the evangel — the "good news of great joy" (Luke 2:10). Tell of Christ's life, Christ's ministry, Christ's death and resurrection, Christ's ascension and coronation. Preach Jesus.

PREACHING AS TEACHING

Biblically, preaching and teaching are twin brothers, but not identical twins. There are differences both in content and audience. Generally speaking, to preach is to announce the news about Christ to those outside the believing community and to teach is to instruct, explain and nurture the Christians in Christ.

Alexander Campbell, C.H. Dodd and many others were clear on the dissimilarities between κηρύσσω and διδάσκω, preach and teach. Where preaching the good news preceded the baptism of converts (Mark 16:16), "teaching them," immediately and continually after their baptism, followed (Matthew 28:18-20). Had not the Jewish converts on Pentecost opted for baptism after Peter preached his sermon on Jesus as "Lord and Christ" (Acts 2:36-41)? Did not these baptized believers then devote themselves "to the apostles' teaching" (Acts 2:42)?

Some argue that the distinction between preach and teach is overstated. They point to supposed instances in the Gospels where an activity of Christ, that one Evangelist calls teaching, another terms preaching (cp. Matthew 4:23; Mark 1:39 and Luke 4:44). Yet, most everyone agrees that the teaching of the New Testament was missionary in nature, addressing the world. However, instruction of the converts contained many recollections of the story as first heard (cp. I Corinthians 15:1-4). It would be fair to say that Colossians 3 and 4 are *didache* addressed to believers, who were reminded in Colossians 1 and 2 of the *kerygma* that had brought them into the church. Always the order in the book of Acts, plus the book of experience, is that the progression must be to evangelize, baptize, catechize. It should be no surprise that, while some are given "to be evangelists" and others "teachers" (Ephesians 4:11), many like Paul will be "appointed a herald . . . and a teacher" (I Timothy 2:7) rolled into one. Did not Jesus, our example, minister in "teaching" as well as "preaching" (Matthew 9:35) wherever He went? Was not the "evangelist" Timothy (II Timothy 4:5) admonished to both "teach" (I Timothy 4:11; 6:2; II Timothy 2:2) and "preach" (II Timothy 4:2)?

It doesn't take much reading between the lines to see that preaching can be didactic, while it is evangelistic; and teaching can build on the convert's past evangelistic encounter, in the future development of his Christian character and Scriptural knowledge. Any "Timothy" is well-advised to devote himself "to preaching and to teaching" (I Timothy 4:13). Any elder is "worthy of double honor . . . whose work is preaching and teaching" (I Timothy 5:17). Any Paul and Barnabas will be well-remembered that has "taught and preached the word of the Lord" (Acts 15:35). The make-up of the audience will determine the emphasis.

PREACHING AS ENTREATING

You have been introduced to *kerygma* (preaching) and *didache* (teaching). It is time to meet *paraklesis* (exhortation). Παρακαλέω has various shades of meaning from beseech to comfort. Sometimes an audience needs not only instruction but a renewal of heart — an encouragement.

The best way to grasp the variant ideas in this word for preaching is to remember that the Holy Spirit is called the *paraclete*. Some translators call Him the Counselor (John 14:16), others the Comforter (K.J.V.). Each choice of an English word carries a portion of the meaning. Παρά means "along side" and καλέω means "to call;" therefore a παράκλητος is one we would call to our side to help us. A man with a legal problem will invite a lawyer to aid him. A person with health difficulties will ask for a doctor's assistance. Another individual, needing business, marital or personal help, will seek out one with expertise in the area of difficulty. Jesus could meet any need and the Holy Spirit, "another Counselor," would do the same.

How does this affect the preacher? It helps define his

preaching ministry. Like the Christ he represents and the Spirit that enables him, he too is to go about preaching, teaching and encouraging. Like Jesus' messages to the people, the minister's sermons are to have the sound of good news, the edifying power of clear instruction and the uplifting refreshment that revives a discouraged soul. Let the words that flow from the herald's mouth be evangelistic, didactic and therapeutic. Let the voice of Christ be heard as the human tongue makes the "appeal" in words that "implore" reconciliation with God (II Corinthians 5:20).

PREACHING AS WITNESSING

No one is more certain than I am that no one today can be a witness of Christ in the way the apostles were, who had walked and talked with Jesus. Only a resident of the first century A.D. might claim to be an "eyewitness" (Luke 1:2). Only men of that time could write: "That . . . which we have heard, which we have seen with our eyes, which we have looked at and our hands have touched — this we proclaim concerning the Word of life. This life appeared; we have seen it and testify to it" (I John 1:1-2). Almost exclusively the word witness in the Acts of the Apostles is reserved for the Twelve and Paul (Acts 1:3,21-22; 10:40-41; 22:14-15; 26:16).

As true as that is, a preacher of the apostolic gospel, in another sense, must be speaking out of experience. No, he cannot claim with Peter and his associates to be "eyewitnesses of his majesty" (II Peter 1:16), nor with Paul affirm "Have I not seen Jesus our Lord?" (I Corinthians 9:1). But, he must know the joy of salvation, the thrill of answered prayer and the experience of growth toward Christlikeness.

Μαρτυρέω has the meaning of bearing witness or testifying to something that has happened. The disciples we meet in the Gospels could testify to Christ being crucified, buried, raised and seen (I Corinthians 15:3-7). The disciples we meet in our world today have not had that experience, but they have experienced conversion and the blessing of serving under the Lord's supervision.

The world would rather follow, through treacherous terrain, a guide who has gone the road before. Few want to follow the voice of a stranger, who sounds like he does not understand the question much less have any sure answer. All this is to say that the preacher will experience success to the degree his listeners grow confident that the proclaimer's experience in the Word has clearly marked the way. Let the sound of confidence, born of experience, be in the voice that tells others the way to go.

Even when admitting that on one level preaching can have the nature of witnessing, a caution flag must be raised. The message we bear is always greater than any person's understanding or appropriation of it. One's own experience is likely but a touching the hem of the garment regarding the reality available. Therefore, one is well-advised to preach Christ rather than one's own religious story. What happened to Jesus in history is of more significance than what has happened to the preacher thus far in his journey.

PREACHING AS PROPHESYING

The words "prophetic preaching" mean different things to different people. Προφητεύω is a verb, meaning to declare in the name of God and προφήτης is the noun for prophet. Since some translators define the action as preaching and the actor as preacher, some clarification is vital.

The word prophet (προφήτης) has two components. The last five letters carry the idea of speaking and the first three mean "for" or "on behalf of." Thus, a prophet is one who speaks for God. In the Old Testament the Hebrew word was *nabhi*, which meant "one who is called" by God.

I am hesitant to follow *The Living Bible Paraphrased* (Wheaton, Illinois: Tyndale House Publishers, 1971) that equates the "some to be prophets" of Ephesians 4:11 with "the gift of being able to preach well." This ignores the vital distinction that a prophet received his message directly from God, with the consequence that a disagreement with a prophet's understanding of God's will would be defiance of God Himself. A preacher does not receive direct revelation from heaven but, rather, studies the message given of old through the prophets and passes it on. It is legitimate for listeners to question on occasion the preacher's understanding of the passage. The former brings new truth. The latter takes the given text provided by the former and teaches it to the best of his ability.

PREACHING AS SERMONIZING

Thus far in defining words, we have spoken only of the words the Bible has used. The word "sermon," while not found in the Bible concordances, describes messages that are found there. It is common parlance to refer to Jesus' Sermon on the Mount or to Paul's Sermon on Mars Hill. What is a sermon?

"Sermon" is a word from the Latin *sermo* that refers to a talk, a speech or discourse. A widely accepted understanding of what today is known as a sermon is the classical definition by the late Austen Phelps of Andover. He wrote, "A sermon is an oral address to the popular mind upon religious truth as contained in the Scriptures, and it is elaborately treated with a view to persuasion"[5]

A "homily" is a less formal explanation of a Biblical text. The Greek ὁμιλια means a familiar conversation or an informal discussion. This is the word used to describe what the two from Em-

---

5. *The Theory of Preaching* (New York: Charles Scribner's Sons, 1895). p. 21.

maus were doing as they were "talking with each other about everything that had happened" (Luke 24:14) and the sessions Felix had with Paul when he "frequently . . . talked with him" (Acts 24:26). The familiar word homiletics comes from ὁμο (the same) and λέγω (to say or speak). Hence, homiletics is that science which strives to produce messages which "say the same thing" as the Biblical passage does. When the words of the preacher have the characteristic of a running commentary on some Scripture read, or they become an informal discussion on some aspect of Christian doctrine or life, the word homily is appropriate. The earliest instance of homily may be when the Levites "read from the Book of the Law of God, making it clear and giving the meaning so that the people could understand what was being read" (Nehemiah 8:8). When the message takes on formal structure, the term sermon is more exact. At its best, a sermon is the most serious form that either speech or literature can assume. The thoughts of God channeled through the mind of a man with the goal of bringing other minds to God — that is a sermon. For such an event to be possible, not only must a man construct a message, God has to build a man. Both take time. Neither are ever perfect. God has the hardest job.

Part One
THE MOORINGS

1

GOD, THE GREAT COMMUNICATOR

Preaching comes in for its share of criticism today. Cynics question its value. Doubters are unconvinced of its claimed power to transform. How strong are the cables that secure the good ship "Proclamation"? Is preaching fixed firmly in its moorings by strong ropes that reach to heaven?

Where a seaman casts his anchor downward into the blue waters beneath to make his ship firm and secure, the believer's fellowship and worship find "anchor for the soul" in moorage found beyond the blue sky — "the inner sanctuary" of heaven (Hebrews 6:19).

Priscilla J. Owen's hymn not only raised the question, "Will your anchor hold in the storms of life?", it answered, "We have an anchor that keeps the soul Steadfast and sure while the billows roll, Fastened to the Rock which cannot move, Grounded firm and deep in the Saviour's love."

Preaching is likewise anchored in God. The Deity of Scripture is the Great Communicator. That should be no surprise, for "God is love" (I John 4:8) and it is the nature of love to share with the ones loved. We know that "God is light" (I John 1:5) and it is the nature of light to shine forth, dispelling darkness. If God is addressed in prayer as "Our Father in heaven" (Matthew 6:9), is he not a father who communicates with his children? Is it not written in the Prophets: "They shall all be taught by God" (John 6:45)?

The God of the Bible is a personal God, who wills to reveal himself to the persons he has created in his own image. What a contrast is the true God to the false gods of idolatry. Paul reminds the Corinthian Christians of their elevation from serving inanimate deities of stone to serving a living God that reveals himself. The apostle glories in I Corinthians 12 that this God has gifted the church with gifts of revelation ("wisdom," "knowledge," "prophecy") and communication ("the ability to speak in different kinds of tongues," "the interpretation of tongues"). Before their conversion, as pagans, these Corinthians were "led astray to dumb idols." They are "dumb" in that they neither speak nor communicate.

The Psalmist praises the Lord that he is not like the "idols of the nations" that "have mouths, but cannot speak, eyes, but they cannot see; they have ears, but cannot hear, nor is there breath in their mouths" (Psalms 135:15-17). The prophet scathes idolaters with sarcastic queries: "Of what value is an idol, since a man has carved it? . . . he makes idols that cannot speak. Woe to him who says . . . to lifeless stone, 'Wake up!' Can it give guidance?" (Habakkuk 1:18-19). Isaiah challenges, "Bring in your idols to tell us what is going to happen. Tell us what the former things were. . . . Or declare to us things to come, tell us what the future holds" (Isaiah 4:22-23).

What an obvious contrast. Idols do not speak. The Lord of heaven and earth communicates. The God of the Bible not only "spoke to our forefathers through the prophets," he did so "at many times and in various ways" (Hebrews 1:1). "Thus said the LORD," "This is what the LORD said," or some equivalent phrase is found not just hundreds of times but over two thousand times in the Scripture. Do not only remember the phrase or the number, but recall the fact that the living God reveals himself to men. The record of Scripture is not of human discoveries about religion but of a God seeking to unfold himself before men.

A prophet may begin, "Hear, O heaven! Listen, O earth! For the LORD has spoken" (Isaiah 1:2) and he may continue, "Hear the word of the LORD" (1:10). A psalmist may sing, "The Lord announced the word, and great was the company of those who proclaimed it" (Psalms 68:11). A worshiper might pray, "O God, do not keep silent; be not quiet, O God, be not still" (Psalms 83:1). A reader of the Torah might be interested in how many times the phrase "The LORD said to Moses" rises off the pages of Exodus (12:43; 13:1; 14:1,15; 16:4,11,34; 17:5,14; 19:9,10,21,24; 30:11,17,22,34; 31:1,12,18; 32:7,33; 33:1,5,14,17,19,21; 34:1,10,27; 40:1). He might be even more surprised to learn that the words of the ten commandments, including their preamble begin, "And God spoke all these words" (20:1).

Regarding Abraham, we learn "God spoke to him" (Acts 7:6). His religious descendants look upon God as their teacher (I Kings 8:36). They ask, "Who is a teacher like him?" (Job 36:22). They pray "Teach me your way, O LORD" (Psalm 27:11; 86:11) and express gratitude to God in the words, "You yourself have taught me" (Psalm 119:102) and in the hope, "All your (Israel's) sons will be taught by the LORD" (Isaiah 54:13).

It is not only through the prophets that God spoke of old time. It was also through His creation that He made known "his eternal power and divine nature" (Romans 1:20). For "the heavens declare the glory of God; his skies proclaim the work of his hands. Day after day they pour forth speech; night after night they display knowledge. There is no speech or language where their voice is not heard. Their voice goes out into all the earth, their words to the ends of the world" (Psalm 19:1-4). Job heard the world around him speak and he admonished his friends, "But ask the animals, and they will teach you, or the birds of the air, and they will tell you; or speak to the earth, and it will teach you, or let the fish of the sea inform you" (Job 12:7-8). Even out of lightning "comes the sound of his roar; he thunders with his majestic voice," says Elihu. Job's friend adds, "When his voice thunders he holds nothing back. God's voice thunders in marvelous ways" (Job 37:4-5).

While it can be said that God has revealed himself in his world, he has made his ways more clearly known through his word. There were the spoken words of prophets that became the written words of Scripture and then, finally — and in the fullest revelation — the incarnate Word, Christ himself. The author of Hebrews notes how "in the past God spoke," but now "in these last days he has spoken to us by his Son" who "is the radiance of God's glory and the exact representation of his being" (Hebrews 1:1-3). This Son of God assured his Father, "I gave them the words you gave to me and they accepted them . . . your word is truth" (John 17:8,14).

The Bible begins with God speaking the universe into existence. "God said, 'Let there be light . . . an expense between the waters . . . the water under the sky . . . gathered to one place . . . the land produce vegetation . . . lights in the expanse of the sky to separate the day from the night . . . living creatures.' " After seven paragraphs beginning "And God said" (Genesis 1:3,6,9,11,14,20,24), the octave begins, "Then God said, 'Let us make man' " (Genesis 1:26). Then follows the long story of God making his will known to Adam, Noah, Abraham and his descendants, until finally he speaks to all the world in his Son. The Sacred Book from beginning to end is the story of the Divine Shepherd calling his sheep. It is not a record of man's search for God, but God's search for man. The redemption story is that of God, the Great Communicator, speaking to his world of his love and the resulting scheme of redemption. All consequent preaching grows out of the Father proclaiming to prodigal sons that the dead can be alive again and the lost found (Luke 15:32).

If disciples of Jesus refuse to preach the grace — "if they keep quiet. the stones will cry out" (Luke 19:40). If prophets of Israel become "befuddled with wine" and fail to proclaim, then "with foreign lips and strange tongues God will speak to this people" (Isaiah 28:7,11). "The rod of his mouth; with the breath of his lips . . . will slay the wicked" (Isaiah 11:4), or say "come, . . . take the free gift of the water of life" (Revelation 22:17). Preaching is the business of the church, for it is the nature of the God of the church to make known "to us by his Spirit" what "No eye has seen, nor ear heard, no mind has conceived," regarding God's plans "for those who love him" (I Corinthians 2:9-10). The personal God wants personal fellowship with persons who love him, so he sends persons to speak to persons, as he has always sought to do. The Communicator uses communicators to share in the mission of communicating the gospel.

2

GOD'S SON, THE PREACHER'S SUPREME EXAMPLE

The preacher can learn about communication from God, the Father. He also will do well to study at the feet of the Son of God who received from all who heard him the reputation of being the Master Preacher. To firm up the ropes of your teaching, find moorage in the preaching of Jesus.

No title for Jesus in the Gospels is more frequently given by both friends and enemies than that of "teacher." In Matthew he is addressed as teacher (12:38; 17:24; 19:16; 22:16,24,36; 26:18), as he was in Mark (5:35; 9:17,38; 10:17,20; 12:14,19,32; 13:1; 14:14) and in Luke (8:49; 10:25; 11:45; 19:39; 20:27,39; 21:7; 22:11). As in the Synoptics, John also recalls incidents where our Lord was addressed as teacher (2:2,10; 8:4; 10:35; 11:28; 13:13-14; 14:14).

The Gospel accounts of Christ's acts and teachings preserve the Hebrew title "Rabbi" in several places (Matthew 26:49; Mark

9:5; 10:51; 14:45; John 1:38,49; 3:2,26; 4:31; 6:25; 9:2; 11:8) and the Aramaic "Rabboni" in John 20:16. Some called him "the prophet from Nazareth" (Matthew 21:11, cp. 16:14; 21:46; Mark 6:15; 8:28; Luke 7:16; 9:19; 24:19; John 4:19; 6:14; 7:40; 9:17) and knew him to be that specific prophet that Moses had foretold (Acts 7:37).

While the title "Preacher" was not used of him, the work of preaching is said to have been his task. Upon the incident of John the Baptist's imprisonment, it is written "From that time on Jesus began to preach" (Matthew 4:17), "proclaiming the good news of God" (Mark 1:14). He was adept at both "teaching" and "preaching" (Matthew 4:23; 9:35; 11:1).

In all his speaking, the authority by which he spoke "amazed" all who heard him (Matthew 7:28-29). That was true when he was but twelve years of age (Luke 2:47). It continued true in the years of his ministry (Luke 4:32). The projection of his voice and the articulation of his words enabled "crowds" of thousands to hear him with understanding (Matthew 5:1; Mark 6:34; Luke 6:17; John 6:2). In Synagogues, or on hill sides, the listeners heard "gracious words . . . from his lips" (Luke 4:22). Only the self-hardened felt the stinging rebuke: "You brood of vipers" (Matthew 12:34). The others bathed in the warm invitation, "Come to me . . . I will give you rest" (Matthew 11:28). Most opinion polls, regarding preaching power, recorded votes being cast for Jesus. They stated, "No one ever spoke the way this man does" (John 7:46). Luke went so far as to say, "everyone praised him" (Luke 4:15).

The importance of Jesus' preaching cannot be overstated, for he himself declared, "Let us go somewhere else — to the nearby villages — so I can preach there also. That is why I have come" (Mark 1:38, cp. Luke 4:44). Since Jesus came to preach, what should be the prayer of all who follow in his steps? Again, let Jesus answer. He declared, "A student is not above his teacher. . . . It is enough for the student to be like his teacher" (Matthew 10:24-25; Luke 6:40).

JESUS SPOKE ON MAJESTIC THEMES

The Master Preacher dealt with issues that had eternal consequences. His topics belonged to his time, our time and every time. His subjects answered the questions that lie deep in the human breast about life's meaning, about God's nature as loving Father and about man's place in the scheme of things. Can man live beyond the grave? Is the assurance of salvation plain? What is life on earth to be under the realm of heaven?

Jesus knew of the eventual time when even heaven and earth would pass away. Both by avoiding themes suggested by fads that would soon fade into oblivion and by selecting eternal verities founded in ancient Scripture, he spoke words that will never lose their power. They may pass into songs and literature, dramas and contatas, laws and ethical norms, but they "will never pass away" (Matthew 24:35).

The Lord spoke of faith and love and hope. He dealt with prayer and almsgiving. He was neither one to be soft on either sin or injustice, nor a teacher that left hearers unsure as to either the way or the hope of salvation. He spoke with urgency rather than aloof objectivity when he spoke of coming judgment and the certainties of hell and lostness. To Jesus doctrine mattered. To Jesus duty, sincerity and forgiveness were required courses rather than electives for instruction. To this Rabbi information without transformation would be a poor teaching objective.

A major theme taught by Jesus was the kingdom of God and the gospel of that kingdom. Once it was clear to his followers that he was the long-expected Messiah, he "began to explain to his disciples that he must go to Jerusalem and suffer many things at the hands of the elders, chief priests and teachers of the law, and that he must be killed and on the third day be raised to life" (Matthew 16:21). That redemptive gospel of Christ's death, burial, resurrection and appearances became the told and retold story of the church (I Corinthians 15:1-8). "All that Jesus began to do and teach" (Acts 1:1) became the continuing message of those later gospel proclaimers who were held securely in his right hand (Revelation 1:20; 2:1). "The sharp, double-edged sword" of his mouth (Revelation 1:16; 2:12; 19:15), still captivates minds and conquers hearts. Never can the message of Christ, "who is the First and the Last" (Revelation 2:8), become dated, out-moded or *passe*. The "key of David" (Revelation 3:7) continues to open the scientific minds of this century, as it did the doubting minds of the time when Jesus lived incarnate in Galilee.

JESUS SPOKE IN A MASTERFUL STYLE

No person sitting at the feet of Jesus went away complaining that the sermon was too long or the topic monotonous. No criticism accused him of being too general in his applications or too learned in his words and phrases.

When Jesus expounded a text, the disciple could but respond, "Rabbi, we know you are a teacher who has come from God" (John 3:2). As he worked his way through the Bible "beginning with Moses and all the Prophets, he explained . . . what was said in all the Scriptures concerning himself" (Luke 24:27). The hearers left knowing that he had "opened the Scriptures" (Luke 24:32) and that he had brought "out of his storeroom new treasures as well as old" (Matthew 13:52).

Christ, who later came to be called "the Word" (John 1:1,14), had in his memory bank the written word always available for use. With logic and simplicity, his messages responded to the people's questions. Is divorce lawful? What command is the greatest? Will few be saved? Who is my neighbor? Why was this man born blind? In answer to the many queries the masses put to him, there came practical rather than theoretical replies. As our Great Physician, Jesus skillfully and helpfully applied the balm of Gilead. As our Advocate with the Father, he understood the Law book and could handle the toughest case. As our Master Teacher, he fully knew the text revealed from heaven as well as the pupils before him, "for he knew what was in a man" (John 2:25).

Nicodemus was asked a question that could never be leveled at Jesus: "You are Israel's teacher . . . and do you not understand these things? (John 3:10). Jesus knew his Bible both *verbatim*, as to content, and comprehensively, as to its historic and religious meaning. He could take either peasants or Pharisees and lift them beyond the inked pages of a scroll to the very presence of the God that had inspired the messengers to write their revelations.

JESUS SPOKE USING MIGHTY ILLUSTRATIONS

The teacher from Nazareth had a different sound than a philosopher from Athens or even a Jewish lawyer from Jerusalem. His language was picturesque. There was place for the figurative descriptions of hypocrisy as leaven (Mark 8:15), false teachers as wolves in sheep's clothing (Matthew 7:15) and preaching to closed minds as hurling pearls to swine (Matthew 7:6). There were proverbial forget-me-nots like "The Sabbath was made for man, not man for the Sabbath" (Mark 2:27) or "Give to Caesar what is Caesar's and to God what is God's" (Mark 12:17). Best remembered are his illustrations known as parables.

Matthew writes that "Jesus spoke all these things to the crowd in parables; he did not say anything to them without using a parable" (Matthew 13:34). Jesus' stories were unforgettable for they were drawn from common life. He spoke of lilies and leaven, seeds and sowers, boats and brides, ships and sparrows. It is no wonder that large crowds "listened to him with delight" (Mark 12:37). There was no sense of trying to watch a football game during a dense London fog. There was rather the experience of viewing a formerly clouded truth under the bright skies of a crystal-clear day. The audience might leave disliking what he said, but never wondering where he stood on an issue.

Who could hear of the prodigal son and not stand amazed at the love of God, the Father (Luke 15:11-32)? Who could listen to the masterpiece of the good Samaritan and fail to see the value of true religion over empty ritual (Luke 10: 25-37)? Who could miss the contrast of the God who longs to answer prayer and the unjust judge who has to be pestered to respond to a widow's cry for help (Luke 18:1-8)? Who could forget the fascinating stories of straying sheep (Luke 15:3-7), foolish bridesmaids (Matthew 25:1-13), lost money (Luke 15:8-10) or buried treasure (Matthew 13:44)? Jesus knew that stories gain attention and hold truths firmly in retention. To remember the story is to remember the lesson and put it in a form easy to pass on to others.

JESUS SPOKE WITH A MARVELOUS SPIRIT

The captivating power of Christ's sermons was not only in his stories, subjects and style but in his sympathy, support and sincerity. Listeners sensed empathy and saw tears. They knew they were loved. It came through to them that this teacher cared for their souls. His tone of voice, his body language and his outstretched hands communicated the magnetism of his heart.

Joyous hope, human concern and proffered help clothed every word. It was not just what he said, but the way he said it. Truth was ever dressed in love. The harshest critique was made easier to swallow because of the sugar-coating of graciousness. The Master Preacher cared. That was beyond doubt. The coming cross, with its total self-giving, would but accent the love present in every earlier sermon he preached.

No technique of message delivery can make up for a lack in caring for the listeners. A bit of sham here, or of faking there, may get by without total audience scrutiny, but a gap in love cannot escape detection. Isaiah foretold how the Messiah would be anointed by the "Spirit of the Sovereign LORD . . . to preach good news" (Isaiah 61:1) and he further defined that the Spirit that would rest on him would be "the Spirit of wisdom and of understanding, the Spirit of counsel and of power, the Spirit of knowledge and of the fear of the LORD" (Isaiah 11:2). The sweetness of his voice, the gracefulness of his words and the purity of his life sprang from the deep wells of his marvelous Spirit. Clarity mingled with charity was warp and woof in every discourse. The sound was joyful, the tidings glad and the news good, for they were the fruit of the Spirit in the preacher. All sermons rise out of a proclaimer's inner self. The invisible soul becomes transparent in the tone of the voice and the expressions of the face.

The object lesson of washing a disciple's feet, or healing a sufferer's blindness, gave body to the love that drove the speaker to speak. If the "lost chord" of love is missing when the organ of the human voice peals out the song of redemption, the converting power will be gone. It was never missing in the teaching of Jesus. It always was heard in the background, even as he brought lessons of "teaching, rebuking, correcting and training" (II Timothy 3:16).

HE SPOKE THROUGH A MAGNIFICENT LIFE

Jesus knew God. His sermons were evidence that he knew the Father by more than just hearsay. The messages from heaven, that he had stowed in his heart and sowed in his world, showed in his life. He could say openly, "I am telling you what I have seen in the Father's presence" (John 8:38). The Revelator could speak of him as "Jesus Christ . . . the faithful witness" (Revelation 1:5), "the Amen . . . and true witness" (Revelation 3:14), because he never failed to back his words with transparent living. He "showed them the full extent of his love" (John 13:1). By washing their feet, bearing their burdens and healing their hurts, he "set . . . an example" for others, in that no messenger is greater than the one who sent him" (John 13:15-16).

"In these last days (God) has spoken to us by his Son" (Hebrews 1:2) and he has never spoken with greater volume than in this life that spoke more loudly than the words. Many who lived in first century Galilee were privileged to hear his strong, full and resonant voice. Small children on his lap and guilty malefactors by his cross heard his kind and encouraging words. Blind eyes and fallen corpses felt the power in his gentle hands. Yet, the greatest inspiration of all was the knowledge that no hypocrisy in living sapped his teaching of any of its strength. The human ears that heard God and the human eyes that beheld him knew that "anyone who has seen (him) has seen the Father" (John 14:9).

Would you like heaven to be "well-pleased" with any teaching or preaching you attempt? Then, "Listen to him!" (Matthew 17:5). He may use many one-syllable words but they can change the life-style of a Zachaeus, bring tears to the eyes of a Mary Magdalene and alter the course of human history. He may at times condescend to speak to a crowd consisting of but one woman at a well, and yet bear fruit among many Samaritans. Every speaker needs a model. There is none better than the Master of everything. Learn preaching from God's "one and only Son" who was "full of grace and truth" (John 1:14). He stands throughout all ages as the preacher *par excellence*. He did not eat only locusts and wild honey. His sermons did not wear sackcloth nor scatter ashes. They glowed with hope and radiated with joy. No wonder it is written, "The whole town gathered at the door" (Mark 1:33) and "So many gathered that there was no room left, not even outside the door, and he preached the word to them" (Mark 2:2).

3

GOD'S SPIRIT, THE PREACHER'S ENABLING POWER

Luke paints a vivid picture of a small ship on the Adriatic Sea driven by winds of hurricane force that endangered the lives of the preacher Paul and all that were with him. The ship's log reads: "Fearing that we would be dashed against the rocks, they dropped four anchors from the stern and prayed for daylight" (Acts 27:29). A broken-hearted preacher, here and there, may feel that this word-picture of a tumultuous scene describes precisely his precarious ministry on the corners of 6th Avenue and G Street ever since the last board-meeting. Are there anchors he can cast to save the lives of all concerned? The Bible tells of "four anchors" that securely moor the ministry of the Word. We have named two (God, as the Great Communicator, and God's Son as the Master Preacher). Now we suggest the third (God's Spirit as the Enabler).

A New Testament term, often used of the Holy Spirit's work, is that of *paraclete*. It is many times translated Counselor or Comforter (KJV). These are facets of the meaning in the Greek word παράκλητος. The first part of the word παρά means "alongside." Our words "parade" or "parable" refer to men marching "alongside" one another, or a story placed "alongside" a truth to clarify its meaning. The κλητός portion of the Greek παράκλητος is from the verb καλέω meaning to "call." That being true, the full word speaks of someone you might call to your side to assist you in some need. If that need is for advice, "counselor" would give the meaning. If the need is for help during a time of sadness, "comforter" would be the better translation. This rich word could include doctors, attorneys, strong men, *etc.* depending on whether the problem behind the call for help was health, legal difficulty, need of protection *et al.* Perhaps "Helper" is the best term to describe the Holy Spirit's ministry to preachers.

PREACHERS HAVE PROMISED HELP FROM GOD

It is of tremendous encouragement to remember that preaching is a partnership. He who said, "make disciples of all nations," also spoke the words, "And surely I will be with you always" (Matthew 28:19-20). The Carpenter of Nazareth invited, "Take my yoke upon you" (Matthew 11:29). The people nodded assent, with joy, for who wants to bear burdens alone? Happier is he who is yoked together with a strong one. Christ's Spirit is the preacher's enabling power.

Jesus, who came preaching in his ministry (Mark 1:14) and commissioned preaching at the climax of that incarnate ministry (Mark 16:15), makes possible the fulfillment of our ministries by the personal presence of his Spirit. The object of preaching is salvation. The saved become the channel of salvation to others and their spoken words the instrument God will use. These saved men who preach, plus their messages, become empowered in their work by the Holy Spirit.

The "Spirit of the LORD came upon Gideon," reads Judges

6:34. More literally, "The Spirit *clothed* himself with Gideon." To obtain his objectives the Spirit attires himself in men. The "Spirit of the LORD" came upon Samson in power, so that with "a jawbone of a donkey, he . . . struck down a thousand men" (Judges 15:14-15). Is it too much to conclude that, if God can clothe himself with a man and use the jaw of an animal to win a victory, the success of the divine mission lies more in the power of the God who goes to battle than the persons or implements he chooses to use along the way?

The motley crew that Jesus gathered and trained to preach were a success because of his strength, not theirs. Upon arrest, these apostles were encouraged, "Do not worry about what to say, for it will not be you speaking, but the Spirit of your Father speaking through you" (Matthew 10:19-20 cp. Mark 13:11; Luke 12:11-12). They were promised, "I will give you words of wisdom that none of your adversaries will be able to resist or contradict" (Luke 21:15).

These words were given to the specific men called to witness regarding Christ's teaching and resurrection — the apostles. Their ears alone in the upper room heard Jesus say to them, "the Holy Spirit . . . will teach you all things and will remind you of everything I have said to you" (John 14:26). They alone were present at the Last Supper as their Master spoke the words, "But when he, the Spirit of Truth comes, he will guide you into all truth" (John 16:13). It would be a violation of sound hermeneutical principles to conclude that a promise given to one person or group in the church would, of necessity, apply to all other people or units of that church both now and forevermore. But, it would be an equal misuse of logic to assume that, although God cared deeply about the inspiration and preservation of the Scriptural documents, his same Spirit offers no assistance to those who seek faithfully to interpret and proclaim the Bible's contents to the world.

Let the preacher say with Isaiah, "The Spirit of the Sovereign LORD is on me, because the LORD has anointed me to preach"

(61:1 cp. Luke 4:18). Let the spokesman for God hear with Jeremiah the heavenly assurance, "Do not be afraid . . . for I am with you" (1:8). Let the gospel proclaimer be emboldened by the transforming words to Saul, "The Spirit of the LORD will come upon you in power, and you will prophesy; . . . and you will be changed into a different person" (I Samuel 10:6). Let the minister of the Word experience with Paul the strengthening vision from God, "Do not be afraid; keep on speaking, do not be silent. For I am with you"(Acts 18:9-10 cp, 27:24). Let later historians write of today's preaching disciples, as Mark recorded regarding yesterday's apostolic band, "the disciples went out and preached everywhere, and the Lord worked with them" (Mark 16:20). Let some reporter speak of you, as Jesus said of the Psalmist, that David himself was "speaking by the Holy Spirit" when he declared his message (Mark 12:36 cp. Acts 4:25).

It was said of Jesus that he gave "instructions through the Holy Spirit" (Acts 1:2). It was written of the twelve that they "were filled with the Holy Spirit and began to speak . . . as the Spirit enabled them" (Acts 2:4). It was stated of Paul's missionary preaching: "our gospel came to you not simply with words, but also with power, with the Holy Spirit and with deep conviction" (I Thessalonians 1:5). It was counselled to young preacher Timothy regarding the pattern of sound teaching, "Guard the good deposit that was entrusted to you . . . with the help of the Holy Spirit" (II Timothy 1:14). If no voice for God in the early days of the church spoke out without the help of the Holy Spirit, would not the preacher become mute, dumb and unable to speak in our time without the same Spirit's aid?

God's Spirit, said Jesus, "will testify about me; but you also must testify" (John 15:26). The apostles echoed that truth when they delared, "We are witnesses of these things, and so is the Holy Spirit" (Acts 5:32). So across the Christian centuries, together (and not separately), "The Spirit and the bride say 'Come!' " (Revelation 22:17). His strength is joined to our weakness and the result is adequacy in proclamation.

Do you grasp God's plan? God's treasure has been placed, intentionally, "in jars of clay to show that this all-surpassing power is from God and not from us" (II Corinthians 4:7). It is "with the help of our God we . . . tell . . . his gospel" (I Thessalonians 2:2). It is because of his power that a minister can look back on difficult times and affirm with Paul, "But the Lord stood at my side and gave me strength, so that through me the message might be fully proclaimed" (II Timothy 4:17). Do you not know that "the anointing you received from him remains in you" (I John 2:27)? Are you unaware that to reject the message by some deacon, like Stephen, is to "resist the Holy Spirit" (Acts 7:51)? In the team effort called preaching, a Paul may plant, an Apollos may water, but it will be God that makes it grow. There is but "one purpose . . . we are God's fellow workers" (I Corinthians 3:6-9). No preacher is ever going solo. Each messenger of Christ — each evangelist — is a "star" held in the Lord's "right hand" (Revelation 1:16,20; 2:1). Those words were written to put backbone into all who rise to speak of Christ.

PREACHERS HAVE PROMISED HELP THROUGH PRAYER

Philosophers rely on the wisdom of their minds. Orators lean heavily on the elegance of their style. Debaters often count on the cleverness of some ploy. Preachers, knowing that pulpit power comes only from above, seek the help found in prayer. A sermon is preceded by prayer, permeated with prayer and perpetuated by prayer. The more a message is saturated with supplication, the more it is slated for success.

The prayer of the apostolic church was, "Enable your servants to speak your word with great boldness" (Acts 4:29). Did anything happen? Was the intercession of the congregation to any avail? Luke records that, "After they prayed . . . they were all filled with the Holy Spirit and spoke the word of God boldly" (Acts 4:31). To preach with power requires being in touch with the power source. He best speaks to men for God who regularly talks to God about men, message and mission.

Wise disciples came to Jesus with the request, "Lord, teach us to pray" (Luke 11:1). They were not asking for a course in how to preach, but how to pray. The teaching sought was not even how to heal. They seemed to know that the Master's power to heal without failure and to preach with persuasive success was based on his closeness to the Father. Could they but learn to pray, they could be ministers unashamed. They were not asking, "Lord teach us that we ought to pray." They already knew that. They were not requesting, "Lord teach us a prayer" — some words to learn by rote. An intimate fellowship with God, that would transform them into vessels he could use, was what they sought. A life bathed in prayer prepares a voice that can penetrate a heart. Prayer changes things, thoughts, lives and all else.

The apostles had learned the importance of keeping perspective on priorities from Jesus. As the early church grew, they saw that "it would not be right . . . to neglect the ministry of the word of God in order to wait on tables. . . . We will turn this responsibility over . . . and will give our attention to prayer and the ministry of the word" (Acts 6:2-4). I admit that, had I been writing the account, my order might have been, first preaching, then tables and finally, prayer. The Twelve prioritized, first prayer, next preaching and, lastly, tables.

Apostles, convinced of the power in prayer, called on the congregations, "pray for us that the message of the Lord may spread rapidly and be honored" (II Thessalonians 3:1). Paul admonished the Ephesians, "Pray also for me that whenever I open my mouth, words may be given so that I will fearlessly make known the mystery of the gospel. . . . Pray that I may declare it fearlessly as I should" (Ephesians 6:19-20). He also sought the supportive undergirding of the Colossians in prayer "that God may open a door for our message." He specifically requested, "Pray that I may proclaim it clearly" (Colossians 4:3-4).

It is written of Moses that "his face was radiant because he had spoken with the LORD" (Exodus 34:29). It is written of Stephen that, as he rose to address the Sanhedrin, "his face was like the face of an angel" (Acts 6:15). It is the experience of the centuries that when men go from the closet of prayer to the podium of proclamation, the audience senses the glint of heaven in the eye and the sound of glory in the voice. Years ago I heard the story of the black preacher from Washington, D.C., who was asked the secret of his pulpit power. I have never forgotten his answer: "I read myself full, think myself clear, pray myself hot and then let myself go."

To take on a God-given task, without receiving the God-given power for that task, is the height of foolishness. The most important part of sermon preparation is prayer — prayer for the people, prayer for the messenger, prayer for understanding and guidance. A spokesman would do well to begin with David's prayer," O LORD . . . examine my heart and my mind" (Psalm 26:2) and to conclude with his heaven-directed request, "May the words of my mouth and the meditation of my heart be pleasing in your sight, O LORD, my Rock and my Redeemer" (Psalm 19:14). When it comes to the ever-present question of what to preach, Jesus is the "Wonderful Counselor" Isaiah prophesied (9:6) and the Holy Spirit is the "Counselor" (John 14:26) Jesus predicted for the church age.

PREACHERS HAVE PROMISED HELP IN SPEAKING

If "evil spirits that looked like frogs" can come "out of the mouth of the dragon, out of the mouth of the beast and out of the mouth of the false prophet" in the picture book of Revelation (16:13), can the Holy Spirit, that acts like Jesus, come out of the mouths of gospel preachers and teachers in the real life of today? If in Decapolis Jesus could help a man that "could hardly talk," and by a touch of "the man's tongue" and the utterance of the word "Ephphatha" find "his tongue . . . loosened" so he could "speak plainly" (Mark 7:31-35), is there Christ's available help to men who want to tell his story in this decade?

We have seen opposers of the message of God's grace, as preached by Stephen, defeated in argument, for "they could not stand up against his wisdom or the Spirit by which he spoke" (Acts 6:10). We have read of Paul praying to "proclaim . . . clearly" (Colossians 4:4) and "declare . . . fearlessly" (Ephesians 6:20). A survey of his missionary journeys and a counting of his converts reveal these prayers were answered. Sometimes he and his workers were "kept by the Holy Spirit from preaching" in a certain place, or not allowed by "the Spirit of Jesus" to evangelize another area, but at other times they found a wide-open door, "concluding God had called" for gospel peaching to that group (Acts 16:6-10).

Jesus still "holds the key of David. What he opens, no one can shut; and what he shuts, no one can open" (Revelation 3:7). After two thousand years, it still can be said, "a great door for effective work has opened to me, and there are many who oppose me" (I Corinthians 16:9 cp. II Corinthians 2:12). The last seven of these words are often joined to the prior ten. Satan will ever cause opposition. The Holy Spirit will always bring victory. Let those on whom the mantle of Paul and Barnabas have fallen enter only that work to which God has called them, knowing that they are "sent on their way by the Holy Spirit" (Acts 13:3-4). Let evangelists like Philip seek the Spirit's counsel as to which chariot to turn into a pulpit (Acts 8:29), or, as to which towns to enter for a preaching ministry (Acts 8:39-40). Let each proclaimer of the message, like Peter before Cornelius, find the Holy Spirit coming "on all who heard the message" (Acts 10:44) even as the speaking begins (Acts 11:15).

How can a speaker perfect his art? A perfect sermon is yet to be produced by any man, for no man is perfect. James hit the bull's eye when he observed, "If anyone is never at fault in what he says, he is a perfect man" (James 3:2). A second arrow from his quiver also hits the center of the target when he writes, "no man can tame the tongue" (James 3:8). Instead of a word of discouragement, that is meant as a word of counsel. No man can tame the tongue, but God can! The wild horse of the tongue can buck the preacher off. Let him get out of the saddle and give Christ's Spirit the reins. Let him rejoice with the Psalmist, "The LORD is with me; I will not be afraid. . . . The LORD is with me; he is my helper" (Psalm 118:6-7). Old Testament prophets "spoke of the grace to come" by "the Spirit of Christ in them" (I Peter 1:10-11). New Testament apostles "preached the gospel . . . by the Holy Spirit sent from heaven" (I Peter 1:12). Modern preachers of that Holy Spirit-revealed message are not given a new or altered revelation, but they can count on divine aid to comprehend and deliver the old, old story.

God "breathed into man's (Adam's) nostrils the breath of life, and man became a living being" (Genesis 2:7). When his Spirit inspires a man's message it, too, comes to life. Count on God to bring light out of darkness, man out of dust and sermons out of men. The human part is to offer the cup. The divine part is to fill it. The preacher is the vessel ready to be used. The Holy Spirit is the enabler. Let the proclaimer empty his life of all else and desire to "be filled with the Spirit" (Ephesians 5:19).

4

GOD'S SCRIPTURE, THE PREACHER'S UNFAILING RESOURCE

The only Biblical reference to a "pulpit of wood" is the KJV wording of Nehemiah 8:4. The NIV calls it "a high wooden platform built for the occasion." As Ezra stood to read, he knew he had under him a solid foundation that would bear his weight. All preachers stand up to speak on a spiritual platform with the four undergirdings of heaven — the Father, the Son, the Spirit and the Scriptures.

Let all who take up the communicating work of the Father, follow the example of the Son and rely on the strength of the Spirit. And let them also use the unfailing resource of the Scripture. The Bible is a well that will never run dry. It is a bank with such abundant riches that it will never fail. It is a food supply so adequately stocked that no preacher who goes there will leave unsatisfied. The Scripture is a medicine cabinet with remedies for every imaginable ill. It is a tool shed so completely supplied "that the man of God may be thoroughly equipped for every good work" (II Timothy 3:17).

Jesus never intended for any of his preachers to resemble the desperate lady in the parable found in Luke 11:5-8. Imagine an unprepared preacher on some Saturday midnight dialing up a fellow-minister with the plea, "Friend, lend me three sermon ideas, because Sunday is coming, the congregation will gather, and I have nothing to set before them.'"

The late Halford E. Luccock admonished homileticians to avoid turning to the newspapers or another's sermon books for pulpit ideas, when the Bible itself was so readily available and so richly stocked. He wrote of preachers, "They began to be in want. Then they came to themselves and said, 'In my father's Book are texts enough and to spare.' And they said, 'I will arise and go to the Bible.' "[1]

The Bible is what the listeners want. It is what the Holy Spirit uses. It is the well from which the preacher should draw the living water of his sermons. His people would rather hear a mediocre sermon on a great Bible truth than an eloquent address on a topic of trivial concern. The Chinese proverb contains wise advice to to the sermonizer, "You cannot carve rotten wood." Whittle sermons from the eternal words of God that will outlast the passing heaven and earth (Matthew 24:35). "The living and enduring word of God" is the church's message. "The grass withers and the flowers fall, but the word of the Lord stands forever" (I Peter 1:23-25).

THE BIBLE IS RICH IN THEMES

The Master Preacher found his Old Testament Bible a "storeroom" from which anyone "instructed in the kingdom of heaven" could bring out "new treasures as well as old" (Matthew

---

1. *In the Minister's Workshop* (Nashville: Abingdon Press, 1944), p. 148.

13:52). Men of modern times wrestle with the same sins, desires and perplexities as did those of ancient days. The listeners may care a great deal about what will happen to them and very little about what did happen to the Jebusites. The man who knows his Bible, however, can start with a present need and whet the appetite of the hearer to learn how that problem was solved by God in an aged story.

Every topic that touches human life now was of consequence before. Family issues, social concerns, theological questions and future hopes are the flesh-and-blood themes of the prophets of Israel and the apostles of the church. Today's congregations do not gather to be moved by the inspiration of some successor of the Greek orator. They rather assemble to hear the revelation of some believer in the Hebrew prophets and their apostolic successors. They do not, with the Athenians, desire to listen to "the latest ideas" or "some new thing" (KJV Acts 17:21). Novelty is not what their ears crave. They long for a fresh restatement of first century teaching in twenty-first century terms.

The disciples of Jesus are known as the people of the Book. The earnest Christian has no greater desire than to grow like Apollos to deserve the epithet, "mighty in the Scriptures" (Acts 18:24 KJV). Woe to that preacher that, when the children ask for bread from heaven, gives a stone (Matthew 7:9). Woe to that teacher who plants a lifeless rock in the garden of the heart, while the Scripture says, "The seed is the word of God" (Luke 8:11). Blessed is that congregation that has a preacher dedicated to making them Bible students, knowledgeable on every Scriptural theme. Happy is that preacher whose head has become a Bible concordance. When a problem is seen, the appropriate Scripture rushes to his mind. When an illustration is needed, the Bible story that fits the need flashes into his memory.

The extent to which the Bible is used shows the honor and respect in which the Scripture is held. Once the preacher is led in his educational pursuits to see that on the pages of Holy Writ is nothing but human record of man's religious thought, and no longer God's revelation to man, his sermons will lose their thrust. An amplified voice can never make up for a lost conviction. Once the question of Biblical authority is settled at the deepest level, the trumpet will no longer give an uncertain sound (I Corinthians 14:8). The preachers in Acts quoted from their Old Testament with assurance and told its historical record with confidence. Ten percent of the New Testament and the teachings of Jesus are Old Testament quotations. To recover the old power and revitalize the new pulpit, let the old Book be the rich mine from which a preacher's sermons are dug and the abundant source by which his life is fed. Familiarity with ancient Scripture breeds contemporary sermons. The Bible in the preacher antedates the Bible in the preaching.

"The prophets are but wind" ("windbags" Moffatt) when "the word is not in them" (Jeremiah 5:13). "Let the word of Christ dwell in you richly as you teach and admonish" (Colossians 3:16). That is the sound advice to anyone who wants his messages to be kept from being only sound with no content. A herald is to know his monarch's mind.

THE BIBLE IS RICH IN TEXTS

That the Sacred Book is rich in texts in an old discovery. Philip heard the Eunuch from Ethiopia read the passage Isaiah 53:7 and 8. "Then Philip began with that very passage of Scripture and told him the good news about Jesus" (Acts 8:32-35). In Nazareth Jesus read Isaiah 61:1 and 2 and began his synagogue remarks, "Today this scripture is fulfilled in your hearing" (Luke 4:18-21). Paul from town to town, after the Sabbath reading "from the Law and the Prophets," would stand up to speak once the synagogue rulers had invited, "Brothers, if you have a message of encouragement for the people, please speak" (Acts 13:15).

In the Jewish synagogues a discourse consisted in the explanation of the text for the day. After the Babylonian captivity, not only was the synagogue born, so also there developed gradually a carefully arranged lectionary that allowed for the entire Torah to be publicly read in about three to three and a half years. The use of the text reflected the high respect in which the Bible was held. The purpose of the lesson was to explain the Scripture portion.

Our word "textile" comes from the Latin, *textum*, meaning that which is woven. In the "text" God has provided the yarn out of which the sermon is to be woven. Ronald E. Sleeth warns that the topical preacher starts with his own ideas and, after the fact, seeks for a text to be used as a pretext. He calls it "jacking up the sermon and running a text under it."[2] The better way is to love the Book from God as a lover clings to the letter from a sweetheart, reading it again and again until every thought has been relished. If Jacob wrestles with an angel in the night until he gains his blessing, a preacher can struggle with his text not releasing it until its sermonic truth is given up (Genesis 32:22-32).

One homiletics professor suggests that the chosen text should be "long enough to be rich, and short enough to be recalled."[3] A text can be too short, tempting the teacher to exercise his human wisdom and personal eloquence to fill the gap. Or, it can be too long, especially if it is read without vocal interpretation, losing the listener before half way through the reading. Whatever the length, let the reading of the text be done so effectively that it escapes Fred B. Craddock's indictment of being so poorly done it is a misdemeanor, if not a felony."[4]

The use of a text lifts the Bible to a position of authority and reminds the people that what is to be remembered is God's word and not the human effort called the sermon. The use of a text

---

2. *Proclaiming the Word* (New York: Abingdon Press, 1964), p. 37.

3. Stanley D. Schneider, *As One Who Speaks for God* (Minneapolis: Augsburg Publishing House, 1965), p. 59.

4. *Preaching* (Nashville: Abingdon Press, 1985), p. 104.

helps create a people of Biblical literacy. It can serve as an introduction and create in the audience anticipation for the message to follow.

When God has his way, the Bible will be read interpretively, quoted authoritatively, expounded intelligently, organized clearly and applied practically, so it can be lived fruitfully. Let every man marching behind Timothy in the preacher's parade, devote himself "to the public reading of Scripture, to preaching and to teaching" (I Timothy 4:13).

THE BIBLE IS RICH IN TERMS

"Grace," "redemption," and "forgiveness" are words in the vocabulary of the church. "Predestined," "saved" and "sealed" are common parlance among the redeemed. They are terms found in the rich storehouse of revelation and are not to be evaded or avoided as theological jargon from antiquity. These Biblical gems in the treasure-box of Scripture are of too great a value to be cast aside. Let the preacher through his study shake off the dust and wipe off the cobwebs, so that the full beauty of the priceless truths can be seen in all their glory.

Man lives "on every word that comes from the mouth of God" (Matthew 4:4). The believing community has "been entrusted with the very words of God" (Romans 3:2). The apostles spoke of their preaching with this description, "This is what we speak, not in words taught us by human wisdom but in words taught by the Spirit, expressing spiritual truths in spiritual words" (I Corinthians 2:13). Since "every word of God is flawless" (Proverbs 30:5), one is well advised to use Bible words for Bible things. Is it possible to improve on the Holy Spirit?

As the last book in the Bible was being penned, an angel said, "These words are trustworthy and true" (Revelation 22:6). As Peter helped the church face false teaching, he wrote, "I want you to recall the words spoken in the past by the holy prophets" and those given "by our Lord and Savior through your apostles" (II Peter 3:2).

Words from God are "living words to pass on" (Acts 7:38). As Paul said, "everything that was written in the past was written to teach us, so that" we might have "the encouragement of the Scriptures" (Romans 15:4). The words revealed through Scripture are not idle words that accomplish nothing. They are each filled with power. They are worthy of meditation day and night. They are valuables to be stored in the heart and mind. They are well worth citing. A "thus saith the Lord" is always more telling in result that a "this is what I think."

Part Two
THE MESSENGER
(THE WHO'S WHO OF PREACHING)

5

THE PREACHER'S CALL

Preaching has been said to be the poorest of trades but the highest of callings. To what degree is it a "calling"?

I have proclaimed the gospel with joy for fifty years and hope to remain in Christ's glad service for many years yet to come. But, let me relate a recent experience. Eating with a lovely older couple after a morning preaching service, the lady of the house phrased to me a question out of her Baptist background. It took me off guard. She inquired, "When did you receive your call to preach?" Had she asked the time of my baptism, I could have responded without a pause, giving the place and time. But, regarding my call to preach, I was speechless as to any specifics. I have total confidence that I am doing what Christ wants me to do. I would have no inner satisfaction doing anything else. Yet there was no voice heard — no vision seen. What was my call?

"Tell us by what authority you are doing these things. . . . Who gave you this authority?" (Luke 20:2). That is a legitimate question. John records that the congregation in Thyatira tolerated "Jezebel, who calls herself a prophetess" (Revelation 2:20). That is a needed observation, showing self appointment is not the same as divine appointment. Jesus "appointed twelve . . . to preach" (Mark 3:14), immediately after having ordered the evil spirits "not to tell who he was" (Mark 3:11-12 cp. Luke 4:41). It mattered to the Lord then and matters now not only what is proclaimed, but by whom it is made known. As the Bible warns regarding the high priest of olden days, "No one takes this honor upon himself; he must be called by God, just as Aaron was" (Hebrews 5:4).

Frank Hamilton Marshall, former Dean of Phillips University, would advise his students, "Don't preach if you can help it." When I first set out to study for the preaching ministry at Northwest Christian College, several chapel speakers said, "Only preach, if you can't do anything else." It rather seemed to me that, if a dedicated Christian could be a success at something else, that was the kind of person we needed in the pulpit. I have come to see what those who addressed the student-body were meaning. They were saying that all spokesmen for God must have such compulsion to make Christ known that they could not find satisfaction in doing anything else. The secret of pulpit power is the inner assurance of knowing that one is doing what God wills.

One vital Bible discovery is that there are different levels of call. For one not called directly, as were apostles and prophets, is not to be discouraged from service, because one's call may come indirectly through the church. Not all those who serve local congregations in the ministry of elder, or deacon or preacher have had an experience to which they can point. I know I am called not by any voices from the blue, but rather by many verses from the Bible. My call was known to me, not by several tickles in my tummy, but by several texts in my New Testament. I hear no voice. I do not speak infallibly. I perform no miracles to confirm my message. But I strive to pass on faithfully the infallible message given through the divinely called apostles, who did have their teaching confirmed "by the signs that accompanied" (Mark 16:20).

THE CALL OF APOSTLES AND PROPHETS

Christ "gave some to be apostles, some to be prophets, some to be evangelists, and some to be pastors and teachers" (Ephesians 4:11). The apostles and prophets served the church universal. The evangelists and those that pastor and teach serve the churches local. The former did a work once-for-all in the service of congregations of every time and place. The latter take that apostolic and prophetic word, once given, and apply it to their particular day and area. The call of the first group is direct and immediate. That of the second is indirect and mediated.

The apostle (Greek: ἀπόστολος) is "one sent" from God — i.e., "a godsend." Of Jesus' many disciples, he "chose twelve of them, whom he also designated apostles" (Luke 6:13). Paul, the special apostle to the Gentiles, also spoke of himself as "called to be an apostle" (Romans 1:1 cp Galatians 1:1). The book of Acts refers to him as God's "chosen instrument" (9:15; 12:14) to do the task given by Jesus (20:24) wherever sent (22:21). He was appointed as a "witness" (Acts 26:16) to carry out "the ministry of reconciliation" (II Corinthians 5:18).

Each apostle of Christ was an eyewitness of Jesus after his resurrection from the dead (Acts 1:3,21-22; 10:40-41; 22:14-15; 26:16; I Corinthians 9:1; I John 1:1; 4:14; Revelation 1:9). That requirement for apostleship could not be expected of all other ministers (Luke 1:2). Neither could the mark of miracle-worker. That was a must for an apostle. It could not be required of all other servants of the Word. (Matthew 10:1,8; II Corinthians 12:12; Hebrews 2:3-4; Acts 2:43).

The office of apostle was unique and allowed for no successors. Since their mission was to reveal infallibly the words and works of Jesus, the church of post-apostolic times needed no new message to replace or alter their testimony. That was "once for all entrusted to the saints" (Jude 3). Since the apostles were guided "into all truth" (John 16:13), no lack was left for later generations to fill. Since the promised Holy Spirit taught and reminded the men at the last supper "of everything" (John 14:26), then the apostles' teaching was destined to be the adequate revelation for the church until time was to be no more.

The church is "built on the foundation of the apostles and prophets" (Ephesians 2:20). Both apostles and prophets received their messages directly from God. To substitute the word "preacher" for the word "prophet" would be to mix categories and confuse calls. The prophet gives original revelation from God. The preacher applies that earlier given message to his audience. The prophet was called directly to his mission. Not necessarily so, was the preacher of the prophetic and apostolic message.

Does it cause concern that some preacher fills the pulpit that cannot witness to a vision like Isaiah's of seeing "the Lord seated on a throne, high and exalted" (Isaiah 6:1) or hearing God's voice command "Go and tell this people" (Isaiah 6:9 cp. II Kings 20:4; II Chronicles 32:20)? Why did Ezekiel have the experience of the Lord's voice calling, "Son of man, I am sending you to the Israelites" (Ezekiel 2:3), and no sound from heaven has reached your or my ears?

The Bible says, "the word of the LORD came to Abram" (Genesis 15:1). It tells how, "the LORD spoke to Moses" (Numbers 1:1)[1] and to Joshua (Joshua 1:1).[2] It leaves no doubt

---

1. Exodus 13:1; 14:1,15,26; 16:4,11,34; 17:5,14; 19:9-10,21,24; 20:22; 25:1; 30:11,17,22,34; 31:1,12,18; 32:7,33; 33:1,5,14,17,19,21; 34:1,10,27; 40:1; Leviticus 1:1-2; 5:14; 6:1,8,19,24; 7:22,28; 8:1; 11:1; 12:1; 13:1; 14:1,33; 15:1; 16:1-2; 17:1; 18:1; 19:1; 20:1; 21:1; 22:1,17,26; 23:1,9,23,33; 24:1,13; 25:1; 27:1,34; Numbers 1:1,19; 2:1,34; 3:14,44; 4:1,17; 5:1,5; 6:1,22; 7:89; 8:5,23; 9:1,9; 10:1; 11:16,23; 12:2,4,6-8,14; 13:1,3; 14:11,20,26; 15:1,17; 16:36; 17:1,10; 18:1,8,25; 19:1; 20:7,9,12; 21:8,34; 34:1; 35:9; 36:13; Deuteronomy 2:31; 4:14; 34:10-11.

2. 4:15; 5:2,9; 6:2; 7:10; 8:1,18; 11:6; 20:1.

that "the LORD called Samuel" (I Samuel 3:4), that "the word of the LORD came to Nathan" (II Samuel 7:4) and that "the Spirit of the Lord spoke through (David)" (II Samuel 23:2). From the major prophets to the minor prophets, each spokesman begins by telling of his call before he gives the burden of his revelation (Jeremiah 1:4; Ezekiel 1:3; Hosea 1:1; Joel 1:1; Amos 1:1 and 2:11; 7:14-15; Jonah 1:1; 3:1; Micah 1:1; Nahum 1:1; Habakkuk 1:1; cp. 3:1; Zephaniah 1:1; Haggai 1:1 cp. 2:10,20; Zechariah 1:1 cp. 4:9; 6:11; 7:4,8: 8:1; Malachi 1:1). Shemaiah was called (I Kings 12:22). Elijah was called (I Kings 18:1; 21:17,28). Azariah was called (II Chronicles 15:1). Nathan was called (II Chronicles 29:25). Huldah was called (II Chronicles 34:22). So were Jeremiah (Jeremiah 1:4)[3] and Ezekiel (Ezekiel 1:3).[4]

The New Testament Scriptures made it clear that John the Baptist was "a man who was sent from God" (John 1:6). The Gospels tell of the call by Jesus to four by the Sea of Galilee to follow and be made "fishers of men" (Matthew 4:19 cp. Mark 1:17,20). Paul's call is highlighted in his epistles from Romans (1:1) to the Pastorals (I Timothy 2:7; II Timothy 1:11; Titus 1:3). It is pointed to from early letters like Galatians (1:15) after the first missionary journey to epistles like I Corinthians (1:17) from his third journey. His call is lifted up in the shorter correspondence written during the Roman imprisonment (cp. Colossians 1:25).

Was not Jesus, the sender of the apostles, also one that was sent? John records many occasions when Jesus talks of himself as the "sent" one (John 7:16; 8:26; 12:49; 13:20). If Christ was called and the prophets and apostles called, then must not all preachers have to experience a similar call?

It is both humbling and helpful to recognize that a preacher is

---

3. 7:1; 11:1; 14:11,14,17; 15:1; 16:1; 18:1,5; 21:1; 24:4; 25:1,4,15,27; 27:2; 29:30; 30:1; 32:1,6,26; 33:1,19,23; 34:8,12; 35:1; 40:11; 42:7; 43:8; 44:1; 46:1,13; 47:1.

4. 2:1-3; 6:1; 7:1; 11:13; 12:1,17,21; 13:1; 15:1; 16:1; 17:1,11; 18:1; 20:45; 21:1,8,18; 22:1,17,23; 23:1; 24:15,20; 27:1; 28:1,11,20; 29:1,17; 30:1; 31:1; 33:1,22-23; 35:1; 36:16; 37:15; 38:1.

neither called to be the Messiah of the church nor the Savior of the world. His is a vital ministry but of far less significance than that of Jesus. The preacher has not been called to bring new revelation for either ancient Israel or the New Israel, which is the church. The preacher's mission is simply to pass on, interpret and apply that divinely-inspired revelation that came through the prophets. With a lesser task comes a lesser call. But, denying "the road to Damascus" type of call that Saul of Tarsus experienced to all who evangelize or teach, is not to deny the certain call that comes over the centuries to all who rise up to preach the apostolic gospel. In each spokesman of heaven's message there must be a hearty sense of vocation. There must be more than the decision that, since one will be at the church gatherings anyway, he might as well be the talker rather than one of the listeners.

THE CALL OF MINISTERS

Does the Biblical idea of the priesthood of all believers carry the connotation of the preacherhood of all in the church? Jesus' ministry began at his baptism. Was our baptism our ordination into the ministry?

Paul's answer in Romans 6 is "yes" — "Thanks be to God that, though you used to be slaves (servants KJV) to sin, you wholeheartedly obeyed the form of teaching to which you were entrusted. You have been set free from sin and have become slaves to righteousness" (vv. 17-18). Paul's response is the same "yes" in Ephesians 4, where he clarifies that the purpose of the workers from apostles through teachers is "to prepare God's people for works of service (ministry KJV)" (v. 12).

Our call to be a follower of Jesus was through the church. All members of the Lord's church "have been called according to his purpose" and as the "called" they will be "justified" and "glorified" (Romans 8:28,30 cp. 9:24; I Peter 1:15; 2:9). Each is to "take hold of the eternal life to which (he is) called" (I Timothy

6:12). To the Thessalonian congregation it was written, "He called you to this through our gospel" (II Thessalonians 2:14; Romans 1:6). How do you get both teachers of children and of adults in your congregation? How do you get deacons and elders? Do you wait until Jesus calls them directly, or is it within the responsibility of a congregation to recruit and train the helpers it needs? The author of the Epistle to the Hebrews, expected that over a period of time a convert ought to be adequately equipped to instruct others. He wrote, "by this time you ought to be teachers" (5:12).

Luke tells of early persecution striking "the church at Jerusalem, and all except the apostles were scattered." He speaks of "men and women" being imprisoned and immediately adds, "those who had been scattered preached the word wherever they went" (Acts 8:1-4). It sounds at first reading that every believer of both sexes and varied ages took responsibility in spreading their faith. If preaching is one person confronting another person with the gospel, then no believer is exempt from the call. David Lipscomb in his book *Queries and Answers* (Nashville: Gospel Advocate, 1963, reprint) on page 347 writes, "All Christians in their spheres are preachers." On this liberals, conservatives and moderates agree.

No less than John Wesley is reported to have remarked, "Give me one hundred preachers who fear nothing but sin and desire nothing but God, and I care not a straw whether they be clergymen or laymen, such alone will shake the gates of hell and set up the Kingdom of God upon the earth." No follower of the Master is exempt from the responsibility of sharing Christ with someone — children, parents, neighbors, co-workers, etc.

In ancient Israel parents were teachers to their own offspring. Moses told the nation, "Impress them (the commandments) on your children. Talk about them when you sit at home and when you walk along the road" (Deuteronomy 6:7 cp. 6:20-21; 11:19-21). Asaph in the Psalms wrote, "things we have heard and known, things our fathers have told us. We will not hide them from their children; we will tell the next generation . . . even the children yet to be born, and they in turn would tell their children" (Psalm 78:3-6).

A priest "ought to preserve knowledge, and from his mouth men should seek instruction — because he is the messenger of the LORD almighty" wrote Malachi (2:7). In addition to priests, God wanted wise men (Proverbs 13:14) and prophets (Jeremiah 25:4) to teach his Old Testament people. At a local and home level, all Jews were to share in the education of others. If the Old Covenant people could sing, "Let the redeemed of the LORD say this" (Psalm 107:2), is not the Christian community to affirm in unison, "through God's mercy we have this ministry" (II Corinthians 4:1), even the ministry of preaching to the lost and teaching the saved?

THE CALL OF EVANGELISTS AND PASTORS

In the sense of "gossiping the gospel," all Christians are to preach. Acts 8:4 makes that clear. But are we to conclude that all disciples of Jesus are to give their full time to preaching? Ephesians 4:11 makes evident that only "some (are) to be evangelists, and some to be pastors and teachers." Paul speaks of certain workers who "are worthy of double honor, especially those whose work is preaching and teaching" (I Timothy 5:17). "Not many should presume to be teachers" is the advice of James (James 3:1). "Are all teachers?" is a legitimate question that anticipates a negative reply (I Corinthians 12:29). The I Corinthian letter is filled with the division of labor concept in the church. Read, "the Lord has assigned to each his task" (3:5). Note, "In the church God has appointed . . . third teachers" (12:28).

Experience is a great teacher and one of its lessons is this: While all have the right and responsibility to make Jesus known, the job gets done only where there is a preacher ever reminding the people in the pews of their ministry. Let all members "always be prepared to give an answer to everyone who asks . . . the reason for the hope that (they) have" (I Peter 3:15). Let all teachers and preachers "Prepare God's people for works of service" (Ephesians 4:12).

This brings us to the question that can not be dodged. All Christians are called to function in the body of Christ, so how does each one find his ministry? How is the believer to find if his niche is the preacher niche? What is the "call" to function as a preacher?

We are not asking about the role of an apostle, who serves the church universal, but of a minister of lower rank, who serves a local flock. We are asking about the functionary who, while far below an apostle, is a cut above the other believers that also win souls as they carry out their bread and butter occupations.

Everyone is under the great commission. Those who ought to become ministers of the Word should examine also the call of the great need and the call of great abilities. In the face of need, should not those capable of meeting the need consider if they are not being called to that work? Christ pointed his disciples to a need not being met. Moved with compassion for the harassed and helpless crowds who were "like sheep without a shepherd," Jesus said to his disciples, "The harvest is plentiful but the workers are few. Ask the Lord of the harvest, therefore, to send out workers into his harvest field" (Matthew 9:36-38). The very next verses of the text tell of Jesus sending his twelve on a preaching mission. He led them to see the need — the great need — and to care about the people to the point of earnest prayer. At that moment, when they saw the need and looked within to see if they had abilities to meet such a need, they realized they were called to do so. Need, plus ability, equals responsibility.

Paul, called by Christ on the Damascus Road to be an apostle, called upon Timothy to do the work of an evangelist. Toward the end of Paul's life, he urged this young preacher to recruit other-such workers in the gospel. He wrote from the confinement of a Roman prison, "The things you have heard me say in the presence of many witnesses entrust to reliable men who will also be qualified to teach others" (II Timothy 2:2). The need was never greater. It was urgent that, as one spokesman would soon fall in the line of duty, others be recruited and trained to fill the ranks. "Reliable" and "qualified," or "faithful" and "able" are the demands. In the light of the Christ's commission to his church and in the awareness of the world's desperate need, let each man examine his abilities to see if he should volunteer.

"Christ's love compels us," spoke Paul long ago (II Corinthians 5:14). "Christ's love compels us," have said missionaries and preachers across the centuries. Today the first question ought not be "Why go?" The primary inquiry of all the baptized should be rather, "Why not go?" In the wars fought by men and nations every person of military age and fitness is conscripted for active service. Who ought to remain away from the battle-front? They alone who can serve their country better in another capacity. Not everyone who volunteers is accepted, and not everyone should preach. This is where the congregation is involved.

The apostolic argument runs that salvation is open to all who call on the Lord, but believing precedes calling, preaching comes before believing and sending is prior to it all. "How can they preach unless they are sent," reads Romans 10:15. This sending is an act of the church. If the congregation that knows your faithfulness and recognizes your abilities, encourages you to train for the task, don't feel a need for more of a call than that.

The call of the church is vital, for preaching is not an individual act. It is the act of the church. The man in the pulpit is the voice of a congregation. He represents their beliefs and convictions before the community. The sermon is to be not the word of the proclaimer but that of the church and its Lord. The message is not person to people on a horizontal level. It is God through his church by its preacher speaking to the masses.

Each congregation, for its well-being, needs elders to pastor and teach the flock. And each body of believers is blessed, if it has at least one of their number who can "do the work of an evangelist" (I Timothy 6:5). Doubly blessed is that flock whose spokesman cries from the heart, "I am compelled to preach. Woe to me if I do not preach the gospel" (I Corinthians 9:16). Triply happy is that body of believers whose proclaimer shouts, "I am obligated . . . that is why I am eager to preach the gospel" (Romans 1:14-15). Grateful beyond measure is the church, where the gospel herald expresses the compulsion, "his word is in my heart like a burning fire" (Jeremiah 20:9).

With Moses, "I wish that all the LORD'S people were prophets" (Numbers 11:29). With Isaiah, I agree, "How beautiful on the mountain are the feet of those who bring good news, who proclaim peace, who bring good tidings, who proclaim salvation, who say in Zion, 'Your God reigns!' " (Isaiah 52:7). With Luke, I pray that every preacher have vision and get ready, "concluding that God had called (him) to preach the gospel" (Acts 16:10).

6

THE PREACHER'S REQUIREMENTS

"A man ought to examine himself" (I Corinthians 11:28). He ought to inquire whether he has been called. Next he should ask if he meets the requirements. "Here is a trustworthy saying: If anyone sets his heart on being an overseer (and I add, a preacher), he desires a noble task. Now the overseer (and again I add, the preacher) must be above reproach" (I Timothy 3:1-2).

The Lord we strive to serve was not happy with the religious leaders of his day. He who charged the teachers of the law with not practicing what they preached (Matthew 23:3), will have even harsher words for those who preach his gospel but do not live his life. Seven times in one chapter of Matthew he cries, "Woe to you, teachers of the law and Pharisees, you hypocrites!" (23:13,15,16,23,25,,27,29). To his own disciples, Jesus warned, "Be on your guard against the yeast of the Pharisees, which is hypocrisy" (Luke 12:1). From his one disciple Paul he heard words that he desires to hear from all his workers: "my way of life in Christ Jesus . . . agrees with what I teach everywhere in every church" (I Corinthians 4:17). To all who preach, the Lord revealed the key to pulpit power saying, "out of the overflow of his heart his mouth speaks" (Luke 6:45).

The world expects genuine sincerity from the ministers of God's word. Its concept of what the "man of God" ought to be was well expressed by William Cowper (1731-1800) in "The Task" Book II. He wrote:

> I venerate the man whose heart is warm,
> Whose hands are pure, whose doctrine and whose life,
> Coincident, exhibit lucid proof
> That he is honest in the sacred cause (line 372).
>
> Would I describe a preacher, . . .
> I would express him simple, grave, sincere;
> In doctrine uncorrupt; in language plain,
> And plain in manner; decent, solemn, chaste.
> And natural in gesture; much impress'd
> Himself, as conscious of his awful charge.
> And anxious mainly that the flock he feeds
> May feel it too; affectionate in look,
> And tender in address, as well becomes
> A messenger of grace to guilty men (line 394).

The terminology "man of God" is not a title to be worn lightly. The evangelist Timothy, made aware of hirelings who do not model the true shepherds, is admonished, "But you, man of God, flee from all this and pursue righteousness, godliness, faith, love, endurance and gentleness" (I Timothy 6:11). To be considered a "man of God" (I Kings 12:22; II Kings 4:16,21,22,27,40; 5:8,13; 6:6,9,10,12,15,16; 8:7,11) is to be expected always to be a "*holy* man of God" (II Kings 4:9).

THE MORAL REQUIREMENT

All Timothies are to "set an example for the believers in

speech, in life, in love, in faith and in purity" (I Timothy 4:12). They are to be representative Christians. There is much more to preaching than Sunday mornings and Wednesday nights. There is the around-the-clock and throughout-the-calendar living of the message. A transformed life is the best visual aid that can be imagined.

George Macdonald once said, " 'The words of the wise are . . . as nails,' but their examples are as the hammers that drive the nails home." P.T. Forsyth, in giving the Lyman Beecher Lectures on Preaching at Yale University in 1907, followed a nine point outline. His first point held priority above all his other wise counsel to preachers. This topic that led the list was "The Preacher and his Character." (*Positive Preaching and the Modern Mind*, New York: A.C. Armstrong and Son, 1908).

People have eyes as well as ears. They see what we are as well as hear what we say. The doctrine we preach is ratified or denied by the lives that we live. We color the message. Heretical conduct can be as damaging as heretical doctrine. Shall the teacher of others unsay with his life what he declares with his lips? Shall a preacher immediately diminish his influence for right by doing wrong? We do not need to hear the full sermon to be grasped by the lesson of the day. The message to which I refer bore the title, "Slightly Soiled, Greatly Reduced in Price."

Hear this word: "The LORD said to Moses, 'Say to Aaron: For the generations to come none of your descendants who has a defect may come near to offer the food of his God' " (Leviticus 21:16). Hear this word: "Depart, depart, go out from there! Touch no unclean thing! Come out from it and be pure, you who carry the vessels of the LORD" (Isaiah 52:11).

What surgeon goes to the operating room without wearing his antiseptic gown? It would be deadly to flout hospital procedure and thus transmit germs by one's careless touch. Should not those who touch souls have clean hands? As Paul asked long ago, "You, then, who teach others, do you not teach yourself? You who preach against stealing, do you steal? You that say that people should not commit adultery, do you commit adultery?" Such inconsistency has a sure result: "God's name is blasphemed among the Gentiles because of you" (Romans 2:21-24).

The note of holiness is not to be silenced in the major chord written into the Divine Script. "We who teach," writes James, "will be judged more strictly" (3:1). The Lord's half-brother cringes under a present condition when "out of the same mouth come praise and cursing." His plea is, "My brothers, this should not be" (3:10).

James' predecessor, Isaiah the prophet, was disappointed to see "priests and prophets stagger from beer and (be) befuddled with wine" (28:7). So did Jeremiah have a "heart broken" (23:9) within him, seeing "prophets follow an evil course" (23:10), "commit adultery and live a lie" (23:14). He could explain the siege of the holy city in the words, "it happened because of the sins of her prophets" (Lamentations 4:13).

For the spokesman of God, only godly living "will refute every tongue that accuses" (Isaiah 54:17). To the question, "Who of us can dwell with everlasting burning?" The answer is "He who walks righteously and speaks what is right" (Isaiah 33:14-15). To the nagging condition, bothering every preacher who knows that "all have sinned," is the question "Is no one to preach?" The paradox is that the sense of one's unworthiness to preach is his prerequisite to do preaching. Isaiah, in the awareness of God's holiness, cried out, "Woe is me! . . . I am ruined! For I am a man of unclean lips" (6:5). So all other proclaimers need the prophet's experience of cleansing. They need to testify, "He touched my mouth and said, 'See, this has touched your lips; your guilt is taken away and your sin atoned for. . . . Go and tell this people' " (6:7-9). What Samuel said to Saul regarding the procession of prophets he would meet, God says to his preachers, "The Spirit of the LORD will come upon you in power, and you will prophesy with them; and you will be changed into a different person" (I Samuel 10:5-6).

Let every speaker in the pulpit on Sunday remember his

message will be magnified or diminished — strengthened or weakened — by his life-style Monday morning through Saturday night. The time-worn joke is that no marriages take place in heaven because no preachers make it there to perform the wedding ceremonies. The truer fact is that the water of life can only come in "jars of clay" ("earthen vessels" KJV of II Corinthians 4:7). The forgiven are the chosen instruments to announce God's unmerited forgiveness. But, let those uncondemned by Christ "go . . . and leave (the) life of sin" (John 8:11). He who believes the salvation he preaches must evidence it in the life he lives. Actions can not be separated from sermons.

Horrid Herod knew John the Baptist "to be a righteous and holy man . . . yet he liked to listen to him" (Mark 6:20). Our world only likes to listen about God from one who has been in the Lord's presence. Those who do not control their bodies are "disqualified" from preaching (I Corinthians 9:27). That is not in any sense easy, but "the kingdom of God is not a matter of talk but of power" (I Corinthians 4:20). Apostles have every right to rebuke those "not acting in line with the truth of the gospel" (Galatians 2:14). "How to live in order to please God" (I Thessalonians 4:1) is a required course for every minister. A graduate from the school of holiness "cleanses himself" and becomes "an instrument for noble purposes, made holy, useful to the Master and prepared to do any good work" (II Timothy 2:21). If pagan husbands "may be won over without talk by the behavior of their wives, when they see the purity and reverence of . . . lives" (I Peter 3:1-2), so may all people be convinced by the logic of a preacher's transformation. "Keep yourself pure" (I Timothy 5:22). Hold a "good conscience" (I Timothy 1:19). "Flee the evil desires of youth" (II Timothy 2:22). "Train yourself to be godly" (I Timothy 4:7).

THE INTELLECTUAL REQUIREMENTS

God used Moses. He "was educated in all the wisdom of the Egyptians and was powerful in speech and action" (Acts 7:22).

God used Paul. Close to the last words that missionary ever wrote were, "Come to me quickly. . . . When you come, bring . . . my scrolls (books KJV) especially the parchments" (II Timothy 4:9,13). No preacher can deliver messages of weight without a library of books. Sorcerers ought to burn their books (Acts 19:19), but preachers should amass helpful ones that serve useful tools in the carpenter shop of sermon construction.

The young gospel preacher needs the nudging to "devote (himself) to the public reading of Scripture" (I Timothy 4:13). "Give heed to reading" (KJV). He needs the challenge, "Do your best to present yourself to God as one approved, a workman who does not need to be ashamed and who correctly handles the word of truth" (II Timothy 2:15). How else will he be "able to teach" (II Timothy 2:24)? He will need, with his sound body and sound morals, a sound mind. As we have noted, the gospel is entrusted to persons "qualified to teach others" (II Timothy 2:2).

He who preaches must believe every word he speaks. It is intellectual dishonesty to have a faith washed thin in seminary studies and yet retain the pulpit of a believing assembly. The preacher is the voice of a congregation. "It is written: 'I believed; therefore I have spoken.' With the same spirit of faith we also believe and therefore speak" (II Corinthians 4:13).

A solid blow cannot be struck for the gospel, when its proponents have their fingers crossed. The church grows where what is preached is confident faith and not wavering doubt. When Matthew wrote of Jesus' virgin birth, he spoke in the bold confidence that comes from standing on the solid ground of revelation. When apostles spoke of the Lord's incarnation, atoning death, bodily resurrection, coronation and certain return, they did not wink with secret skepticism.

The early church teachers were graduates of the "I am not ashamed" school. They received their doctoral diplomas at the "I am convinced" seminary (cp. II Timothy 1:12). They have the "distinguishing mark" (II Thessalonians 3:17) of the Master Teacher, "who taught as one who had authority, and not as their teachers of the law" (Matthew 7:29). They were believers to the man. Not one skeptical voice marred their witness. Doubting Thomas and Vacillating Peter had moved from sinking sand to solid rock.

THE EMOTIONAL REQUIREMENTS

The price to be paid for success in the pulpit will not come down. The life of the preacher must be transparent, his mind must be disciplined and his heart must be sensitive. To be effective in preaching, sympathy with people is a must. Paul was right, "If I speak in the tongues of men and of angels, but have not love, I am only a resounding gong or a clanging cymbal" (I Corinthians 13:1). The preacher with every other homiletical skill, but lacking in genuine care about people, will find his message falling on deaf ears. There must be the caring for the flock before the sharing of the fodder with the sheep.

A preacher can not fake love. Many a convert to Christianity, by way of the Sunday School, can testify that he first learned to love his teacher, next that teacher's Bible and finally that teacher's Christ. A good teacher not only opens his mouth and teaches God's love, he opens his heart and demonstrates that love.

An effective preacher, as "the Lord's servant must not quarrel; instead he must be kind to everyone . . . he must gently instruct" (II Timothy 3:24-25). He must "Preach the Word . . . with great patience" (II Timothy 4:2). Jesus did not just preach. The records say he was "preaching the gospel and healing people everywhere" (Luke 9:6). Nothing is more healing — more cathartic — than "speaking the truth in love" (Ephesians 4:15). Give the people your heart as well as your head. "Rejoice with those who rejoice; mourn with those who mourn" (Romans 12:15).

Shepherds and hirelings have many things in common. Both

are with the sheep guiding, feeding, mending fences and doing the many other duties that go with the task. Both are paid, so that is not the difference. The wide gulf that separates shepherds from hirelings is that the shepherd loves his sheep and shows genuine care in his duties. To not care and to not manifest love is to be a "mortician's delight." The preacher's wife and children will know best how real is the love this husband and daddy talks about from his pulpit.

Helmut Thielicke, in his book *The Trouble with the Church* (New York: Harper and Row, 1965), contrasts the preacher with a druggist. He makes the case that people do not especially care about whether the man filling their prescription loves or hates, is envious or is not. What matters is that he gets the right medicine. With the preacher who delivers God's message, however, his actions belie the most well-chosen words of Scripture.

Paul holds up the "true . . . noble . . . right . . . pure . . . lovely . . . (and) admirable." Then he adds the pertinent words, "Whatever you have learned or received or heard from me, or seen in me" (Phillipians 4:8-9). Whatever your listeners hear from you is likewise to be seen in you. As a good salesman your samples are more convincing than your spiel. The potential customer is more apt to buy when he finds you earnest, sincere, humble and sympathetic, bearing the fruit of the Spirit.

Elders are prudent to ask, as their title implies, "Am I acting maturely?" Childlikeness and childishness are not the same. "Put childish ways behind" (I Corinthians 13:11). A mature person is one of enlarged horizons, experience, wisdom and controlled emotions. Pastors are wise to examine their shepherding. Are they seeking the strays? feeding the sheep? caring for the lambs? The response evidences whether they "truly love" (John 21:15-16). Evangelists must measure their love for the world by the passion of Christ. To pass the moral and intellectual tests for the preacher is not enough. The emotion test demands an A grade. All preachers must answer: "Christ's love compels us" (II Corinthians 5:14).

THE SPIRITUAL REQUIREMENT

"A man is not a Jew if he is only one outwardly. . . . No, a man is a Jew if he is one inwardly" (Romans 2:28-29). The same is true regarding the Christian. Let the preacher, especially, use his Bible as a full-length mirror (cp. James 1:22-25). Let him look at himself. Then let him be reminded that, before he goes into the community and tells the people he represents Christ and the church, he needs to look himself over and see if he truly does.

Jesus' words to his disciples were first "follow me" (Matthew 4:19). Only later did he send them out with the instruction, "go, preach" (Matthew 10:7). At the end of Christ's ministry he did order his followers to "go . . . preach the good news" (Mark 16:15), but earlier in that ministry the disciples were instructed, "go into your room, close the door and pray" (Matthew 6:6). The order is intentional. First be a follower, then a proclaimer. First go into your closet and only then from the place of prayer go out to preach. The preacher at Colossae is a good model to follow. Paul writes of Epaphras, "He is always wrestling in prayer for you; that you may stand firm in all the will of God, mature and fully assured" (Colossians 4:12).

Those who speak for God to people need to know both parties well. A brilliant mind, a gift of communication and a radiant personality will not make up for the lack of a personal walk with God. Have you ever heard a school teacher tell of another country — its language, costumes and customs — and yet you were very aware that he or she had never been there? E. Stanley Jones used to compare some preachers to workers at the Railway Station who kept calling out the names of towns where a train would be going and yet they had never travelled there themselves.

Words apart from lives are empty. Lives apart from words are unclear. He who walks the Calvary Road day by day, makes a better guide than a total stranger to the Way of the Cross. Let him, who says "Lord, Lord," be a doer of what is said (Luke 6:46). Let him, who speaks Christ's words, "put them into practice" (Luke 6:49). Let each Timothy hear Paul's instruction, "Be diligent in these matters; give yourself wholly to them, so that everyone may see your progress" (I Timothy 4:15). To those who see that "progress," a Timothy has earned his right to speak to them. The apostle had captured Timothy's allegiance, for he could write, "You . . . know all about my teaching, my way of life" (II Timothy 3:10). Teaching and life are interlaced together. They are separated only at great loss. "Live according to the teaching" (II Thessalonians 3:6). See that the gospel comes "not simply with words" (I Thessalonians 1:5). Let the preaching be accompanied "with a demonstration of the Spirit's power" (I Corinthians 2:4). Let the Word become flesh and live among us (John 1:14). Then the congregation's ears can become eyes and they can see Christ, as well as hear his name.

Actors in the theater can play parts, for they are not known personally by their audiences. Congregations know the man who talks to them from the podium. He can not be a play actor. He must be the real thing.

7

THE PREACHER'S PREPARATION

"Be prepared" was in my younger years only a Boy Scout Motto. Since I have become a preacher, it is the basic essential of every day. "Always be prepared" (I Peter 3:15) has been the continual advice of the one who preached the sermon on Pentecost the day the church began.

Jesus spoke of a student being "fully trained" to "be like his teacher" (Luke 6:40). That "full" training is a life-long pursuit for anyone who would preach like the Master Preacher. The greatest message any world has ever received deserves the best presentation any spokesman can ever give.

The gospel preacher can learn from every experience with sorrow, every wrestling with texts of Scripture and every exposure to books and to people. The Psalmist could not imagine that "he who teaches man (would) lack knowledge" (93:10). It would have been unthinkable to Solomon to send "a message by the hand of a fool." That would be "like cutting off one's feet"

(Proverbs 26:6). God used Moses, who "was educated in all the wisdom of the Egyptians" (Acts 7:22). God used Apollos, who "was a learned man with a thorough knowledge of the Scriptures" (Acts 18:24). God used Paul, who was respected as a man of "great learning" (Acts 26:24). God stood ready to use any persons that Timothy would recruit, as long as they were "qualified to teach others" (II Timothy 2:2). The Lord will use you, if you follow his order, "Get yourself ready!" (Jeremiah 1:17). He ever has used each person that has "devoted himself to the study and observance of the Law of the LORD, and to teaching its decrees" (Ezra 7:10).

No one who speaks for God can be too educated, but woe to that preacher whose degrees are in skepticism rather than faith. Upon hearing a clergyman speak, who had a string of intellectual degrees but little conviction, a parishioner left the service with the comment, "He has degrees all right — ten below zero!" A missionary to Africa, named Charlie Studd, observed, "It is not the degree of B.A., or D.D., that makes a good missionary; it is the degree of sacrifice. There must be a heart hot for Jesus. Give me people with a boiling heart for Jesus. Any old turnip will do for a head." That is an overstatement, but it does draw emphasis to the importance of keeping one's feet on solid ground while one's head is reaching toward the clouds.

A street preacher was heard to tell his open air crowd, "I have not been to college, but I have been to Calvary." Dwight L. Moody is remembered for saying every preacher needed two degrees — the B.A. and the O.O. He meant Born Again and Out and Out! As true as that is, the sharper your axe, the more trees you can fell.

STUDY IN THE SCHOOL OF CHRIST

No matter from whom you study, let Jesus remain your major professor in training for ministry. Ask yourself how the disciples learned to preach. The evident answer is that they listened to Jesus. They observed how he related to people and how he spoke to them. The Gospels read, "After Jesus had finished instructing his twelve disciples, he went on from there to teach and preach" (Matthew 11:1). There was instruction, followed by modeling. Excellent educational procedure in anyone's school.

When Luke reports the Sanhedrin's charge that Christ's disciples were "unschooled, ordinary men" (Acts 4:13), he makes evident that they needed to learn that they had in Jesus the best possible teacher for both theology and homiletics. Many of the world's greatest musicians and artists began their careers imitating the masters in their field. Can not learning by example prove as effective as learning by reading rules? The Sanhedrin's conclusion was unavoidable: "They were astonished and they took note that these men had been with Jesus." They had experienced earlier the same difficulty to account for Jesus' preaching power, asking, "How did this man get such learning without having studied?" (John 7:15).

To preach well, study Jesus. Learn by listening to what he teaches and how he talks. Remember his promise to those he calls, "I will make you fishers of men" (Matthew 4:19; Mark 1:17). The potter is telling the clay that yields to his touch, "I will make you." Your part is to be pliable. His part is to mold the instrument that will carry his gospel. He who told his apostles, "it will not be you speaking, but the Spirit of your Father speaking through you" (Matthew 10:20; Mark 13:11 cp. Luke 12:12), will not be AWOL when lesser workmen attempt the faithful delivery of the apostolic word.

Hands on experience must accompany the studying of books. Who ever learned to swim by reading books on swimming or staying out of the water? Jesus' technique was to appoint men "that they might be with him and that he might send them out to preach" (Mark 3:14 cp. Luke 8:1; Mark 6:7-8). "With him," they could observe preaching at its best. Then "sent out," they could try their own hands at it. They were taught by Jesus, then taught by experience. The earliest disciples turned the world upside down. They learned well how to preach. Latter day disciples, instructed by the same teacher, can anticipate the same results.

STUDY TO THINK CLEARLY

James Moffatt's translation of Proverbs 13:17 speaks volumes: "A careless messenger is a calamity." To avoid such a calamity, "Do not be quick with your mouth" (Ecclesiastes 5:2), "be slow to speak" (James 1:19). Only open your mouth when you can say, "The Sovereign LORD has given me an instructed tongue" (Isaiah 50:4).

Thinking precedes speaking or regret follows it. Prior to the commission, "go preach," were the many occasions when Christ took "the Twelve aside" (Matthew 10:33). Quiet occasions without distraction were necessary for clarity of message. The records read, "Jesus did not want anyone to know where they were, because he was teaching his disciples" (Matthew 9:30-31). A "gift of gab" can be a curse. Gifts of knowledge, wisdom and discernment can be a blessing. Only the latter gains the respect of the people. Let your ears and eyes get their full-week's exercise before your mouth begins its Sunday morning jog. Hours of serious reflection will enhance the minutes of pulpit projection. To go on and on with fluent speech, while not first gaining lucid clarity of thought, is to say nothing of substance and to accomplish no goal of significance. Unless the preacher has fed his own soul with inner enrichment, the flock will disperse at the benediction not having enjoyed the expected refreshments from God's "green pastures" or "quiet waters" (Psalm 23:2).

Let him speak "who correctly handles the word of truth" (II Timothy 2:15). That demands a thorough hermeneutical grasp by thinking through a text's literary and historical context in the light of the teaching of the whole Bible. Let him "Preach the Word" who is "prepared" (II Timothy 4:2) and "thoroughly equipped" (II Timothy 3:17). That requires endless hours, following Jesus' early example of "sitting among the teachers, listening to them and asking them questions" (Luke 2:46). It also demands following the apostles' awareness that it would never be "right . . . to neglect the ministry of the word of God" (Acts 6:4).

The people of the world do not trust an amateur to play surgeon, when a critical and life-threatening operation faces them. The people in the pew want no half-prepared person dealing with their eternal souls. They want a preacher who manifests evidence that he is "God . . . approved" and a "workman who does not need to be ashamed" (II Timothy 2:15).

STUDY TO SPEAK ACCURATELY

If there is even a slim chance that Matthew 12:36-37 will be used at the final judgment, preachers had better shape up. It reads, "I tell you that men will have to give account on the day of judgment for every careless word they have spoken. For by your words you will be acquitted, and by your words you will be condemned." Preachers work with words, like craftsmen work with tools. Is there a professional golfer that is not careful in his choice of clubs, or an avid fisherman that does not carefully select his lures? Words are the sum and substance of sermons. They are to be selected with precision.

Sloven English, faulty grammar, poorly chosen terms and incorrect pronunciation are the four horsemen announcing apocalyptic-doom to any message that contains them. There will be times when men with closed minds will label each of God's best prophets as a "fool" or "maniac" (Hosea 9:7), but don't let the charge stick. Even Paul felt the criticism of the so-called "super apostles" for not being "a trained speaker" (II Corinthians 11:6), but history lists him among the world's great orators. Moses also felt himself "never (to have) been eloquent," but ever to have been "slow of speech and tongue" (Exodus 4:10), yet three world religions (Judaism, Christianity, Islam) look to him as God's mouthpiece.

What are we to conclude as we see who God has used in Old Testament, New Testament and modern times? "Not many . . . were wise by human standards. . . . But God chose the foolish things of the world to shame the wise . . . so that no one may boast" (I Corinthians 1:26-29). That means Christ's sufficiency makes up for our lacks. That means you and I can be used. But, let us develop and make the most of the few talents we have. He is able to mold a preacher out of you. He made Adam out of a handful of dust. Dwight L. Moody heard that the world was waiting to see what God could do out of a man totally dedicated to him. Moody's determination was to be that man. He doesn't need to be the only one.

8

THE PREACHER'S ORDINATION

Many are the questions each embrionic preacher asks. Have I been called? Do I meet the requirements? Am I properly trained? Is the church ready for me? Can I be ordained?

To ask what the Bible says about ordination is to ask a Herculean question and to only find a midget answer. There is very little said. But like an atom that is not large but has world shaking power, so is the small amount of New Testament material on "the laying on of hands."

THE OLD TESTAMENT BACKGROUND

In Jewish tradition the laying on of hands seemed to illustrate either the transference of (1) guilt, or (2) blessing, or (3) responsibility.

(1) Guilt. In making a sin offering Aaron and his sons were to

"bring the bull to the front of the Tent of Meeting, and . . . lay their hands on its head" (Exodus 29:10). Israelites were to present burnt offerings of a male without defect from their herds with the order, "to lay his hand on the head of the burnt offering, and it will be accepted in his behalf to make atonement for him" (Leviticus 1:4 cp. 4:4). If a people can transfer their guilt symbolically to one who will represent them, it is not difficult to see how that same people can transfer, by the same symbol of laying on of hands, a ministry to a representative person.

(2) Blessing. The earliest of the Old Testament books relates the incident of Jacob blessing Joseph's sons Ephraim and Manasseh. The account reads, "Israel reached out his right hand and put it on Ephraim's head, though he was the younger, and crossing his arms put his left hand on Manasseh's head, even though Manasseh was the firstborn" (Genesis 48:14). The first portion of the New Testament, the Gospels, shows Jesus carrying on the practice of blessing children by the laying on of his hands. Matthew tells how "little children were brought to Jesus for him to place his hands on them and pray for them" (19:13,15 cp. Mark 10:13). Mark gives the tender account that "he took the children in his arms, put his hands on them and blessed them" (10:16).

It was not only children that felt his touch. Even in skeptical Nazareth, Jesus did "lay his hands on a few sick people and heal them" (Mark 6:5). At Bethesda a blind man "begged Jesus to touch him" and the touch of his hands brought the blessing of sight (Mark 8:22-25). In a synagogue a woman crippled for eighteen years found the blessing of a straightened back because "he put his hands on her" (Luke 13:10-13). Lepers, with whom men tried avoiding the contaminating touch, found cure at the touch of Jesus' compassionate heart and healing hands (Mark 1:41-42). Let the records show that "various kinds of sickness" can be healed by Christ's "laying his hands on each one" (Luke 4:40). And let the mind grasp that the "laying on of hands" often symbolizes the reception of blessing, even the highest blessing of the privilege of ministry.

(3) Responsibility. A third significance in the Old Testament of the laying on of hands was to symbolize induction into office or consecration for service. The Lord instructed Moses, "You are to bring the Levites before the LORD, and the Israelites are to lay their hands on them . . . so that they may be ready to do the work of the LORD" (Numbers 8:10-11). Later Moses was directed, "Take Joshua son of Nun, a man in whom is the spirit, and lay your hand on him" (Numbers 27:18,23; Deuteronomy 34:9). Did that practice flow over into the time of the early church? Jewish rabbis came to lay hands on their pupils when they were considered ready to teach. How was it in the Christian community?

THE NEW TESTAMENT PASSAGES

A book in a series titled *What the Bible Says* can not reach into either Roman Catholic or Protestant traditions. It ought to examine the pure water at its New Testament source before the pollutants of time make a mix with the impurities of other sectarian traditions and practices.

Other religions from the prophets of Baal to the priests of modern sects have their clergy. These are marked to the eye by special robes and to the ear by special titles. The Lord of the church warned his disciples: "Beware of the teachers of the law. They like to walk in flowing robes" (Luke 20:46). There was a perceived danger in coveting special greeting in the streets and special seats of honor at banquets. To make "phylacteries wide and . . . tassels of . . . prayer shawls long" and to love the title "Rabbi," was to walk near the edge of a fatal precipice (Matthew 23:7-10). We say Jesus was a convincing speaker, but a modern glance down the halls of Christendom leaves the impression that not everyone that calls Jesus Lord has paid close attention to what he taught on this matter.

The New Testament reveals a division of labor in the church.

Hands were laid on deacons (Acts 6:6), elders (Acts 14:23), evangelists (I Timothy 4:13) and missionaries (Acts 13:3). They did the work assigned but seemed to be known more for the tasks accomplished than the titles worn — more for the lives they lived than the attire in which they were garbed.

The incidences of laying on of hands, installing a believer to a particular work, seem not to have qualified a man for his task but to have been a recognition that he was considered by the church as qualified for the job. The "deacons" in Acts 6 did not become recipients of the Holy Spirit at their ordination, but rather received the laying on of hands because the Jerusalem church selected them on the grounds that they were "known to be full of the Spirit" (Acts 6:3,5). As surely as the early church baptized converts, not to make them penitent believers but because they saw them to be such, so they "sent" out workers in whom they recognized the essential marks of ministry (Romans 10:15).

The inner call of God's Holy Spirit, recognized by the external call of God's church, is what we today call ordination. To be "sent" is to enter a work with the support of the church community. Not every member of the Antioch church could touch Barnabas and Saul, when they were "set apart for the work to which (they were) called;" but the ones who with fasting and prayer did place "their hands on them," were representative of all the others (Acts 13:2-3). What a powerful asset the worker has who goes to his task knowing he has the undergirding of a praying congregation. One hesitates to call Paul's commissioning to do mission work among Gentiles an "ordination," for he had been preaching for years. Installation to a special work it was. He had been "appointed a herald" (I Timothy 2:7) long years before. We might say he had church hands laid on him at Antioch, but he had nail-pierced hands touch him on the road to Damascus. Yet the human hands that sent him on a journey to Cyprus and Galatia had become folded hands of supplication during his missionary journey. Hence at the end of the mission, Paul and Barnabas "sailed back to Antioch, where they had been committed to the grace of God for the work they had now completed" (Acts 14:26).

The clearest text on the ordination of a preacher is I Timothy 4:14. It speaks of "the body of elders" laying hands on Timothy. At that very occasion, the Apostle Paul conferred a miraculous gift. Paul writes that this gift was in Timothy "through the laying on of (his) hands" (II Timothy 1:6). It is important to note that elders' hands can make a community aware that a person is being set aside to "do the work of an evangelist" (II Timothy 4:5). It is essential to observe that only apostolic hands could give miraculous powers (cp. Acts 6:6,8; 8:18; 19:6).

"The laying on of hands" is included in "the elementary teachings about Christ" (Hebrews 6:2). It is a serious act and not one to be done lightly. Good advice, that will keep the church from bad days, is, "Do not be hasty in the laying on of hands" (I Timothy 5:22). When it is done regarding deacon, preacher or elder, it does not have to be for life. Our limited Scriptures on the subject lead to the belief that a congregation is justified in setting aside workers for greater or lesser amounts of time, with greater or lesser amounts of remuneration. Each congregation is left with a great amount of freedom. No detailed pattern exists. But let the train be kept moving down the track on the solid rails of "fitting" and "orderly" (I Corinthians 14:40).

9

THE PREACHER'S LIMITATIONS

Are there limitations in my Bible or my culture as to who may preach? Must one be of a certain race, a certain age, a certain marital status or a certain gender?

That is a question of more than academic interest. Over five billion people live on our planet and their salvation depends on preaching (Romans 10:15). Just who can legitimately train for such a task?

More than half the world's population are Hindus, Muslims or Chinese. By the year 2000, if present rates continue, only 16% of our world will be Christian. What if an unmarried man wants to help reach the million converts needed each four or five days to just hold our own? Would that be Scriptural? What if your granddaughter set out to train for teaching on a mission field and assist in winning the one soul per second needed over thirty-two years if at least one billion of earth's people could know Jesus? Would that be a sin?

If Paul can say to young preacher Timothy, "Don't let anyone look down on you because you are young" (I Timothy 4:12), could he say to Titus, "Don't let anyone look down on you because you are an uncircumcised Greek?" Would it be right to tell missionary Paul himself, "Don't let anyone look down on you because you are single rather than married?" Dare anyone whisper to a potential Euodia or Syntyche desiring to contend "in the cause of the gospel" (Philippians 4:2-3), "Don't let anyone look down on you because of your femininity?"

Jeremiah faced the age-question and objected to God's call, arguing, "I do not know how to speak, I am only a child." The Lord responded, "Do not say, 'I am only a child.' You must go to everyone I send you to" (Jeremiah 1:6-7). Elihu's conversation with Job reflects the accepted norm that wisdom comes with age. He said, "I am young in years, and you are old; and that is why I was fearful, not daring to tell you what I know. I thought, 'Age should speak; advanced years should teach wisdom.' But it is the spirit in a man, the breath of the Almighty, that gives him understanding. It is not only the old who are wise, nor only the aged who understand what is right. Therefore I say: Listen to me; I too will tell you what I know" (Job 32:6-10). Peter's sermon, on the first day of the church, announced the fulfillment of Joel's prophecy (2:28) of "the last days" (the Christian era), when "sons and daughters" would prophesy from the "young men" to the "old men" (Acts 2:16-17). There would be spheres in which every age level could teach the new faith. But, what of the part of that prophecy that told of God's Spirit falling on "women" and their joining in the work of prophesying (Acts 2:18)? That is the question of all questions in our day.

I preached sixteen years in a church started by a woman. Did she do wrong in preaching to the few who gathered in her home during the congregation's earliest years? I recently visited a wonderfully fruitful missionary work in a foreign land started by two single girls forty years before. Had they done the right thing, or should they have waited until men rose up and volunteered for the task? Several Bible colleges have potential preachers receiving their training in ministry from women professors. Is such a school under God's curse or blessing?

Let's seek our answer from the Scripture in three steps. First let us note the prominence of women in the New Testament, then the seeming prohibitions against women in Paul's writings and lastly the proper place for women in today's church.

THE PROMINENCE OF WOMEN IN THE NEW TESTAMENT

The soil into which the gospel seed was first planted was hard soil, resistant to the idea that "in Christ" there would no longer be "Jew nor Greek, slave nor free, male nor female" (Galatians 3:28). Every Jewish boy had learned from his father to thank God each morning that he was neither born a Gentile, nor a slave, nor a woman. His visits to the Jerusalem temple revealed to him its special area named the Court of the Women. There mothers and sisters had to remain behind, while only the men could ascend steps leading to the Court of Israel. That same distinction was echoed in every local Synagogue, where some special removed section — often the gallery — was to hold the females and separate them from view. It was unheard of for a female to have a part in leadership at a Sabbath service. Only males read the Scriptures, for the women were not allowed to learn the Law. It was not for them to teach in the Synagogue school, even though the students were children.

In spite of the low status of women in Israel, it was several notches above that of their sisters in the Greek world. A Jewish woman might be one step above a "thing" to be used as a husband or father willed. But remember Corinth, where the Temple of Aphrodite used a thousand girls at a time for sacred prostitution and recall Ephesus where the Temple of Diana similarly consumed a hundred priestesses in similar activity.

The whole world of Bible times let women be in the background, often not eating with the male members of their family. At least God's Old Covenant people had received his laws for women's protection, knew a better lot than their neighbors in Mesopotamia, Arabia and Egypt and found praise for their success in being "a wife of noble character" (Proverbs 31:10). Did not the Jew's Bible tell of Huldah (II Kings 22:14; II Chronicles 34:22-23), Abigail (I Samuel 25:3) and Noadiah (Nehemiah 6:14)? As the sun was about to set on the old dispensation and Jesus was born, God still used "a prophetess, Anna" (Luke 2:36) as well as a prophet, John (Matthew 21:6).

Then came Jesus with no "patriarchal ax to grind or . . . 'male ego' to defend," according to Dorothy Sayers in her book, *Are Women Human*? Jesus had the Twelve travel with him "from one town and village to another, proclaiming the good news of the kingdom of God." Not only were " the Twelve with him . . . also some women" were (Luke 8:1-3). Jesus could be found "talking with a woman" (John 4:27) and his Gospels tell of many Samaritans coming to faith by a "woman's testimony" (John 4:39). A Martha may play a helpful role in the kitchen, but a Mary can be commended for choosing spiritual instruction above material serving (Luke 10:42).

In Matthew, Mark, Luke and John women are not only mentioned favorably, they take a prominent part. Christ taught women openly and healed them by his touch. He chose to let Mary bring him into the world at birth. He felt the comfort of women, who stood by as he suffered from the cross. He appeared after his resurrection first to women and asked their help in getting the resurrection fact known to his men.

It is, therefore, no wonder to read that the first church in all the world grows out of a prayer-meeting of one hundred and twenty that consisted of the eleven apostles "along with the women and Mary the mother of Jesus" (Acts 1:14). If Sapphira came into the church with her husband Ananias (Acts 5:1), it is reasonable to conclude that many wives were following their husband's lead into the Christian faith. Luke records the fact that "more and more men and women believed in the Lord and were added to their number" (Acts 5:14). Saul of Tarsus, the persecutor, was dragging into prison "men and women" (Acts 8:3) and Philip the evangelist was baptizing "both men and women" (Acts 8:12).

Prominent on the pages of Acts are women like Dorcas (9:41), Mary, the mother of Mark (12:12), Rhoda, the servant girl (12:13), Lydia, the seller of purple dye (16:14), Priscilla, wife of Aquila (18:26), Philip the evangelist's daughters (21:9) and the "prominent women" of Thessalonica (17:4) and Berea (17:12). The greetings that fill most of the last chapter of Romans call Phoebe "a servant of the church" (16:1), Priscilla a "fellow worker" (16:3) and Mary a "hard" worker (16:6) along with Tryphena, Tryphosa and Persis (16:12). He also names Julia and the sister of Nereus (16:15). Euodia and Syntyche are added to the list of New Testament "women who have contended . . . in the cause of the gospel" (Philippians 4:3). Paul would never leave out Eunice and Lois, who got Timothy started out right (II Timothy 1:5).

With all this pro-women talk in the New Testament, why the question: "to speak or not to speak?" Women have sensitivity and feeling for people. They today do not fall behind men in Biblical understanding, mental astuteness and speaking ability. Was Samuel Johnson (1709-1784) reflecting Biblical truth or masculine prejuduce when he railed, according to Boswell's *Life of Johnson*, "Sir, a woman preaching is like a dog's walking on his hind legs. It is not done well; but you are surprised to find it done at all!" Or, was George E. Sweazey closer to the truth when he wrote, on page 302 of his *Preaching the Good News* (Englewood Cliffs, New Jersey: Prentiss Hall Inc., 1976), "The Church has been impoverished by not using for its preaching the mental and spiritual endowments of half its members." We need to turn to "What the Bible Says" and not to "How do I feel about it?"

THE PROHIBITIONS AGAINST WOMEN SPEAKING IN PAUL'S WRITINGS

Just last year I heard a speaker argue that women were to have no place of leadership or speaking in a church assembly. He spoke of two New Testament passages as "un-get-around-able." There was the "women should remain silent in the churches" of I Corinthians 14:34 and the "I do not permit a woman to teach or to have authority over a man" of I Timothy 2:12.

A study of most any dozen or so commentaries will reveal instantly that, while the texts may well be "un-get-around-able," many scholars give it a noble try. But, leaving the scholars aside, my friends on both sides of the issue have no desire to get around the Bible's teaching, but rather sincerely want to be clear on what that teaching is. They are searching to find what light the literary and historical contexts throw on the passage. They also want to discover if the English translators gave the exact meaning of the Greek words Paul wrote.

Take I Corinthians 14:33-36 first of all. The paragraph reads: "As in all the congregations of the saints, women should remain silent in the churches. They are not allowed to speak, but must be in submission, as the Law says. If they want to inquire about something, they should ask their own husbands at home; for it is disgraceful for a woman to speak in the church. Did the word of God originate with you? Or are you the only people it has reached?"

Contextually Paul is dealing one by one with problems in the Corinthian church. Chapters 12-14 speak to problems relating to charismatic gifts and the previous chapter 11 has to do with worship gatherings. In 11:5 women are instructed how to attire themselves when they pray and prophesy.

The main topic of 11:2-16 is the veil. Should Corinthian women defy convention and shock their neighbors? Without the veil would Greeks classify them as *hetairae*, or loose women? Paul with missionary concern, asked the women coming to assembly to abide by the custom of their society. He appealed to theology (vv. 3-8), common sense (v. 13), nature (vv. 14-15) and to custom (v. 16). Let no one be "contentious about this" was Paul's bottom line. He did not approve of their breaking custom and added, "nor do the churches of God." Let the women pray and prophesy veiled.

Hard questions rise. Do we insist on the required silence of Chapter 14? Were they both part of the temporary customs or of the eternal gospel? If the women were praying and prophesying in the earlier chapter, why is total silence demanded in the later? Did Paul change his mind? If the Holy Spirit gives his gifts "just as he determines" (I Corinthians 12:11), why would he give the gift of prophecy to a woman, if she is not to do any speaking?

Which option shall we choose? Option one is that in every church gathering women are to be silent. Option two is to call the verses 34 and 35 spurious and not written by Paul. Codex Bezae and its related Western manuscripts have the verses at the close of the 14th chapter. Could the words be a marginal gloss — an addition by a later writer? Option three is that the Apostle Paul is inconsistent, denying in chapter 14 what he allowed in chapter 11. Option four is that two different kinds of meetings are under discussion, with the earlier chapter dealing with an informal gathering of some believers (perhaps segregated according to sex) and the later with the regular assembly of the entire congregation. Option five is to relegate the teaching to the first century, when cultural customs were different. Option six is that Paul could be quoting a view of the Corinthians, to which he would respond. If 14:34-35 is what Corinthians were saying to Paul, then verse 36 would be his reply.

If the words are Paul's in 14:34-35, and they very well could be, what were they asking? As the apostle dealt with the spiritual gifts issue, his concern was that everything contribute to mutual edification and nothing to congregational confusion. "God is not a God of disorder but of peace" (I Corinthians 14:33). A God-given gift to edify the body must never be misused, so that it become an opportunity for private exhibition.

Paul had already called on tongue speakers to recognize times they are to "keep quiet" (v. 28) and for prophets to "stop" (v. 30). He next asked women to "remain silent" (v. 34). There was a proper time and place for persons from each group to speak. There were other occasions when it would be "not allowed" (v. 34). Noise control would enable the gospel to be heard without interference.

Visualize the situation. Women were seated apart from their husbands, as was the custom. A revelation was being given by a prophet. Women were chattering, calling to their children and the prophet's wife was embarrasing her husband by calling for him to explain something he or the previous prophet had said. She may even have been teaching an alternate view by the questions she was pressing or the interjected remarks she was making. The Greek of the word "ask" means to interrogate as in cross-examination. Her repeated question after question was dominating the learning situation, as if she were the teacher.

Order could be restored if the woman would grill her husband at home. Her questions were important and her learning was vital, but the home with its privacy would be the better learning situation. The edification of the larger body was to take precedence and she was to hush. It was "disgraceful" to disrupt worship and violate the community's established decorum.

It is hard to envision a similar situation in today's church in our part of the world. Women no longer sit veiled in a separate part of the building where saints assemble. Gifts of revelation are not coming at each gathering. Ever since the apostolic age closed, the gospel has been fully revealed for all time. Single girls, widowed wives and Biblically illiterate women have no knowledgeable "husbands at home" to ask. Is the unique problem of this temporary situation to prohibit all women of every time to ever utter a sound? The "remain silent," enjoined in I Corinthians 14:34, means act quietly. "Act quietly" is the meaning of σιγάω and an orderly service is the result.

The most "un-get-around-able" of the "un-get-around-able" texts is I Timothy 2:11-15. It reads, "A woman should learn in quietness and full submission. I do not permit a woman to teach or to have authority over a man; she must be silent. For Adam was formed first, then Eve. And Adam was not the one who was deceived; it was the woman who was deceived and became a sinner. But women will be kept safe through childbirth, if they continue in faith, love and holiness with propriety." Timothy throughout Asia, like Titus throughout Crete, was to "straighten out" or "set in order" (KJV) the work of every congregation (Titus 1:5). The written document in hand would give apostolic authorization for the corrective work of Timothy. He was to examine the public worship (chapter 2) and the qualified leadership (3).

Paul struck out at an attidude that was rising in some that would harm the church. Instead of the beauty of "quietness," there was the ugliness of a dominating spirit. He would not permit αὐθενέω over men. This word, used only here in all the Bible, is translated "have authority over," or "dictate to" (Moffatt), or "domineer over" (NEB). It is not fitting that women take absolute power over men, as some in Ephesus were proposing. Subjection to one another and a quiet, peaceful humble spirit offered the better way. The modest dress of verses 9 and 10 better fit a woman whose interest was worshiping God rather than capturing attention to self. The excercise of voluntary self-restraint would bring both glory to God and converts to Christ faster than shocking the heathen neighborhood.

Eve, created to be a help-meet for her husband, when taking to herself the leadership position, became responsible for evil to get a foothold. She "was deceived" and the result was fatal. The seeking to be "over a man" was the Satanic lure.

Women can teach and have authority, according to other Scriptures. They could "teach what is good . . . (and) train younger women" (Titus 2:3-4). The "men" Timothy was to recruit for qualified teaching were people of either gender. (He used the generic ἄνθρωπος not the specific ἀνήρ, II Timothy 2:2.) He was looking for faithful persons. Women were needed to teach but were not, autocratically nor ostentatiously to usurp a man's position.

There is something good to be said for "quietness" (ἡσυχία and for living "peaceful and quiet lives" (I Timothy 2:2). Paul takes aim at extravagances that resulted from Christ's emancipation of women. Let them remember Eve's God-given role of a "suitable helper" to Adam (Genesis 2:20). Let them not forget that no role imagined could top the joy and responsibility of bringing children into the world and nurturing them. Such was a higher calling that attending meetings and addressing them. Let them avoid like a plague the self-assertive attitude that demanded the eye of the world rather than the heart of God.

THE PLACE OF WOMEN IN TODAY'S CHURCH

It is a fact that no women wrote any portion of the Old or New Testaments. It is a fact that, in choosing his twelve apostles, Jesus' selections were male. It is a fact that, when Christ picked the special apostle for the uncircumcised, his choice was a Paul and not a Pauline. It is a fact that the elders of the Christian congregations in Apostolic times were men.

These facts still leave us with the question "Why?" Was it Jesus' intention to reveal that this was the way God wanted it to be over the future centuries of the church, whatever the social changes? Or was it, rather, the best route to take in light of the cultural mores of the day and the evangelistic urgencies of the hour?

Upon coming to a decision on whether women should be ordained as preachers today, at the very least there must be consistency. Can we reject "veils" and still opt only for "males?" That is, can we label one instruction by Paul cultural and the other eternal without a clearer reason than one's own feelings on the matter?

Culture is under and not over the gospel. Christianity laid the very foundation for social changes. The message of freedom in Christ was the planted seed that brought forth the emancipation of slaves and womankind. As the church moved across the world, it met some cultures it rejected, some it modified and some it embraced. Can a Jew preach to a Gentile? Paul is God's answer to that question. Can a Gentile bring the good-news to a Jew? Luke is God's answer. Can youth tell the story to persons of older years? Timothy is God's reply.

There are parts of our world today where the culture would put limits on women leading in Christian worship. That is a different issue from heaven sent limitations. Where an Apollos needs instruction, let some Priscilla not hesitate to invite him to her home and explain "the way of God more adequately" (Acts 18:26). When God gifts daughters of some evangelist to teach, let them use their gift modestly and effectively rather than bury it unused (Acts 21:8). There is always enough work in the gospel to be done to keep every sister busy in the sphere her culture allows without murmuring about the limitations set. The gospel "is the power of God for the salvation of everyone who believes" (Romans 1:16), whether the voice that speaks it in sound is soprano or bass and whether it is proclaimed publicly or privately. There are also more ways to help spread the life-saving message than in public discourse. To "manage" one's home is church work (I Timothy 5:14). To "train the younger women to love their husbands and children" is church work (Titus 2:4). To travel with and be supportive of a preaching husband is church work (I Corinthians 9:5). To bring a lesson or pray on behalf of a congregation, when asked by its elders, is church work. The only Scriptural limitation is never to domineer "over a man" (I Timothy 2:11). The attitude of servanthood is ever welcomed. The love "to be first" is ever unfitting (III John 9). Stand ready to enter any field of service "the body of elders" (I Timothy 4:14) request. There is division of labor in the body of Christ, but not hierarchy of importance. "Obey your leaders and submit to their authority"

(Hebrews 13:17) was and is excellent advice. Seek to serve and not to gain power. Prudence suggests each person to act for the good of Christ's cause and for the need of our age.

In a world so desperate for the saving gospel, what Christian is not glad to sing the ancient Psalm, "The LORD gives the word: the women that publish the tidings are a great host" (68:11).

Part Three
THE MESSAGE
(THE WHAT'S WHAT OF PREACHING)

10

PROCLAIMING THE TRUTH

"What shall I preach?" is not an unanswered question in the Bible. God not only commissions men to preach, He tells them what to say. When the Lord sent Jonah to the city of Nineveh His order was specific: "Proclaim to it the message I give you" (Jonah 3:2). That God-given message to today's church and for today's world can be phrased in a variety of ways. We preach "the good news of God" (Mark 1:15) and of His "kingdom" (Luke 16:16). That means we herald the story of "Christ crucified" (I Corinthians 1:23) and "in Jesus the resurrection of the dead" (Acts 4:2). To "preach the Word" (II Timothy 4:2) is "preaching the faith" (Galatians 1:23) and "telling . . the way to be saved" (Acts 16:17). "Repentance and forgiveness of sins" is "preached in his (Christ's) name" (Luke 24:47), as is "peace" (Ephesians 2:17) and "the unsearchable riches of Christ" (Ephesians 3:8).

A reading of the New Testament underscores that doctrine matters to the One who commissions messengers to preach. A herald needs a strong voice, but the greater requirement is a strong and sound theology. "Sound doctrine" was a must for Titus (Titus 2:1) and "sound teaching" an essential for Timothy (II Timothy 1:13). "False doctrines," that do "not agree to the sound instruction of our Lord Jesus Christ" (I Timothy 6:3), are not to be heard from any Christian pulpit.

The greatest teacher of all time often punctuated His messages with "verily I say unto you." The ἀμήν or "amen" means "truly," approving that what is being said is the truth. Count how many times in Matthew's Gospel Jesus began "I tell you the truth" (18:18; 19:23,28; 21:31; 23:36; 24:34,47; 26:34,68). Reading the same are the Gospels of Mark (9:1,41; 10:15,29; 12:43; 14:9,30), of Luke (4:24; 12:44; 18:29; 21:32) and of John (1:51; 3:3,5; 5:19,24,25; 6:53; 8:34,51,58; 13:16,21; 14:12; 16:7,20,23; 21:18). How could Christ's messages contain anything but truth, when He Himself claimed to be "the way and the truth and the life" (John 14:6)? How could Jesus' apostles preach any lie or half-truth, while filled by His Spirit — "the Spirit of truth" (John 14:17)?

Paul affirmed, "I speak the truth in Christ — I am not lying, my conscience confirms it in the Holy Spirit" (Romans 9:1). He commended himself to all hearers "in truthful speech" (II Corinthians 6:7). He labeled his words, "sound doctrine" (I Timothy 1:10) or the "trustworthy message" (Titus 1:9). Angels, agreeing with what all apostles taught, shouted, "These words are trustworthy and true" (Revelation 22:6).

God speaks to all who preach in His name, "Let the one who had my word speak it faithfully. For what has straw to do with grain" (Jeremiah 23:28)? Let every herald of Christ say with Job, "My tongue will utter no deceit" (Job 27:4) and with Elihu, "Be assured that my words are not false" (Job 36:4). Let each congregation of Christ, remember the warning of their Messiah, "Watch out for false prophets" (Matthew 7:15). Let the church be cognizant that believers, who do not walk defensively, can "be carried away by all kinds of strange teachings" (Hebrews 13:9).

How can "we recognize the Spirit of truth and the spirit of falsehood" (I John 4:6)? There is a distinctive difference and *"Vive la difference!"*

THE DIFFERENT SOURCE

Truth is single. Error is multiple. If one doctrine on a subject is right, then all other doctrines are wrong. Listen to John: "Dear friends, do not believe every spirit, but test the spirits to see whether they are from God, because many false prophets have gone out into the world. This is how you can recognize the Spirit of God: Every spirit that acknowledges that Jesus Christ has come in the flesh is from God" (I John 4:1-2). Contrasting the false teachers with the preachers of the gospel, John continues, "They are from the world and therefore speak from the viewpoint of the world, and the world listens to them. We are from God, and whoever knows God listens to us; but whoever is not from God does not listen to us. This is how we recognize the Spirit of truth and the spirit of falsehood" (I John 4:5-6).

Nothing could be clearer. The source of truth is God. The origin of error is Satan. The truth is the revelation of God brought to the world by the incarnate Jesus. His apostles, of which John is the last, have passed that revelation of God's grace on to the church. The error of substitute gospels is the work of antichrists. Their alternative teachings are legion to better confound the unwary.

Jesus taught that, when Satan "lies, he speaks his native language, for he is a liar and the father of lies" (John 8:44). In contrast the Son of God did "but speak just what the Father has taught" (John 8:28). Describing His true follower, Jesus made this distinction: "His (Christ's) sheep follow him because they know his voice. But they will never follow a stranger; in fact, they will run away from him because they do not recognize a stranger's voice" (John 10:4-5,16). Those who "teach the way of God in accordance with the truth" (Matthew 22:16 cp. Mark 12:14), are following their Lord's example. They recognize, as did He, that "rules taught by men" and "traditions of men" can "nullify the word of God" (Mark 7:7-8,13).

To make his Satanic substitutes more palatable, the Devil labels the products "the wisdom of this age" (I Corinthians 2:6). But peel away the veneer and the Serpent's work is clear, the main product is lies. The foolish soul trades the genuine "truths of the faith and of the good teaching" for "godless myths and old wives' tales" (I Timothy 4:6-7). The wiser person "will pay no attention to Jewish myths" (Titus 1:14) and will "not follow cleverly invented stories" (II Peter 1:16). Why follow some Jezebel just because she "calls herself a prophetess" and claims to have "learned Satan's so-called deep secrets" (Revelation 2:20,24)? Why go the way of "Baal," in order to "commit adultery and live a lie" (Jeremiah 23:13-14)?

Not all preachers are true preachers any more than all prophets in Israel were true prophets. Some even declare, " 'This is what the Sovereign LORD says' — when the LORD has not spoken" (Ezekiel 22:28). The fact of the matter is they "Prophesy out of their own imagination" and "follow their own spirit (and) . . . their visions" are "false and their divinations a lie" (Ezekiel 13:2-3,6). Jeremiah, a voice for God, could say of his time, "The prophets prophesy lies" (5:31). He could reveal that he knew of men claiming to be a voice for Jehovah, yet God Himself was rejecting their messages with the refutation, "I did not send them" (Jeremiah 14:15). The clear ringing warning from God to Israel was, "Do not listen to what the (false) prophets are prophesying to you . . . they speak visions from their own minds, not from the mouth of the LORD. . . . I did not send these prophets, yet they have run with their message; I did not speak to them, yet they have prophesied" (Jeremiah 23:16,21). They are men "who steal words from one another supposedly from (God) . . . who wag their own tongues and yet declare, 'The LORD declares' " (Jeremiah 23:30-31). Hananiah was one such prophet that "Persuaded this nation (Israel) to trust in lies" (Jeremiah 28:15).

Add to the warnings of Jeremiah those of Isaiah. In light of the fact that truth comes from heaven and error from hell, where ought God's people to turn? Here is Isaiah's sign-post, pointing the way: "When men tell you to consult mediums and spirits, who whisper and mutter, should not a people inquire of their God? . . . to the law and to the testimony?" (8:19-20). Turning to astrology, or to the stars, is the depth and height of foolishness. Astrology can be spelled astray-ology, as far as the Christian is concerned. The only "ology" that leads to God is Christology.

Preacher, pay attention. It matters what you preach. Truth is to be taught. Error is to be refuted. Once the source is recognized, the distinction in message is apparent. Declare with Paul, "the gospel I preached is not something that man made up" (Galatians 1:11). Shout with Balaam, "I must speak only what God puts in my mouth" Numbers 22:38). State with Jesus, "I came . . . to testify to the truth" (John 18:37). Before you communicate, learn the message worthy of communication. Before you seek to be relevant, know the Lord's truth that deserves to be made relevant. Then, instead of being "infants, tossed back and forth by the waves, and blown here and there by every wind of teaching . . . (be) speaking the truth in love" (Ephesians 4:14-15).

THE DIFFERENT RESULT

The reason Jesus told His disciples "to guard against . . . the teaching of the Pharisees and Sadducees" (Matthew 16:12) was that the consequence of what is taught cannot be avoided. "Blind guides" (Matthew 23:16) would not lead their followers to safety. As Paul instructed Timothy, "Watch your . . . doctrine closely . . . because if you do, you will save both yourself and your hearers" (I Timothy 4:16). Peter was right in labeling the teaching of the false prophets "destructive heresies" and he was correct in revealing the end result of error, as bringing "the way of truth into disrepute" (II Peter 2:1-2). Instead of it not mattering what one teaches, John warns that error does "lead you astray" (I John 2:26). Paul agrees that errorists "deceive . . . with empty words" (Ephesians 5:6).

May it never be written of you that "by your teaching (you) have caused many to stumble" (Malachi 2:8). All who do preach error "will bear their guilt" (Ezekiel 14:10). Determine with Solomon "to speak what is right" (Proverbs 8:6), knowing full well that "the LORD detests lying lips" (Proverbs 12:22). Such a one "who pours out lies will perish" (Proverbs 19:9).

Why such a harsh penalty for those "teaching things they ought not to teach" (Titus 1:11)? Such teaching is not innocent. It "ruins those who listen" and it does "spread like gangrene," with the result that it does "destroy the faith of some" (II Timothy 2:14-18). "False and misleading" (Lamentations 2:14) sermons, by "prophets who teach lies" (Isaiah 9:14), deserve God's judgment. His will is that the one who represents Him be a messenger "who speaks from his heart" (Psalm 15:2) and who "speaks what is right" (Isaiah 33:15). Let each preacher "be careful how he builds" each message, for "fire will test the quality of each man's work" (I Corinthians 3:10,13). God has declared, "no one who speaks falsely will stand in my presence" (Psalm 101:7).

THE DIFFERENT NATURE

Once the determination is made to speak truth because its source is God and its consequence is blessing, the need becomes to learn the traits of error. The reason for that is so it quickly can be shunned. Once one recognizes the nature of truth, it firmly can be embraced. Jesus is the norm of truth. Satan is the model of error.

Be careful here. "Satan himself masquerades as an angel of

light. It is not surprising, then, if his servants masquerade as servants of righteousness" (II Corinthians 11:14-15). The arch-deceiver can best lead "the whole world astray" (Revelation 12:9) by assuming the role of the gospel preacher. Disguised as a spokesman for God, the devil dupes the naive who do not look beyond the outward appearance. Deception is the Devil's specialty.

Jesus' words of warning to His followers must not fall on deaf ears. He said, "Watch out that no one deceives you . . . many false prophets will appear and deceive many people" (Matthew 24:11,24). He even called for alertness against some who would profess to prophesy in His name and report to have performed many miracles (Matthew 7:22). All that can be faked. The "fruit" of Christ-like lives, produced over time by the message, is the test of genuineness.

Unable to stop holiness of character, the Serpent sets out to "deceive . . . by fine sounding arguments" (Colossians 2:4). He makes a case by "godless chatter and . . . what is falsely called knowledge" (I Timothy 6:20). With "speech . . . smoother than oil" (Proverbs 5:3), a false teacher "disguises himself with his lips" and uses "speech (that) is charming" (Proverbs 26:24-25). There will always be customers for the product of lies. Rebellious hearts cry to their prophets, "Tell us pleasant things, prophesy illusions . . . stop confronting us with the Holy One of Israel" (Isaiah 30:10-11). They are eager to be filled "with false hopes" (Jeremiah 23:16) and avid to be led by "deceitful men . . . with lying togues" (Psalm 109:2). The advocates of truth can deny "trying to trick" their audiences and can assure them that they "never use flattery . . . (as) a mask to cover up greed" (I Thessalonians 2:3,5). The proponents of error even forge letters in an apostle's name to get recognition of their peculiar doctrines (II Thessalonians 2:2).

Error is marked by deceit and also by distortion. Twisting Scriptures to make them fit a foreign theology is an art among heretics and sectarians. "They distort . . . Scriptures, to their own destruction" (II Peter 3:16). It is a crime to "distort the words of the living God" (Jeremiah 23:36). Gnostics took Old Testament "genealogies" (Titus 3:9) and warped them into allegories to promote their own philosophies. Even from within the Ephesian eldership rose men, who did "distort the truth in order to draw away disciples after them" (Acts 20:30). In true Pauline fashion, the genuine teachers affirm, "we do not use deception, nor do we distort the word of God. On the contrary, by setting forth the truth plainly, we commend ourselves to every man's conscience in the sight of God" (II Corinthians 4:2).

Add to deceit and distortion doubt and denial for a fuller picture of the advocate of error. Following the Serpent's trail from the garden of Eden, one finds the insinuation of the incredibility of God's word. "Did God really say?" (Genesis 3:1) is the questioner's ploy. The gospel herald's assurance of faith has the opposite ring: "As surely as God is faithful, our message to you is not 'Yes' and 'No.' For the Son of God, Jesus Christ, who was preached among you by me . . . was not 'Yes' and 'No,' but in him it has always been 'Yes' " (II Corinthians 1:18-19). Some, in Peter's day and ours, go so far as "denying the sovereign Lord who bought them" (II Peter 2:1). "The elementary truths of God's word" (Hebrews 6:12) demand proclamation, not challenge or denial.

"The wisdom of the wise; the intelligence of the intelligent" (I Corinthians 1:19) will one day crumble, but Christ's "words will never pass away" (Matthew 24:35). The dependability of Jesus' words is evidenced on occasion after occasion, where events occurred "just as he (Christ) told" (Mark 16:7 cp. Luke 2:20, John 18:9,32).

The nature of truth is found to be dependable, while that of error is discovered to be full of deceit, doubt, denial and distortion. Shall we add that error is different from truth and in no way similar? Oil and water do not mix. Neither do truth and error. The court room requirement of a witness is a must for the church assembly. What is told must be "the truth, the whole truth and nothing but the truth." A half-truth can mislead. An overstated case can perjudice a jury. Truth is not to be added to nor subtracted from.

He who preaches is "to proclaim . . . the whole will of God" (Acts 20:27). He is to report, "I have fully proclaimed the gospel of Christ" (Romans 15:19 cp. II Timothy 4:17). He is "to present . . . the word of God in its fullness" (Colossians 1:25). He is "to say everything (God) commanded" (Exodus 7:2 cp. Deuteronomy 1:3). He is to utter "all the words of the entire revelation" (II Samuel 7:17 cp. Ezekiel 40:4). The full gospel is the only gospel there is. Nothing is to be left out.

The equal truth is that nothing is to be added. The last chapter of the last book in the Bible warns "anyone (who) adds anything . . . and . . . anyone (who) takes words away" will suffer dire consequences (Revelation 22:18-19). First century Pharisees and teachers of the law had added their traditions and human rules, thus nullifying the word of God (Matthew 15:6,9). The creeds of men are like junk food — palatable but not profitable. Christ's body needs the upbuilding that only a healthful diet of God's truth can supply. If a king's recipe for potato salad given to the chef calls for sweet pickles and Miracle Whip salad dressing, it is not pleasing for the chef, at his own discretion, to add mustard or horse radish. When the king orders potato salad, to substitute steak and eggs would be an error. To use the requested mayonnaise but omit the pickles would not please his majesty by the omission. The equal mistake would be to add elements that, by their very presence, produce a different diet than the royal monarch requested. Preachers are not the king. They are only servants. God's menu, not man's preferences or dislikes, should determine the contents of the message to be offered the world.

The instruction book clearly reads: "Every word of God is flawless. . . . Do not add to his words, or he will rebuke you and prove you a liar" (Proverbs 30:6 cp, Deuteronomy 4:2). What ". . . itching ears want to hear" (II Timothy 4:3) is not to be the determining factor. It was not determinative to Ezekiel, as he spoke, "I prophesied as I was commanded" (37:7), it was not to Jeremiah, who had received the instruction, "prophesy all these words" (25:30), "tell them everything I command . . . do not omit a word" (26:2,8 cp. 1:7,17). It was not to Micaiah, who stated, "I can tell . . . only what my God says" (II Chronicles 18:13 cp. I Kings 22:14).

"A thorough knowledge of the Scriptures" was the reason Apollos could teach "about Jesus accurately" (Acts 18:24-25). The Sadducee's failure in teaching was pinpointed by Jesus to be, "You are in error because you do not know the Scriptures" (Matthew 22:29 cp. Mark 12:24). If you would tell the truth, learn that truth from the Bible and then "tell the people the full message of this new life" (Acts 5:20). Do not offer "the teaching of Balaam" nor "the teaching of the Nicolaitans" (Revelation 2:14-15) to the world that needs Christ. Do not follow the Judaizers "to a different gospel — which is really no gospel at all" (Galatians 1:6-7 cp, II Corinthians 11:4). Refuse to be enamored by some "hollow and deceptive philosophy, which depends on human tradition and the basic principles of this world rather than on Christ" (Colossians 2:8).

Why set your hope on "clouds without rain" (Jude 12), when the refreshing showers come from the truths of heaven? Why turn to "springs without water" (II Peter 2:17), when God's wells of truth will never run dry? Why join "men (who) oppose the truth" and become "imposters" (II Timothy 3:8,13) or "false witnesses" (I Corinthians 15:15), when only "the truth will set . . . free" (John 8:32)?

The world is filled with people of many languages, colors, sizes, and shapes, but they have common needs, aspirations and hungers that only God's truth can satisfy. No preacher has a right to ask for the attendance and attention of any of these people, unless he has the truth from heaven to offer their ears. The spread of AIDS, that has plagued our world, is fostered primarily by certain types of humans — those who misuse sex and drugs.

Likewise, the spread of error that has plagued our churches, is fostered by certain types of preachers — those with enlarged egos and unbending wills. They resist being bound by yesterday's convictions. They flaunt their freedom and claim license to do their own thing. "But you, man of God, flee from all this . . . fight the good fight of the faith" (I Timothy 6:11-12). "It is required that those who have been given a trust must prove faithful" (II Corinthians 4:2). "To please men" is "not to be a servant of Christ" (Galatians 1:10).

11

PROCLAIMING THE BIBLE

Pilate asked, "What is truth?" (John 18:38). The preacher, being under orders to speak the truth, needs never question where heaven's truth is to be found. He knows it is in that body of truth that the church has preserved over the centuries — that is, in the Sacred Scriptures. To speak, "Preach the Word" (II Timothy 4:2) is another way of saying "preach the truth."

"Book of Revelation" is not just an appropriate title for the final writing that concludes the New Testament. It is fitting nomenclature for the entire Bible. The Sacred Scriptures, from Moses' Genesis to John's Apocalypse, is revelation from God. Each inspired writing is a message from God to man and not some religious opinions about God from some man. The people of our world are not anxious to consume their precious time hearing only the "think so's" of another human. A "thus saith the Lord" alone is worthy of human attention. That is why the apostolic injunction "Preach the Word" is the abiding order for ministers in every pulpit on earth.

A singer that can't sing probably should not opt for making opera his career. Yet a preacher that can not preach is even more a misplaced person. He that would preach must have something to say. That something of eternal relevance, that cries out to be heralded, is the message of God found in Eternal Writ. That word from heaven for the ears of man is called "the word of faith" (Romans 10:8), "the word of grace" (Acts 20:32), "the word of life" (Philippians 2:16), "the word of Christ" (Colossians 3:16), and "the word of truth' '(II Corinthians 6:7 KJV). One's sermons are more apt to be "the message of wisdom" and "the message of knowledge" (I Corinthians 12:8), when they grow out of the fertile soil of God's written word.

PREACH THE BOOK WITH DIVINE AWARENESS

Every congregation faces its preacher with the words of King Zedekiah on its lips, "Is there any word from the LORD?" (Jeremiah 37:17). General reflections on religious themes by a nice man will not satisfy. The hunger of the human heart is to hear the voice of God. No uncertainty is removed and no waywardness is corrected by sermons that but echo the political, economic or social opinion of the time. But let the light of God's revelation come into the room. When it does, hope, confidence and surety will radiate upon all in the house.

The prophets of the Bible ever pointed to the source of their messages. "This is what the LORD Almighty says" is the constant recurring phrase in the message of Jeremiah.[1] The same "This is what the LORD Almighty says" interspaces also the words of

---

1. 6:6,9,16,21,22; 7:21; 8:4; 9:7; 10:1; 11:21; 12:14; 13:1,9,12; 14:1,10; 17:5; 18:11,13; 19:1,15; 21:4,8; 22:1,6,11,18,24; 23:16; 25:32; 26:2,4,18; 29:4,8,10,32; 31:7,23,35,37; 32:3,14,42; 33:10,12,13,17; 38:3, 17; 39:16; 44:11,25; 45:2; 46:25; 48:1,40,44,47; 49:1,2,5,6,7,12,14,28, 30,32,39; 50:1,10,21,30,40; 51:1,25,26,33,36,39,48,52,53,58.

Ezekiel, Obadiah, Micah, Nahum, Zephaniah, Haggai, Zechariah and Malachi.[2] The listeners at a prophet's feet heard a message that might begin, "Then the LORD reached out his hand and touched my mouth and said to me, 'Now, I have put my words in your mouth' " (Jeremiah 1:9). Each audience was invited to "hear the word of the LORD" (Ezekiel 16:35 cp. 37:4; Jeremiah 2:4; 27:18,21; 31:10; 34:17; Hosea 4:1; Jonah 1:1) or to "come and hear the message that has come from the LORD" (Ezekiel 33:30). The hearers were told, "Open your ears to the words of his (the LORD's) mouth" (Jeremiah 9:20) or they were requested, "Stay here awhile, so that I may give you a message from God" (I Samuel 9:27).

The New Testament apostles unquestionably accepted the "Scripture" as what "the Holy Spirit spoke long ago") Acts 1:16 cp. 2:16; 4:25; 28:25). The disciples had learned from Jesus to "know the Scriptures" as "what God said" (Matthew 22:29,31). They, likewise, determined not "to neglect the ministry of the word of God" (Acts 6:2) and believed their messages to be "not . . . the word of men, but . . . the word of God" (I Thessalonians 2:13). They had a high view of Scripture, believing in its inspiration (Matthew 1:22; 2:5,15,17,23; 3:1-4; 4:4,14; 8:17; 12:17; 13:14; 21:4; 24:15; 26:56; 27:9 cp. Mark 1:2; 7:6; 11:17; Luke 1:70; 3:4). They had a high view of gospel preaching, believing in its transforming power to save (Romans 1:16).

---

2. Ezekiel 2:4; 3:27; 5:5,7,8; 6:11; 7:2,5; 11:5,7,16,17; 12:10,28; 13:3,8,13,18; 14:6,11,21; 15:6; 16:35,59; 17:9,19,22; 20:27,30,47; 21:24,28; 22:28; 23:22,28,32,35,46; 24:3,6,9,21; 25:12,15; 26:7,15,19; 27:3; 28:8; 29:8,13; 30:10,13; 31:10,15; 32:11; 33:27; 34:2,10,11,17,20; 35:3; 36:3,4,6,13,22,33,37; 37:5,9,27; 38:10,17; 39:17,25; 43:18; 45:9, 18; 46:1,16; 47:13; Amos 1:3,5,6,8,9,13,15; 2:1,3,4,6,16; 3:8,11,13,15; 4:5,6,8,9,10,11; 5:3,4,16,17,27; 6:8; 7:1,4,6,17; 8:9,11; 9:8,12,15; Obadiah 1:1,4,8; Micah 3:5; 6:1; Nahum 1:12; Zephaniah 1:3,10; 3:8,20; Haggai 1:2,12,13; 2:1,6,9,11,23; Zechariah 1:2,4,14,16,17: 2:6; 3:6,9,10; 8:2,4,6,7,9,14,17,18,19,20,23; 11:4; 12:1; 13:2,7; Malachi 1:8,9,11,13; 2:2,4,8,16; 3:5,11,13.

When God's word is preached, God is present, working through that word to rescue His people. The preacher, who lets doubt whittle away at his conviction regarding the Bible's uniqueness as God's word, has shorn his sermons of authority and drained them of convincing power. But that messenger of the word, who is committed totally to the Bible's truth and relevancy, has guaranteed that his messages, like God's word itself, "will not return . . . empty, but will . . . achieve (their) purpose" (Isaiah 55:11). Be not "slow of heart to believe all that the prophets have spoken" (Luke 24:25). Join Paul in the confession, "I believe everything that . . . is written in the Prophets" (Acts 24:14), and you are on the road that leads to great preaching and satisfied congregations.

The congregation is a believing assembly. The speaker is to speak for the church as well as to it. He properly acts, when he speaks, not to air his mind, but their mind. His voice is intended to be the voice of the body. Freelancing is out. Christ's entrusted message is the story to be told. The Bible on the pulpit carries the message of the church. Ordaining hands were laid on the spokesman to add the entire church's weight to his single voice. One individual may be speaking, but the entire church of every time and place is confessing its faith through that one personality. Woe to that preacher that rushes to speak, unaware of the church about him, the God above him or the Bible before him.

PREACH THE BOOK WITH AUDIENCE AWARENESS

Where Christians gather can, in accuracy, be called an auditorium. It is a place for hearing. The preacher ought never to forget that it is God's voice the ears ache to hear. The Bible, lying open on the pulpit or held firmly in the preacher's hand, nonverbally, communicates that the message being preached has behind it the authority of Scripture. For the sake of Biblical literacy in a congregation, the public reading of large portions of Psalms, Gospels and Epistles ought not to be done only in the more highly liturgical churches. The early churches made a place for it. Justin Martyr (ca 140 A.D.) describes a service "on the day which is called Sunday." In depicting the service he notes, "The records of the Apostles or the writings of the Prophets are read as long as we have time. Then the reader concludes; and the President verbally instructs and exhorts us to the imitation of these excellent things" (Apology 1:67).

This church practice of Scripture reading grew out of the practice of the synagogues that arose after the Jewish nation's Babylonian captivity. A lectionary of readings from the Law and the Prophets developed, allowing the people to hear their entire Scripture read aloud to them each three years or so. Jesus shared in the custom. In Nazareth "he went into the synagogue, as was his custom. And he stood up to read" (Luke 4:16). Paul took advantage of the opportunity the synagogues offered him. At Antioch "after the reading from the Law and the Prophets, the synagogue rulers" allowed the missionary to bring "a message of encouragement for the people" (Acts 13:15).

Would the reading of lengthy passages lose the attention of the worshipers? Joshua believed the advantages to outweigh disadvantages, so he "read all the words of the law — the blessings and the curses — just as it is written in the Book of the Law. There was not a word of all that Moses had commanded that Joshua did not read to the whole assembly of Israel, including the women and the children, and the aliens who lived among them" (Joshua 8:34-35). Ezra was in favor of reading lengthy Bible passages to "all . . . able to understand," for he read (the Law) aloud from daybreak till noon . . . and all the people listened attentively" (Nehemiah 8:2-3). How could they keep attention so long? The answer given is, "They read from the Book of the Law of God, making it clear and giving the meaning so that the people could understand what was being read" (8:8).

As early as Deuteronomy, Moses gave this order to the sons of Levi, "At the end of every seven years . . . during the Feast of Tabernacles, when all Israel comes to appear before the

LORD . . . read this law before them in their hearing. Assemble the people — men, women and children . . . (they) must hear it and learn to fear the LORD" (Deuteronomy 31:10-13). It will do the Christian good to remember that the New Testament epistles were not distributed to their original recipients in printed form for daily devotional help during the personal quiet times. Rather, they were read to the gathered congregation aloud. Each disciple, "who has an ear to hear," was to hear the apostolic letter (Revelation 2:7). And blessed is said to be both "The one who reads . . . and . . . those who hear it and take heed to what is written" (Revelation 1:3 cp. 22:18). Let the word of God be heard.

Other religions may exist and spread without speakers audibly proclaiming their message, but not the revealed religions of Judaism and Christianity. Faith came then, comes now and will continue to come in the future, "by hearing" (Romans 10:17). As valuable as silent and meditative reading are, the interpretively read text has the advantage. A wise Eunuch from Ethiopia, even by himself on a desert road, was "heard . . . reading Isaiah the prophet" (Acts 8:30). When the messages were first delivered by the prophets, "they spoke from God as they were carried along by the Holy Spirit" (II Peter 1:21). The same Spirit of God works with today's preacher, who proclaims the same message to his own generation. So "take the sword of the Spirit, which is the word of God" (Ephesians 6:17), as you go to battle for souls. It is not the word of man that "is living and active. Sharper than any double-edged sword" (Hebrews 4:12). Unsheath the weapon God has provided. Become skilled in Scripture. Enter the fray with the weapon that "cannot be broken" (John 10:35). "Preach the Word" (II Timothy 4:2).

PREACH THE BOOK WITH HERMENEUTICAL AWARENESS

One homiletician compares the reading of the sermon's text

to the playing of the national anthem at the beginning of a football game. He quips that it gets the game started but is not played again or referred to the rest of the time.[3] Wiser is the preacher who is known as a Biblical expositor. Wise is the one who, in the tradition of Jesus, leaves his listeners saying, "Were not our hearts burning within us while he talked with us . . . and opened the Scriptures to us?" (Luke 24:32).

For a Bible passage to open up like the bud of a flower, revealing its beauty and spreading its fragrance, it must be studied with hermeneutical awareness. Long hours of prayerful pondering over a Scripture text will be rewarded with treasures of truth beyond counting.

What was the historical situation that brought forth the inspired revelation to Israel or the church? To be one "who correctly handles the word of truth" (II Timothy 2:15) that question must be answered. Week by week freshly immerse yourself in God's word in a scholarly and experimental way. Remind yourself of yesterday's situation that brought forth the writing, so that the revelation can be applied correctly to today's condition. Make that clear, and the congregation's grasp of the truth will clarify and make good sense. They will leave the assembly with the path of righteousness plainly in view. They will be saying "I understand it now." A blind adventure through the mist of mysticism would have left the audience ignorant of the Bible and confused by nonsense.

One truth, of high-voltage and many mega-watts of power and light, is the awareness of the distinction between covenants. The law of Moses is not the gospel of Christ. The commandments to Israel at Sinai are not equal in every way to the new covenant inaugurated in Jerusalem after Jesus' death, resurrection, ascension and coronation. The preacher, without historic con-

---

3. Haddon W. Robinson, *Biblical Preaching: The Development and Delivery of Expository Messages* (Grand Rapids, Michigan: Baker Book House, 1980), p. 20.

sciousness, might mix promises or commands to ancient Israel with those to the church. To "pour new wine into old wineskins" (Matthew 9:17) is as foolish as to force the fresh gospel of grace into the brittle rituals and practice of temple and law. No church in Galveston or Galatia is instructed properly in Scripture that does not recognize the historic fact that "now that faith has come, we are no longer under the supervision of the law (Galatians 3:25).

A misused Bible has little advantage over a disused one. The proper use of text calls for finding the literary context, as well as the historical one. A verse preacher may not be a Bible preacher. The whole context of each verse, plus the entire teaching of the Bible, ought to be kept in the interpreter's mind. Serious preaching must be preceded by serious examination of one's chosen text in light of the chapter and the book in which it is found. Otherwise, what may be perceived as biblical preaching is in fact pseudo-biblical. The listeners, instead of receiving "the whole will of God" (Acts 20:27), have more likely received a large amount of the preacher's opinions sandwiched between very thin slices of textual bread. The sermon could be palatable. Then again, it could be mostly baloney.

Let God's words to Ezekiel be His counsel to you: "You must speak my words to them, whether they listen or fail to listen. . . . But you, son of man, listen to what I say to you . . . open your mouth and eat what I give you . . . eat this scroll; then go and speak to the house of Israel" (2:7-8; 3:1). Before you has gathered a flock of Christ's sheep. Their unspoken prayer is that of Zophar, "O how I wish that God would speak, that he would open his lips . . . and disclose . . . the secrets of wisdom" (Job 11:5). Be an answer to their prayer.

PREACH THE BOOK WITH NEED AWARENESS

The man of God, who stands in the pulpit, ought to be not only truth-teller and Bible-expositor. He also must be need-

assessor. His Bible is to be believed confidently, read interpretively, taught correctly and ministered helpfully. Let's face it. People have needs. The Bible has the answers to those needs. Bible sermons are meant to be prescriptions from heaven for the ills of earth. God's spokesman is expected to be expert in Biblical knowledge and human problems. Knowing his people and the Great Physician's Doctor Book, the preacher is to diagnose the hurts and prescribe the balm. A sermon's main business is to solve some spiritual ill. Just ask why a New Testament epistle was written and you become awakened to the fact that the letter was God's answer to some specific need. If the Biblical books arise out of the problems facing the people, the church's sermons can well rise to fulfill the same need.

Those congregations benefit where a problem is stated and dealt with fairly, frankly and helpfully. Modern pedagogy starts with a child to be helped and not just a subject to be taught. Your church is confronted with need. Your Bible has the resources of the Christian faith well stocked on every shelf. Your task is to remember the whence and whither of preaching and is to minister to the perplexities, problems and sins of human life. Your question, calling for answer before the sermon is delivered, is "Does my lesson for the hour minister as Christ would minister?"

An explanation of what happened to the antedeluvians might be accurate, according to Scriptural facts, but deadly, according to Biblical purpose. Preaching is to speak "to men for their strengthening, encouragement and comfort" (I Corinthians 14:3). Contemporary life is not enhanced by preachers who, in Charles Spurgeon's words, are like lions engaged in mouse-hunting. Avoid trivia and talk about what matters. Fred Craddock reminds proclaimers that "pennies polished to a high gloss remain but pennies."[4]

"The holy Scriptures . . . are able to make you wise for salva-

---

4. *Preaching* (Nashville: Abingdon Press, 1985), p.49.

tion" (II Timothy 3:15). The greatest of great preachers "reasoned with them (the Jews) from the Scriptures, explaining and proving" his proclamation of Jesus until many "were persuaded and joined" (Acts 17:2-4). When the need of the people is to be convinced, the Bible contains the evidence. When the need is discouragement, the Scripture has the comforting balm. When the need is false teaching, the Apostolic teaching shows the true way. Whatever the need, "Preach the Word" (II Timothy 4:2).

12

PROCLAIMING THE CHRIST

To leave the Lord's Supper, talking about the texture of the table cloth, is to have missed communion's purpose. "Do this, whenever you drink it, in remembrance of me" were Jesus' instructions (I Corinthians 11:24). To leave the sermon, knowing the text of the Scripture but not knowing the touch of the Savior, is to have mistaken a path for the final destination. When we preach the truth or proclaim the Bible, we are heralding a person. In a Christmas sermon, Martin Luther compared the Bethlehem cradle that held the baby Jesus to the Scriptures. The written Word contained the living Word. In the Bible find Christ. He is the Savior. The book is where He is to be found.

A Gideon friend speaks of his Bible as "the Him book," because its message is about Him. Like the Bible, your sermons ought to be about Him, if you would preach in New Testament style. The gist of Peter's preaching was, "God has made this Jesus . . . both Lord and Christ" (Acts 2:36). Philip's sermon consisted of telling "the good news about Jesus" (Acts 8:35). The records tell that, wherever Philip went, he "proclaimed the Christ there" (Acts 8:5) and "preached the good news . . . of Jesus" (Acts 8:12). No sooner was Paul converted on the Damascus road than "at once he began to preach . . . Jesus" (Acts 9:20), until even enemies began to speak "of Jesus whom Paul preaches" (Acts 19:13). The self-description of preaching by this apostle and his associates was said to be, "Jesus Christ . . . preached among you by me and Silas and Timothy" (II Corinthians 1:19). His call from God was understood to be to "preach him (Christ) among the Gentiles" (Galatians 1:16).

"Preach Christ" is the recurring phrase in Philippians (1:15,17,18). "We proclaim him" that men "may know . . . Christ" is the mission statement in Colossians (1:28; 2:2). "That the message of the Lord may spread rapidly" is the prayer request of II Thessalonians (3:1). "He . . . was preached among the nations" is the victory song of I Timothy (3:16).

Apostles got their orders straight. These heralds of Christ used their Bibles as pointers, but their message was a person and that person was God's Son. Jesus told them, "you will be my witnesses" (Acts 1:8). "The testimony of Jesus Christ" was their mission (Revelation 1:2 cp. 20:4; I Corinthians 1:6). Concerning the Holy Spirit that inspired them, Jesus said, He "will testify about me" (John 15:26). And testify about Jesus the apostles did. "We do not preach ourselves, but Jesus" was their boast (II Corinthians 4:5). John the Baptist, who preceded the apostles, also "came as a witness to testify . . . to the light (Christ)" (John 1:7-8). John's disciples spoke of Jesus to John as "the one you testified about" (John 3:26 cp. 5:32,36).

The determination of that old preacher, who baptized in Jordan, ought to be the vow of young preachers who, timewise, will baptize down stream. He vowed, "He must become greater; I must become less" (John 3:30). As I teach, using screen and projector, students often ask me to step aside, for I am in the way of their seeing the material on the screen. As you preach Christ, do not make it necessary for someone in the pew to have to say, "Down in front! You are keeping me from seeing Jesus." Relating your charismatic experience, or Paul "boasting," regarding his "visions and revelations" (II Corinthians 12:1), may turn attention away from Christ to self. Promoting millennial theories may draw large crowds, but possibly may also draw more attention to modern Israel than to the eternal Jesus. Passing theories, like flickering lamps, do draw attention to themselves. Stay with the eternal flame. Point to the magnificent Lord of glory until your hearers lose sight of you. It is not essential that you even know the name of the Western Union boy who delivers the message. What is essential is that you receive the message. The messenger's only importance is to get that message delivered. "What after all, is Apollos? And what is Paul? Only servants, through whom you came to believe" (I Corinthians 3:5).

PREACH WHO HE IS

To preach Christ is to announce who He is. The samples of sermons in Acts reveal the preachers announcing Jesus' office and deity. Peter proclaimed Him to Jews as "both Lord and Christ" (Acts 2:36) and to Gentiles as "Lord of all" (Acts 10:36). Paul in the synagogues spoke of Jesus as God's "Son" (Acts 13:33) and "the Christ" (Acts 17:3). The record by Luke reads, "Paul devoted himself exclusively to preaching, testifying to the Jews that Jesus was the Christ" (Acts 18:5 cp. 18:28). Before gathered believers the apostle to the Gentiles spoke of their common "Lord Jesus" (Acts 20:21). The Christian confession at its tersest form is to call the Master one's "Lord Jesus Christ." The last line of the document named the Acts of the apostles reads, "Boldly and without hindrance he (Paul) preached . . . the Lord Jesus Christ" (28:31).

Reflecting his sermonic phraseology, Paul in his letters speaks of Jesus as "(God's) Son . . . Jesus Christ our Lord" (Romans

1:3-4 cp. 10:9,17; 16:25; I Corinthians 12:3; II Timothy 1:8). His hope is for that day, when not his tongue alone but "every tongue (would) confess that Jesus Christ is Lord" (Philippians 2:11). The confession at Caesarea Philippi is that Jesus is the Christ, the Son of the living God" (Matthew 16:16). At Jesus' baptism and, again, at His transfiguration, God confesses, "This is my Son" (Matthew 3:17; 17:5). John the Baptist gave amen to the Father's words, affirming, "I testify that this is the Son of God . . . the Lamb of God" (John 1:32,34-36).

That "Jesus is the Christ, the Son of God" (John 20:31) is the underlying conviction of all preaching. When addressing Jews, the message is that the Messiah for which Israel has long awaited has come and His name is Jesus. When speaking to people of all other religious persuasions, the truth proclaimed is that the vision of God and the meaning of life, which human hearts have reached out for, has come to earth in the person of Jesus of Nazareth.

"Everybody ought to know who Jesus is" is the refrain of a popular chorus. That He is the Light of the World, God's only-begotten Son and earth's only Savor must be made known. His uniqueness and all-sufficiency is Biblical fact. The burden of all preaching is to announce His presence. The faithful present-day preacher begins with a Scripture, but preaches Jesus. He begins from a funeral, but preaches Jesus. He starts at a wedding, but preaches Jesus. He may start out from a counseling appointment in his office or a play-time with children on the playground, but he proclaims Christ.

PREACH WHAT HE DID

It is important for people to know who Jesus is and what He has done. Every person freed by the Lord from demonic powers is under Jesus' orders, "Go home to your family and tell them how much the Lord has done for you, and how he has had mercy on you" (Mark 5:19). All preachers ordained to relate the Christian message are under instruction to "preach Christ crucified" (I Corinthians 1:23). Apostles, when they "proclaimed . . . the testimony about God . . . resolved to know nothing . . . except Jesus Christ and him crucified" (I Corinthians 2:1-2). Their picturesque messages of the cross were so descriptive they could say to their hearers, "Before your very eyes Jesus Christ was clearly portrayed as crucified" (Galatians 3:1).

The sermons of the first three decades of the church center on the cross of the Christ and the Christ of the cross. Their final triumphant announcement is that God has raised His Son from the grave just as the prophets foretold and the apostles now testify. Ask what message was heard and the answer would be, "It is preached that Christ has been raised from the dead" (I Corinthians 15:12). Each witness left untold any unique visions he had experienced or world travel sights he had seen. Paul was not excited about the Parthenon in Athens, the Colosseum in Rome or the shipwreck on the Adriatic Sea. All his time was taken in relating the grand story of what God had done in Christ. A news reporter is not to recount his own experiences. He is to tell the news he was commissioned to report. It is not required that the Editor's name be on every tongue in the land. The populace may overlook that. The job assigned is well done, when the news is given clear and adequate coverage.

PREACH WHAT HE TAUGHT

A Gospel, like that of Luke, is the evangel regarding "all that Jesus began to do and to teach" (Acts 1:1). Once a learner knows who Jesus is (Son of God, etc.) and what He has done for his salvation, that embryo Christian is ready to listen to his Lord's teaching (Matthew 28:20). Each time the congregation gathers, the new member of God's family looks beyond the preacher before him in the pulpit to Christ with every hope of hearing his

Master's voice.

"He who listens to you listens to me" (Luke 10:16), was Jesus' encouraging word. Of the prophets it was written that "the Spirit of Christ (was) in them," as they "predicted the sufferings of Christ and the glories that would follow" (I Peter 1:11 cp. Luke 24:27; John 5:39). Of the apostles it was said, they "preached the gospel . . . by the Holy Spirit sent from heaven" (I Peter 1:12). Of the present-day preacher may the audience sense that Christ's Spirit is in you and that it is Christ's words that are falling on their ears (cp. John 10:16). "The testimony of Jesus Christ" (Revelation 1:2) is both about Him and from Him.

Human words in all their glory will pass away and lie forgotten in the cemetery of the past, but Jesus' "words will never pass away" (Matthew 24:35 cp. Luke 21:33). Religious fads perish. Theological systems lie imprisoned in big words and heavy tomes beyond the reach of most men, but "God's word is not chained" (II Timothy 2:9). Allow that the profound but simple teaching from the Master Teacher's lips fall upon the ears before you. As at the communion table, the congregation hears, "This is my body, which is for you" (I Corinthians 11:24), may they, from the sacred desk where you speak, hear the voice of Jesus saying, "This is my teaching, which is for you."

Pray that "grace (be) given . . . to preach . . . the unsearchable riches of Christ, and to make plain to everyone . . . this mystery" (Ephesians 3:8-9). Learn the message of the transfiguration, where Moses (representing the Law) and Elijah (representing the Prophets) vanish from view, and only Christ remains. The voice of God gives the bottom line never to be forgotten by disciples that preach, "Listen to him!" (Matthew 17:4-5). "Continue in the teaching of Christ," for it is "this teaching" that ties one to God (II John 9-10). When Jesus' teaching is openly proclaimed, people are "filled with awe and praise God." They come to realize "God has come to help his people." Let "this good news about Jesus spread" (Luke 7:16-17 cp. Acts 13:12). At the end of your ministry let it be written of you, as it was of the apostles, "They never stopped teaching and proclaiming the good news that Jesus is the Christ" (Acts 5:42). Such words may be written about you one day, if you now know with certainty that you were called "to be a minister of Christ Jesus . . . with the priestly duty of proclaiming the gospel of God" (Romans 15:16).

PREACH WHAT HE OFFERS

When the church sings its gospel songs, hearts are filled with hope by their positive affirmations. It is the same when Christ is preached. That is why opportunity for response by the hearers to God's loving offer followed the first gospel sermon in the Biblical record. "The promise is for you and your children and for all who are far off," rang the appeal of Peter (Acts 2:39). "My brothers, I want you to know that through Jesus the forgiveness of sins is proclaimed to you," was the invitation of Paul (Acts 13:38). John's message, likewise, concluded with the invitation, "That you may believe that Jesus is the Christ, the son of God, and that believing you may have life in his name" (John 20:31).

Preach Christ. Preach for a decision. Tell who He is, what He has done and taught, and what He offers. Then tie a knot in the thread. Otherwise, you will have sewn in vain and all your good work come unravelled. Will a lawyer make a solid case and fail to appeal for a verdict? Will a salesman create an interest in his product and walk away with no attempt to get a signature on the order form? Let the preacher of Christ paint a portrait of Jesus with arms outstretched in welcome, while he speaks Christ's clearly uttered words in bold voice, "Come to me" (Matthew 11:28).

13

PROCLAIMING THE GOSPEL

The Biblical phrase, "As we have already said, so now I say again" (Galatians 1:9), is not a Pauline desire for redundancy but an Apostolic concern for accuracy in proclaiming the gospel of Christ. "A gospel other than the one (apostles) preached" was to be "eternally condemned!" What is preached does matter!

Honing down the content of proclamation, we have found the Bible to call for preaching truth (not error), the Bible (not human wisdom) and Christ (not any other person). Precision is found in calling the true message in the Scripture about Jesus, "The gospel of Christ" (II Corinthians 2:12 cp. Acts 5:42; 8:35,40; 11:20; 14:7; 17:18). When the world asks, "What is this teaching?" (Luke 4:36), the church should be ready to define its gospel. A half-hour bag, crammed with religious words of various sizes, may contain no gospel message at all. To be gospel, or the good news about Jesus, the message must be the telling of what God has done through His incarnate Son, what promise that gives to persons and what demands that places upon them.

News answers the questions who? when? where? what? why? and how? The good-news has to do with an event — a happening in history during the early years of the first century that has eternal consequences and cosmic results. It is the church's story about heavenly promises that are tied to earthly facts. It is about human responses that are to rise from grateful hearts. It is not something that "man" made up (Galatians 1:11).

THE GOSPEL FACTS

To rehearse the mighty deeds of God for man's salvation is preaching in the New Testament sense. The visitors in Jerusalem on the first day of the church described what they heard from the preachers' lips as, "We hear them declaring the wonders of God" (Acts 2:11). Peter's sermon on that day was news about Jesus' miracles, death and resurrection.

The commissioned apostles did not seem burdened to tell everything they knew about the Bible, but they were debtors "obligated . . . to preach the gospel" (Romans 1:14-15) in its fullness, especially "where Christ was not known" (Romans 15:20 cp. II Corinthians 10:16; Colossians 1:23). Their sermons were not heavy with good advice but rather with good news. The old story of Christ crucified and risen for man's redemption was repeated, restated and reiterated both time after time and town after town.

The gospel facts were not good news until they were told. But, praise God, they were told simply, joyfully and faithfully. There was urgency in the preacher's voice and passion in his heart.

Arnold Lunn is correct in his well-known quip, "There is no market for sermons on the text ' God so loved the world that he inspired a certain Jew to inform his contemporaries that there was a great deal to be said for loving one's neighbors.' " The gospel is not moralism, telling people what not to do. It is heralding what God has done. It is more declaring what Christ has achieved than a call to become an achiever. The gospel is not peace of mind. A relaxed piano string can produce no music. Neither is the gospel toleration of every religious view. No true preacher of God's only-begotten Son is ready to evade confrontation by surrendering the gospel's uniqueness for the mush that includes on equal footing the views of Gnostics, Judaizers or Pagan philosophers.

"Good speel" is by its nature the telling of something wonderful that has happened. It is proclamation of an event. It is almost blasphemy to substitute propaganda for Marxism, Socialism or Capitalism for proclaiming the gospel. The eternal gospel stands above all transient systems of men.

"Servants of the word" (Luke 1:2), "Let the word of Christ dwell in you richly as you teach" (Colossians 3:16). How can a surgeon practice medicine, who does not know anatomy? How can an attorney practice law, who is unskilled in jurisprudence? How dare a preacher speak to and for the church, while inept in his grasp of the gospel? What seed is planted, is what crop will grow. Remember as you preach, "the seed is the word of God" (Luke 8:11). The early church "preached the word" (Acts 8:4; 16:6 cp. Mark 2:2). That word was called "the word of the Lord" (Acts 8:25; 13:49; 15:35; 19:10,20), "the word of God" (Acts 12:24; 13:5,7; 18:11; Hebrews 6:5 cp. Luke 5:1), "his word" (Titus 1:3), "the word of his grace" (Acts 20:32) and "the word of truth, the gospel" (Colossians 1:5).

The gospel-word orbits around Christ's death and resurrection. Once Jesus' disciples knew that He was the promised Messiah, the Lord "began to teach them that the Son of Man . . . must be killed and after three days rise again. He spoke plainly about this" (Mark 8:31-32). This He did repeatedly (cp. Mark 9:31; 10:32-34; Luke 18:31-33). After the predictions had become fact, the heralds began to preach the twin events of Jesus' death and resurrection (Acts 1:22; 2:23-24; 3:13-16; 4:2,33; 10:34-44; 13:28-37; 17:3; 23:6; 24:21; 25:19; 26:23).

Apostolic epistles to the churches kept the converts reminded, "we preach Christ crucified" (I Corinthians 1:23). They let it be clear that they had "resolved to know nothing . . . except Jesus Christ . . . crucified" (I Corinthians 2:2 cp. Galatians 3:1; Revelation 2:8). To the Corinthians Paul wrote, "I want to remind you of the gospel I preached to you . . . that Christ died for our sins according to the Scriptures . . . that he was raised on the third day according to the Scriptures" (I Corinthians 15:1-4,11-12,14). Even the Old Testament is the foretelling of "the sufferings of Christ and the glories that would follow" (I Peter 1:11).

The power of early preaching lay in the proclaimer's assurance that it was God who was speaking through him to men about a gospel, where He in Christ, was revealing His love for a lost world both at Calvary and at an open tomb. "The mystery . . . preached among the nations" was that God had appeared in a body" (the incarnate crucified Jesus) and "was vindicated by the Spirit" (through the resurrection) (I Timothy 3:16). This "mystery" (Romans 16:25 cp. Ephesians 3:9; Colossians 1:26) is the "mystery of the gospel" (Ephesians 6:19 or "the mystery of God, namely Christ" (Colossians 2:2 cp. I Corinthians 2:7-16). Paul calls for prayer that he "may proclaim the mystery of Christ" and "proclaim it clearly" (Colossians 4:3-4).

The triumphant joy and irrepressible conviction behind the first century sermons were in the fact that their messages dealt with solid facts of history. The proclaimers were not acting as some master of ceremonies, trying to get the audience to have a mystical and private experience. They were heralds of what Jesus had experienced for men in His suffering for their sins and His conquest of death itself. This made them and us "more than conquerors through him who loves us" (Romans 8:37). How foolish to substitute the powerful gospel of Christ for self-improvement lessons. Shall Christian soldiers enter the battlefield carrying rifles loaded with blanks? There is no life-transforming power in gospel substitutes, but the gospel unchanged is still "the power of God for the salvation of everyone who believes" (Romans 1:16).

THE GOSPEL PROMISES

Linked to what God has done (the facts) are the blessings that come to us because of His goodness (the promises). Martin Luther was quick to observe that the bare fact Christ died would be bad news. What made His death gospel, or good news, was that "Christ died for our sins" (I Corinthians 15:3). The consequence of that past event is my present forgiveness and future eternal life.

"Everyone who believes in him receives forgiveness of sins through his name," was the message shouted to Gentiles (Acts 10:43). "That your sins may be forgiven," was the hope offered Jews at the conclusion of Peter's sermon to Jews on Pentecost (Acts 2:38). When Jesus' forerunner, John the Baptist, began announcing the soon-coming Messiah, he too was "preaching a baptism of repentance for the forgiveness of sins" (Mark 1:4; Luke 3:3). That was rightly called the preaching of "the good news" (Luke 3:18). At the birth of the long-awaited Messiah, even angels were joining in bringing "good news of great joy . . . a Savior" (Luke 2:10-11). When Jesus began His ministry, the populace was "amazed at the gracious words that came from his lips" (Luke 4:22). He could startle critical legalists by saying to a woman with sinful past, "Your sins are forgiven" and He could illustrate by the story of cancelled debts (Luke 7:41-43,48). The message was even "grace" (I Peter 1:10), when it was foretold by the prophets. It remained "grace" (John 1:14), when it was witnessed by the apostle John. It was preached as "the gospel of God's grace," or "the word of his grace," when commended by the aspostle Paul (Acts 20:24,32). It is Christ's hope that "forgiveness of sins will be preached in his name to all the nations" (Luke 24:46).

Words of grace and forgiveness become words of life to sinners. The letter of John states, "we proclaim concerning the word of life" (I John 1:1). He recalls the angelic instruction to "tell the people the full message of this new life" (Acts 5:20). The fatal disease is sin, but the proffered cure is the gospel. Lengthy descriptions of the horrid malady is not the need of a dying man. Clear words of the Great Physician and His certain remedy is the necessity of the hour. The medicine that heals doesn't even taste awful. It is good news, enjoyable to hear. Be "eager to preach the gospel," which makes whole (Romans 1:15). It is "the gospel of God — the gospel promised beforehand" (Romans 1:1-2). It is "the gospel of his Son" (Romans 1:9).

"How beautiful on the mountains are the feet of those who bring good news, who proclaim peace, who bring good tidings" (Isaiah 52:7). To preach peace is to announce that God is not man's enemy. It is to tell "the good news of peace through Jesus Christ" (Acts 10:36). Peace is made between former enemies and reconcilition accomplished "through the cross" of Christ who "preached peace" (Ephesians 2:15-17).

Peace between husband and wife or neighbor and neighbor may be the result of peace between man and God. But the preaching of the psychology of inner peace is to put the cart before the horse. Only a superficial healing can come where the "peace with God through our Lord Jesus Christ" (Romans 5:1) is not first preached. The gospel Paul preached, he called "my gospel" (II Timothy 2:8), "our gospel" (I Thessalonians 1:5), "his (God's) gospel" (I Thessalonians 2:2), "the gospel" (I Thessalonians 2:4; Galatians 2:2; 4:13) or "this gospel" (II Timothy 1:11). But it never was "a different gospel — which is really no gospel at all" (Galatians 1:6-7).

Sermon books by some Norman Vincent Peale, Robert Schuller or Harry Emerson Fosdick could start a young preacher thinking of himself as a helpful leaning-post or a father-figure. He might be led to understand his mission as showing the way to dealing with hate and overcoming fears. Rereading the sermons of Peter, Paul or Stephen might clarify that Christ's gospel goes far beyond Psychiatry and deals with the sin problem that needs curing before the other human failures can find their lasting cure.

Thousands of speeches, that are but moral advice or legal demands, are unmasked and shown not to be real sermons by Biblical study. "Preaching the good news of the kingdom" (Matthew 4:23; 9:35; Luke 4:43; 8:1; 9:2,11; 10:9; Acts 1:3) is to tell of God's reign. John the Baptist prepared hearts for Christ the coming king, announcing: "the kingdom of heaven is near" (Matthew 3:2 cp. 10:7). The king of this kingdom, unlike all others, is to His people a servant and a savior. His subjects are those who by free-will choose to enter that kingdom by His invitation. His laws are the application of the one principle of love applied to all relationships toward both God and man. The earliest history book of the church tells of men like Philip, who "preached the good news of the kingdom of God and the name of Jesus Christ" (Acts 8:12). It also speaks of spokesmen, who "boldly and without hindrance . . . preached the kingdom," like Paul (Acts 28:31 cp. 20:25; 28:23).

Declare a holiday from sermons that "tie up heavy loads and put them on men's shoulders" (Matthew 23:4). Make it a regular practice to vow with David, "I will praise you, O LORD . . . I will tell of all your wonders" (Psalm 9:1). Pledge that you will admonish with Israel's sweet singer to "proclaim among the nations what he has done" (Psalm 9:11 cp. 44:1). Psalm after Psalm admonishes the "telling of all (God's) wonderful deeds" (Psalm 26:7 cp. 119:27) and the "declaring of (God's) splendor" (71:8), "righteousness" (71:15), "mighty acts" (71:16 cp. 73:28; 78:7) and "power" (71:18 cp. 78:4). You will find that "it is good . . . to proclaim (God's) love in the morning and (God's) faithfulness at night" (92:1-2). Instead of facing a new week, knowing another Sunday is coming with the dilemma "What have I to say?", you thank God another Lord's Day will soon be there for there is so much about God that cries out to be told. A mind immersed in Biblical literature prays, "Many, O LORD my God, are the wonders you have done . . . were I to speak and tell of them, they would be too many to declare" (Psalm 40:5). What shall I preach? The answer of the Book is, "Let the redeemed of the LORD say this . . . the LORD . . . is good; his love endures forever" (Psalm 107:1-2 cp. 118:2). What "mighty acts . . . glorious splendor . . . awesome works . . . great deeds" (Psalm 145:4-6)! The spiritual appetite is stirred by the varied homiletical diets in the menu book of heaven.

To preach like Jesus is "to preach good news . . . bind up the broken hearted . . . proclaim freedom . . . release . . . (and) the LORD's favor" (Isaiah 61:1-2 cp. Luke 4:18-19). The hopeful gospel promises are built on the kindly gospel facts. "Make known among the nations what he has done . . . for he has done glorious things; let this be known to all the world" (Isaiah 12:4-5 cp. 40:9).

THE GOSPEL DEMANDS

While the gospel message is not "do good so you can be saved," it is "do good now that you have been saved." Paul's message was about "the kindness and love of God our Savior . . . (who) saved us, not because of righteous things we had done, but because of his mercy" (Titus 3:5). "Doing what is good" (Titus 1:16; 2:14; 3:8) is not a meritorious work that purchases God's approval. Doing good is the natural overflow of gratitude from a life rescued from damning sin by the work of God.

The *kerygma* of the early church, that announced what God had done in Christ for man's salvation, concluded with an appeal to the hearer to make the crucified and risen Jesus "both Lord and Christ" (Acts 2:36). Unconditional surrender was the demand. The call for repentance and baptism was request for both inner and outer acknowledgment of the King's Lordship (Acts 2:38). There were no exceptions. "Those who accepted the message were baptized" (Acts 2:41). It was their signing of the covenant that Jesus had signed in blood. The immersion in water, signifying the total surrender of the total person to the total will of God, was "the pledge" (I Peter 3:21). The missionaries of Christ were envoys of the King of kings, bearing heaven's terms for peace. To submit to baptism was to announce acceptance of Jesus as king, with all the ramifications such acknowledgment would entail.

"John the Baptist came, preaching . . . saying, 'Repent' " (Matthew 3:1-2). "Jesus began to preach, 'Repent' " (Matthew 4:17; Mark 1:14). "Repent" was the call of Peter (Acts 2:38) and Paul (Acts 17:30). "Repent" is the call for decision, the appeal to make up the mind. To obey the great commission is to combine "repentance and forgiveness of sins" (Luke 24:47) in our preaching. Once the gospel facts and promises are known, decision is called for.

Dean Inge caustically remarked that fewer people would be in the churches, if the gospel as given were preached to them. He might have been pleasantly surprised at the opposite outcome. The whole gospel with all its demands might have more appeal than some small glass of bicarbonate of soda for the world's ills being offered in place of the bitter pill called repentance. There can be no cure for sin apart from the cross on Jesus' part and repentance on man's part. Necessity, urgency, immediacy, insistency are words that describe the gospel appeal. Do not be timid to use Paul's words, "We implore you on Christ's behalf: Be reconciled to God" (II Corinthians 5:20). Without the change of mind in "repentance," there will be no change of life in the hearer and no change of destiny in eternity. Jesus' message reverberated with urgency when He said, "unless you repent, you too will all perish" (Luke 13:3,5). Join Martin Luther in preaching as though Jesus was crucified yesterday, risen again from the dead today and coming back tomorrow. Tell the facts, highlight the promises and call for decision.

14

PROCLAIMING CHRISTIAN LIVING

Evangelize, baptize, then catechize is the order. You present the gospel, immerse those who respond to God's call and then begin "teaching them to obey everything (Christ) commanded" (Matthew 28:20). First *kerygma*, then *didache*. First gospel, then application.

Upon accepting the free gift of God, the convert is ready to hear instruction on how to live the Christian life. The foundation of what God has done has been laid. How do we build the superstructure thereon? The indicatives, regarding the Lord's acts on our behalf, call for the imperatives, dealing with a forgiven person's responsibilities. What road is the Christian to walk? Is there a road map pointing out the "paths of righteousness" (Psalm 23:3)? Is there a book of instructions, listing the obligations or ethical demands for those in covenant with Jesus the Lord?

Several of Paul's epistles begin with doctrine and end with application for daily life, likely illustrating what he would do as a preacher as well as a writer. In Romans, for example, after eleven heavy chapters on God justifying man by faith, the last five chapters of application to daily life begin, "Therefore, I urge you, brothers, in view of God's mercy, to offer your bodies as living sacrifices, holy and pleasing to God" (Romans 12:1). The four Gospels, written by men we call evangelists, have been used across the centuries not only to herald what God has done but to instruct disciples in the art of Christian living. Faith conceived is to bring forth fidelity to the Savior. Preaching brought new converts into the fold. Teaching is now to consolidate the gains, so none be lost from that fold.

Under the Old Covenant the Israelites, who had been graciously rescued from bondage, were given Moses as a teacher to "show them the way to live and the duties they (were) to perform" (Exodus 18:20 cp. Deuteronomy 4:1,14; 6:1). Upon Moses' death, the responsibility of instructing Israel in how redeemed people were to act, passed to Joshua. He was told, "Be careful to obey all the law my servant Moses gave you; do not turn from it to the right or to the left . . . meditate on it day and night, so that you may be careful to do everything written in it" (Joshua 1:7-8). Under the New Covenant, those redeemed from sin's bondage by the blood of the Lamb of God are not lawless. While no longer under the law of Moses, the New Israel, the Church, is to "fulfill the law of Christ" (Galatians 6:2).

Paul's missionary technique was not to "win them, dip them and drop them." He wrote to the baptized believers, "We instructed you how to live in order to please God" (I Thessalonians 4:1). He expected them all to "live according to the teaching" (II Thessalonians 3:6) and to "obey . . . instruction" (II Thessalonians 3:14). He sent helpers to "give the people . . . instructions" (I Timothy 5:7) and specified, "These are the things you are to teach and urge on them" (I Timothy 6:2). A chasm of difference lies between the law of Moses and the law of Christ. It is written of the former that Israel "begged that no further word be spoken to them, because they could not bear what was commanded" (Hebrews 12:19-20). It is written of the latter, "Take my (Christ's) yoke upon you and learn from me, for I am gentle and humble in heart, and you will find rest for your souls. For my yoke is easy and my burden is light" (Matthew 11:29-30).

"Teacher, I will follow you wherever you go" (Matthew 8:19) is not a decision to be made lightly. To place oneself, as slave under a master's bidding, demands careful thought. The gospel call is a call to "obey" (Romans 15:18), a call to hear Jesus' words and put them into practice (Luke 6:47,49; 8:21), a call to "keep" or "do as Jesus . . . instructed" (Matthew 21:6). People under Christ's covenant know they have been loved and chosen to belong to Him. As sinners they have heard the unbelievingly kind words, "Neither do I condemn you." But they have also listened to the following declaration, "Go now and leave your life of sin" (John 8:11). The amazing grace of God is not cheap grace. Holy love demands transformation. Forgiveness is the starting point. Christlikeness is the goal. The "evangelists . . . pastors and teachers" work until each believer attains "the whole measure of the fullness of Christ" (Ephesians 4:11,13).

LIVING AS SERVANTS OF THE LORD

Jesus considered Himself the fulfillment of the prophetic announcement regarding a coming *ebed Yahweh* or servant of Jehovah. "For the student to be like his teacher, and the servant like his master" (Matthew 10:25) would then require a disciple of Christ to become a servant of God as Jesus was.

To serve a God, who "so loved the world that he gave his one and only Son" (John 3:16) for man's redemption, calls for service toward that same goal of world redemption. The preacher's job is not finished until those responding to the gospel call of salvation, echo that same call to those they meet in the way. A sinner, reached by the outstretched hand of the Lover of souls, must sense the obligation to become an extension of Christ's arm of love that reaches out for lost and straying souls.

To accept this God, who loves sinners, is to obligate oneself to seek for prodigal sons waiting to be welcomed home. It seems also logical to assume that to respond to the call from a God who "is light; (and) in (whom) there is no darkness at all" (I John 1:5), is to come under the ethical command, "Be holy, because I am holy" (I Peter 1:16). Preaching under the auspices of a holy God, caused John the Baptist's message before Herod to include the warning, "It is not lawful for you to have your brother's wife" (Mark 6:18). Proclaiming under heaven's directives, caused Jesus to rebuke the Pharisees' hypocrisy and it brought their unhappy response, "you insult us" (Luke 11:45). To "proclaim righteousness" (Joel 2:23), often calls for "a wise man's rebuke to a listening ear" (Proverbs 25:12).

Some may respond, "This is a hard teaching. Who can accept it?" (John 6:60). Others will call "the teaching about God our Savior attractive" as "it teaches us to say 'No' to ungodliness and worldly passions, and to live self-controlled, upright and godly lives in the present age" (Titus 2:10,12). The message of Jesus to the woman at the well contained the bitter pill, "You had five husbands, and the man you now have is not your husband" (John 4:18). But, taking the medicine of repentance, she came to know that Jesus "really is the Savior of the World" (John 4:42).

Preaching in the concept of Jesus was not giving psychological counseling on an individual or a group scale, aimed at getting the person or persons to feel better about themselves. He sought to bring His audiences of either one or many to an encounter with the Holy One Himself. A sinner confronted with his sin must decide to repent and cast himself on God's mercy or he must reject heaven's offer of grace, continuing in his sin until the final day of judgment. For any teacher to offer an easy forgiveness, without the repentance Christ required, is to trivialize God. Jesus' death on the cross was the price that had to be paid on God's side and the sinner's death to sin is the cost on the human side.

Servants of the holy God must preach repentance. John the Baptist did so with the result of the "people . . . confessing their sins . . . (and being) baptized by him in the Jordan River" (Matthew 3:1-2,5-6). John was said to be "preaching a baptism of repentance for the forgiveness of sins" (Mark 1:4; Luke 3:3 cp. Acts 13:24). Jesus understood His mission to be that of calling "sinners to repentance" (Luke 5:32). He sent out the twelve who "preached that people should repent" (Mark 6:12). Repentance was their call in Jerusalem (Acts 2:38; 3:19), Judea (Acts 26:20) and Samaria (Acts 8:22), and in the uttermost parts of the earth (Acts 17:30; 20:21). Noah had been called "a preacher of righteousness" (II Peter 2:5). Some, who have weeded old-fashioned words like "repent" out of their sermons, have themselves become "slaves of depravity" (II Peter 2:19).

LIVING AS MEMBERS OF THE CHURCH

Christian living is to be taught to those who respond to the preached gospel. Christlikeness demands teaching evangelism and holiness to converts, for God loves the lost and He has "loved righteousness and hated iniquity" (Hebrews 1:9). Since "God is love" (I John 4:8) and "God is light" (I John 1:5), His preachers are both to proclaim that "God so loved the world" that He sent "his Son . . . to save the world through him" (John 3:16-17); and they are also to preach that "without holiness no one will see the Lord" (Hebrews 12:14). As servants of the Lord, we are to be taught that we "should follow in his steps" (I Peter 2:21), loving the lost and living in holiness. Further, as members of the church, we are to be instructed in our new relationships and responsibility roles in the body.

"This is the message you heard from the beginning: We should love one another" (I John 3:11). As to brotherly love, we "have been taught by God to love each other" (I Thessalonians 4:9). The members of Christ's body, the church, need to learn from the first day that "quarreling about words . . . is of no value" (II Timothy 2:14) but to "love each other deeply . . . covers over a multitude of sins" (I Peter 4:8).

To love as Christ loved is to love the God above us and the brother beside us. To enter Christ is to enter a relationship with the other members of His body, the other children in His family. Unity, then, becomes one of the needed sermons for individuals and congregations to hear over and over again. "Christ loved the church and gave himself up for her . . . he feeds and cares for her" (Ephesians 5:25,29). In that church, "we who are many form one body, and each member belongs to all the others" (Romans 12:5). It is untenable to think that one member could say to any other, "I don't need you!" for all the members "are indispensible" (I Corinthians 12:21-22). Love is the family trait by which "all men will know" who are Christ's disciples (John 13:35).

Congregations need to hear sermons that admonish, "Keep on loving each other as brothers" (Hebrews 13:1). Members need also to hear messages that remind us that "it is required that those who have been given a trust . . . prove faithful" (I Corinthians 4:2). Upon entering the family of God, the believer has entered a ministry requiring faithful stewardship. In the body of believers each member has a relationship to enjoy and a role to fulfill. To be a member in the body is to have a function to perform for the benefit of the other members in that body. The success of one brings joy to all and the failure of one causes pain for all. "Let us not give up meeting together . . . but let us encourage one another" (Hebrews 10:25). Let our "word of exhortation" (Hebrews 13:22) include the admonition, "Be faithful, even to the point of death" (Revelation 2:10), for church membership does not consist in a baptismal certificate alone, but in a life where the believer affirms, "I no longer live, but Christ lives in me" (Galatians 2:20).

The baptism, that pictured the death and burial of the old self, also symbolized a resurrection after which the convert "may live a new life" (Romans 6:4). Paul joins in the doxology of all redeemed men, singing, "Thanks be to God that, though you used to be slaves to sin, you wholeheartedly obeyed the form of teaching to which you were entrusted . . . (and) set free from sin (you) have become slaves to righteousness" (Romans 6:17-18). A life after baptism that was no better than the life before baptism is unheard of on the pages of the New Testament. When the death of repentance precedes the burial of baptism, the old life style is over and the new way begun. The good news calls for turning "from . . . worthless things to the living God" (Acts 14:15). Hearts opened "to respond to . . . (the apostolic) message" (Acts 16:14), lead to converts that "openly confessed their evil deeds." Their transformation included such a decisive break with the past that "a number who had practiced sorcery brought their scrolls together and burned them publicly" (Acts 19:18-19). Those on their way to heaven deemed it fitting to begin allowing the Father's will to "be done on earth as it is in heaven" (Matthew 6:10).

Sermons that include warnings "night and day with tears" (Acts 20:31), or discourses "on righteousness, self-control and the judgment to come" (Acts 24:25), either result in turning to God or in trembling in fear. Neither consequence flows from nice words on sentimental themes that call for no discipline in disciples.

LIVING AS CITIZENS OF THE WORLD

Citizenship in the kingdom of heaven makes the Christian a better citizen of the earthly kingdom of which he is a part. Rendering "to God what is God's," does not annul the giving "to Caesar what is Caesar's" (Matthew 22:21). Those who live lives of Christlikeness, "pay taxes, for authorities are God's servants, who give their full time to governing" (Romans 13:6). Admonition to the newly baptized can call for submission "for the Lord's sake to every authority instituted among men" (I Peter 2:13).

Christian living in this present world calls for helpful teaching regarding the "liberty and justice for all" of which our pledge of allegiance speaks. The God who taught us to pray, "Defend the cause of the weak and fatherless; maintain the rights of the poor and oppressed" (Psalm 82:2), wants His people to work for the same objectives. Shall he who intercedes with God not "speak up for those who cannot speak for themselves" (Proverbs 31:8)? Do we serve a different God than Jeremiah who sent the prophet "to prophesy against this house and this city . . . (saying) 'reform your ways and your actions and obey the LORD your God' " (Jeremiah 26:12-13)? Is the social concern of Amos, bringing forth his "lament" (Amos 5:1), to have no place in the Christian era? When innocent blood is shed and people are killed for unjust gain, should gospel preachers "whitewash these deeds . . . by false visions and lying divinations" (Ezekiel 22:27-28)? Does obedience to the Lord include proclaiming "freedom for your fellow countrymen" (Jeremiah 34:17)?

"Religion that God our Father accepts as pure and faultless" includes both looking "after orphans and widows in their distress" and keeping "oneself from being polluted by the world" (James 1:27). The full gospel has the dimension of social responsibility and personal holiness. The Master Teacher's messages included denouncing the cities "in which most of his miracles had been performed, because they did not repent" (Matthew 11:20). He fulfilled Isaiah's description of the Messiah who would "proclaim justice to the nations" (Matthew 12:18). The forerunner, John the Baptist, preached a good news that included calls for honesty from "the crowd," from "tax collectors" and from "soldiers" (Luke 3:10,12,14,18). We who live after the days of the incarnation, are to preach a gospel that baptized believers will be "saved" and that non-believers will be "condemned" (Mark 16:16).

Preacher, the ancient words of God to Ezekiel stand as present words from Him to you: "Son of man, I have made you a watchman for the house of Israel; so hear the word I speak and give them warning from me. When I say to the wicked, 'O wicked man, you will surely die,' and you do not speak out to dissuade him from his ways, that wicked man will die for his sin, and I will hold you accountable for his blood. But if you do warn the wicked man to turn from his ways, and he does not do so, he will die for his sin, but you will have saved yourself" (Ezekiel 33:7-9).

15

PROCLAIMING THE APOSTOLIC

No one can play tennis, if there are no clearly marked lines on the court. No one can preach the gospel, when there is no understanding as to what constitutes gospel preaching. A sermon can be full of Scriptures from the Bible and yet be barren of the Christian message. Cults and sects of every description cite their favorite proof-texts with expertise and sway those with ears to hear. Can a sermon-craftsman use his hermeneutical tools with such care that his end-product is the gospel of Christ and not simply some unrelated Biblical passages nailed together at whim to fit Sunday's thirty-minute time slot?

The Rabbi in the synagogue down the street and the preacher at the Christian church around the corner may be dealing with the same passage from Isaiah. They both may have advanced degrees from Hebrew Union University and they both may have read the same commentaries, but there ought to be a noticeable difference in their sermons. One has been ordained to proclaim the gospel. The former might ask with the Eunuch regarding Isaiah 53, "Who is the prophet talking about?" (Acts 8:34). The latter with Philip will begin "with that very passage of Scripture and (tell) . . . the good news about Jesus" (Acts 8:35).

Disciples of Christ devoted themselves "to the apostles' teaching" (Acts 2:42). Apostles of Christ admonished their churches, "Stand firm and hold to the teachings we passed on to you, whether by word of mouth or by letter" (II Thessalonians 2:15). They knew their testimony to be "the word of God . . . not . . . the word of men" (II Thessalonians 2:13). Peter spoke of the apostolic tradition as "the command given by our Lord and Savior through your apostles" (II Peter 3:2). Paul praised his churches for "holding to the teachings, just as (he) passed them on" (I Corinthians 11:2). The message that they heard from him, they were to "keep as the pattern of sound teaching" (II Timothy 1:13). He called that entrusted teaching "our message" (II Timothy 4:15), "what you have learned" (3:14) and "the things you have heard me say in the presence of many witnesses" (2:2). John declared the apostles to be from God saying, "Whoever knows God listens to us" (I John 4:6), When you sermonize, be one who "correctly handles the word of truth" (II Timothy 2:15). Follow the gospel blueprint passed on by the Carpenter of Nazareth. Read your Old Testament through His eyes. It is in the writings of the apostles, we learn "the mind of Christ" (I Corinthians 2:16).

APOSTLES PREACHED THE NEW COVENANT, NOT THE OLD

There is a danger that the expository preacher needs to avoid when he works his homiletical way through Old Testament books. His lesson should have the clear sound of a Christian minister who lives on this side of Jesus' death and resurrection. Christ "has made us competent as ministers of a new covenant" (II Corinthians 3:6). Jesus, the prophesied "messenger of the covenant" (Malachi 3:1) spoke of "the new covenant in my (his) blood, which is poured out for you" (Luke 22:20).

Jeremiah was not speaking empty words, when he predicted that the "new covenant" would "not be like the covenant . . . made with (the) forefathers" (Jeremiah 31:31-32 cp. Hebrews 8:8-9). The old covenant between God and Israel[1] had Moses as its mediator. The new covenant between God and the church has Jesus as its mediator (Hebrews 12:24). "The covenant of which he (Christ) is mediator is superior to the old one, and it is founded on better promises" (Hebrews 8:6).

The ten commandments delivered at Mount Sinai were engraved on stone and called the "tablets of the covenant" (Hebrews 9:4). In having called the covenant in Jesus' blood " 'new,' he (God) has made the first one obsolete" (Hebrews 8:13). In an allegory based on the women Hagar and Sarah and their sons Isacc and Ishmael, Paul contrasts the covenants of Mount Sinai and the Jerusalem above. Instead of mixing covenants, as though they were of equal authority, Paul's advice is "Get rid of the slave woman and her son" (Galatians 4:21-31). Judaizers blended into one mix the old and new. The apostolic teaching spoke of their discontinuity. At the feet of Jesus His apostles had learned the lesson neither to tear "a patch from a new garment and (sew) it on an old one," nor to pour "new wine into old wineskins" (Luke 5:36-39). At the Mount of Transfiguration they had seen Moses and Elijah vanish with only Jesus remaining. Heaven's voice, at the disappearance of Moses (the Law) and Elijah (the Prophets), called for listening to Jesus the only personage to remain (Luke 9:28-36).

The preacher must not treat the Bible in all its parts as on a level. The New Testament brings more light than that revealed in the Old Testament. While every Bible book is equally inspired of

---

1. Leviticus 7:23; 11:2; 12:2; 15:2; 17:2,8; 18:2; 19:2; 20:2; 21:1; 22:17; 23:2,9,29; 25:2; 26:46; 27:2,34; Numbers 15:2,18; 18:26,30; 36:13; Deuteronomy 1:1,3; 29:2.

God, not every passage is equally authoritative for the church age. A New Testament church is under a higher covenant than an Old Testament synagogue. Let your sermons from either testament show clearly you know the difference Christ has made. To be "still preaching circumcision" (Galatians 5:11) would be preaching as if Jesus had never set "aside the first to establish the second" (Hebrews 10:9).

APOSTLES PREACHED THE GOSPEL, NOT THE LAW

One Bible reason for preaching is "to contend for the faith that was once for all entrusted to the saints" (Jude 3). It is the gospel and not the law that "has been entrusted to (our) care" (I Timothy 6:20). "For the law was given through Moses; grace and truth came through Jesus Christ" (John 1:17).

The apostolic faith taught "the purpose of the law" was to serve as a tutor. It "was put in charge to lead us to Christ that we might be justified by faith." Does that mean that the ceremonies, food regulations and other statutes are still binding? Paul's answer is, "Now that faith has come, we are no longer under the supervision of the law" (Galatians 3:19,24-25). If "Christ is the end of the law" (Romans 10:4), don't give the impression in your sermons that it is still binding. Since Jesus "canceled the written code, with its regulations . . . nailing it to the cross," don't allow your message from an Old Testament text to leave the audience feeling judged, regarding "meat or drink . . . a religious festival, a New Moon celebration or a Sabbath day" (Colossians 2:14,16-17).

The Gospels often contrast the apostles Jesus sent out with "teachers of the law"[2] or "experts in the law."[3] Jesus' preaching

---

2. Matthew 12:38; 13:52; 16:21; 17:10; 20:18; 23:2,15,23,25,27,29; 26:57; Mark 1:22; 2:6; 3:22; 7:1,5; 8:31; 10:33; 11:18; 12:28,38; 14:1,53; 15:1,31; Luke 5:17,21,30; 9:22; 11:53; 20:1,19,39,46; 22:2; 23:10; John 8:3 cp. Acts 4:5; 5:34; 23:9.

3. Luke 10:25; 11:45.

amazed His audiences, because it had an "authority, not as the teachers of the law" (Mark 1:22). His very death could be laid at the feet of His rejecters, such as "teachers of the law" (Mark 8:31; Luke 9:22). His own disciples heard Him warn, "Watch out for the teachers of the law" (Mark 12:38). Paul as a Christian held out the disclaimer, "I myself am not under the law." But he made it clear he was dedicated "to win those under the law" (I Corinthians 9:20).

Since Jesus sent men out to "preach the good news to all creation" (Mark 16:15), why should some "want to be teachers of the law?" Paul ridicules the Judaizers with the charge, "they do not know what they are talking about, or what they so confidently affirm" (I Timothy 1:7). To avoid such condemnation, "hold firmly to the trustworthy message as it has been taught" (Titus 1:9) and "pay no attention to Jewish myths" (1:13). "Sound doctrine" (2:1) is more firmly held by those who "avoid foolish controversies and genealogies and arguments and quarrels about the law" (3:9). Do you hear the caution? Do you see the flashing amber light of warning? A preacher can take texts from inspired writings of Scripture and still so misuse them that the law of Moses is heard rather than the gospel of Christ. Avoid the error made by "the believers who belonged to the party of the Pharisees (who) stood up and said, 'The Gentiles must be circumcised and required to obey the law of Moses' " (Acts 15:5). Rather agree with Peter's words to the legalists, "Why do you try to test God by putting on the necks of the disciples a yoke that neither we nor our fathers have been able to bear" (Acts 15:11).

It was a false charge against the early deacon, when some said, "We have heard Stephen speak words of blasphemy against Moses" (Acts 6:11) and others testified, "This fellow never stops speaking against the holy place and against the law" (6:13). It was a false charge against the apostle to the uncircumcision, when some accused Paul of "persuading people to worship God in ways contrary to the law" (18:13) or to "teach all men everywhere against our people (Jews) and our law and this place" (21:28). The apostolic teaching was rather that the promised Messiah had come in Jesus, the law of the Jews had been fulfilled, the sacrificial system had found meaning in the death of Christ and He as the Son of David was now conquering the entire world.

The kingdom of God was but an unfulfilled promise before. Now it is a reality (Matthew 11:13). The baptism by John prepared for the coming King. Now King Jesus is reigning from His heavenly throne. The ancient prophets "spoke of the grace that was to come" (I Peter 1:10). Now the apostles are telling the incarnation fact, saying, "We are witnesses of these things" (Acts 5:32 cp. 8:25; 10:40-42; 13:30-31).

APOSTLES PREACHED THE CHRIST, NOT MOSES

Apostolic preaching is covenant-conscious. It is gospel-conscious. It is Christ-conscious. At the Jerusalem council, James, the Lord's half-brother, states the fact, "Moses has been preached in every city from the earliest times and is read in the synagogues on every Sabbath" (Acts 15:21). Early history is quick to describe Christian assemblies on the Lord's Day. There Christ was preached and Bible readings included reading from the Gospels then called the Memoirs of the Apostles (Justin Martyr: *Apologia* 1:67).

The job description for the Twelve was akin to that of the Holy Spirit. Jesus' upper-room discourse reads, "The Spirit of truth . . . will testify about me; but you also must testify, for you have been with us from the beginning" (John 15:26-27). When this band of preachers set out after Pentecost to do their assigned work of making Christ known, they openly affirmed, "We are witnesses of these things, and so is the Holy Spirit" (Acts 5:32). Their writings make the same claim, as they penned, "This is the message we have heard from him and declare to you" (I John 1:5). Their warnings rang out that some would "not continue in the teaching of Christ" (II John 9), but Christ was, is and would ever be the theme of apostolic testimony.

The church of Christ is founded on the apostles' teaching regarding Jesus. "No one can lay any foundation other than the one already laid, which is Jesus Christ" (I Corinthians 3:11). The function of preaching is to lay that foundation in any community where it has not yet been laid. The "apostles' teaching" (Acts 2:41), which is from Christ, about Christ and for Christ, is the norm because it is "the mind of Christ" (I Corinthians 2:16). For that reason an apostle can exhort the Christian worker, "Whatever you have learned or received or heard from me . . . put it into practice" (Philippians 4:9).

No preacher, while doing exposition of Genesis through Deuteronomy, is to preach Moses. Rather hear heaven's guiding word, "Fix your thoughts on Jesus. . . . Jesus has been found worthy of greater honor than Moses. . . . Moses was faithful as a son in all God's house. . . . But Christ is faithful as a son over God's house. And we are his house" (Hebrews 3:1,5-6). As Jesus said, "If you hold my teaching, you are really my disciples" (John 8:31). Disciples of Christ preach Christ. They know the difference between Law and gospel. They see the distinction between Old Covenant and New Covenant. They perceive that type is not the same as antitype.

APOSTLES PREACHED THE SUBSTANCE, NOT THE SHADOW

There is a difference that needs recognition between shadow and reality. "The law is only a shadow of the good things that are coming — not the realities themselves," wrote the author of Hebrews (10:1). Paul, dealing with Old Testament food regulations and holy days, added, "These are a shadow of the things that were to come; the reality, however, is found in Christ" (Colossians 2:16-17).

This is to say that the Law, Prophets and Psalms of the Synagogue constituted the Bible of the earliest church, but there was a difference. Through the eyes of Jesus the apostles had come to see in the ancient writings not only Hebrew history but the story of Jesus and the church in type.

In typology Jesus was the second "Adam" (Romans 5:12-21; I Corinthians 15:22,45), "our Passover lamb" (I Corinthians 5:7) and "the firstfruits" (I Corinthians 15:20,23). Israel's exodus from Egyptian bondage became an analogy for the church's deliverance from Satan's entrapment. Passing through the sea symbolized baptism and eating manna a picture of the Lord's Supper (I Corinthians 10:1-13). Tabernacle furnishings were seen as picture prophecy regarding the church, being called "the copies of the heavenly things" (Hebrews 8:23). The laver was the washing of baptism, the table of shewbread communion, the candelabra the Scripture, incense prayer and the holy of holies heaven (Hebrews 9). Where Leviticus 23 with its festal calendar might be boring to a Gentile Christian, it takes on the glow of excitement when seen as a mural of events in the life of Christ and His church.

Peter used the Noah story of ark and flood to illustrate the saving power of baptism into Christ (I Peter 3:20-22). Jesus had made the familiar story of Jonah in the belly of a huge fish for three days and nights a foretelling of His coming death and resurrection.

The point is that the Old Testament texts are rich in illustrative materials for New Testament preachers. Only remember that, when you find in the Genesis to Malachi material what Jesus and the apostles found, you are on solid ground. When you interpret the old prophecies as the inspired New Testament writers did you are in good company. However, sinking sand and extremely thin ice, await the sermonizer, who finds types at every turn and fantasies on every page, even though no apostle or his Lord noticed them. Another word of caution would be to let the apostles' use of the Old Covenant Scriptures guide you into what passages are significant to the church. It is a good rule of thumb to allow the Gospels and Epistles to interpret the Law and Prophets, rather than *vice versa*.

Part Four
THE MOTIVES
(THE HERE'S WHY OF PREACHING)

16

PREACHING SAVES

If the preaching described in the book of Acts is intended to be normative, sermons will not pass muster that are only pep talks on morality. The evangelists of apostolic days that heralded the evangel gave messages that had an evangelistic sound. They were addressing men regarding life and death matters. They believed that preaching was God's way of reaching the lost. Each spokesman from the apostle Peter to the apostle Paul, or each messenger from the deacon Stephen to the deacon Philip, was bent on winning souls.

These gospelers were not in the order of some of the Old Testament prophets, announcing the bad news of coming doom on a wicked city or nation. Their audiences heard the joyful sound of a Savior that offered the grace of forgiveness. The work of preaching was a serious task for a serious day with a potential glorious ending, if the listener would but respond.

"The ministry of the word" (Acts 6:4) held priority, even over the important social action work of feeding the hungry. Christ's men resisted the temptation in ministry of getting so involved in doing work in so many good organizations that preaching became secondary. Today's spokesmen need to be aware that churches are looking for youth leaders, psychological counselors, fund raisers and capable administrators, but God is still looking for gospel preachers burdened for the salvation of men.

Hear a "thus saith the Lord." "The message of the cross is foolishness to those who are perishing, but to us who are being saved it is the power of God. . . . God was pleased through the foolishness of what was preached to save those who believe" (I Corinthians 1:18,21). Don't fail to miss that "God was pleased" to offer salvation. Do not overlook that χηρύγμα in this sentence is a noun and not a verb. It is not the act of preaching that saves, but the substance of the testimony. It was not talking that the world thought foolish, but the message of the gospel being spoken. Yet, the gospel to be gospel has to be told in order for it to be good news and accomplish redemption.

"Paul," we ask, "why (are you) so eager to preach the gospel?" He answers, "The gospel . . . is the power of God for the salvation of everyone who believes" (Romans 1:15-16). He replies again, "By this gospel you are saved" (I Corinthians 15:2). "God," we inquire, "for what reason are you sending a preacher to me?" He responds, "He will bring you a message through which you and all your household will be saved" (Acts 11:14).

Without the messenger, the people will hear no message. Sinners, whose lives have been changed by the grace of God, are the best proclaimers of the forgiveness that has touched them. Charles H. Spurgeon, moved by the wonder of the gospel, could not understand a preacher who acted like "a lion engaged in mouse-hunting." Such a fate could never happen to the man in the pulpit who has the understanding of preaching's real purpose. In the words of Harold Knott, "To face . . . a congregation, and give them the only message that can lift them out of the transient and the sordid into the eternal and sublime; to tell people in terms of our own experience, the unspeakable joy of communion with the Infinite — is a privilege any one might covet."[1]

THE WONDER OF OUR WORDS

Speaking words can stir up a riot or start a revival. Words, by a comic in a cocktail lounge, can get an audience roaring with laughter. Words, by a minister in a chapel, can bring worshipers face to face with God. The words of John the Baptist brought "many of the people of Israel . . . back to the Lord their God" (Luke 1:16). The words of Peter were given that men "might hear from (his) lips the message of the gospel and believe" (Acts 15:7). The words of Paul enabled men "to come to a knowledge of the truth" (I Timothy 2:4). In preaching, God reveals himself.

Words have power. The words of sermons can disturb a conscience, kindle a mind, strengthen a will and transform a life. Preaching has the awesome power to confront, convict and convert a hearer, for the words are used by God. Sermons confront intellects to inform and convince. They address emotions to stimulate, inspire and persuade. They speak to the will, exhorting, challenging, appealing. The Scriptures remind us that "the word of faith we are proclaiming" brings salvation to believers and that faith can only come to "they (who) hear . . . someone preaching to them . . . (for) faith comes from hearing the message" (Romans 10:8,14,17). Wherever the gospel was preached, "many who heard the message believed" (Acts 4:4, cp. II Thessalonians 1:10). It was so in Samaria, where "they believed Philip as he preached the good news" (Acts 8:12). It was that way in Iconium, as Paul and Barnabas "spoke so effectively that a great number of Jews and Gentiles believed" (Acts 14:1). The cause and effect order continued in Achaia, where "many of

---

1. *How to Prepare a Sermon* (Cincinnati: Standard Publishing Co.), p. 19.

the Corinthians who heard . . . believed" (Acts 18:8). In Jesus' ministry it was said, "even as he spoke, many put their faith in him" (John 8:30). His prayer was, "I pray also for those who will believe in me through their message" (John 17:20).

It should give great encouragement to workers to recall that the same seed sown today will have the same results (cp. Mark 4:26-29). To "have sown spiritual seed" (I Corinthians 9:11) is to have relied on the law of the harvest, that it will be "God (who has) made it grow" (I Corinthians 3:6). If the word of Christ will have enough power to raise the dead at the final day, it has sufficient power to bring life to hearers now (John 5:28-29,25). It is not required of a preacher that he get results, but that he faithfully preach the gospel and leave it to God to give the increase. Depend on the promise: "As the rain and the snow come down from heaven . . . watering the earth and making it bud and flourish . . . so is my word that goes out from my mouth: It will . . . achieve the purpose for which I sent it" (Isaiah 55:10-11).

Discussion groups have their place. Pageants, dramas and movies are allies of the pulpit. But, preaching is the church's mightiest weapon. "Preach the word" (II Timothy 4:2). It is an anomaly to find an "evangelical" with a high view of scriptural inspiration and yet a low view of preaching's power, when that Scripture is said to be "able to make (one) wise for salvation" (II Timothy 3:15).

THE SCOPE OF OUR HOPE

"Salvation which was first announced by the Lord" (Hebrews 2:3), is a diamond of many facets, reflecting light in every direction. So a preacher, telling God's love story day by day, never needs fail in finding fresh ways of describing our hope of salvation. Preaching good news is "to bind up the brokenhearted, to proclaim freedom for the captives and release for the prisoners"

(Isaiah 61:1).

Included in the vast scope of salvation is sin's forgiveness. The preaching of the Baptist was "to give his people the knowledge of salvation through the forgiveness of their sins" (Luke 1:77). It was the expressed will of Jesus that "repentance and forgiveness of sins . . . be preached in his name to all nations, beginning at Jerualem" (Luke 24:47). "Forgiveness of sins through his (Jesus') name" was Peter's "message" (Acts 10:43-44 cp. Acts 2:38). Paul echoed, "Through Jesus the forgiveness of sins is proclaimed to you" (Acts 13:38 cp. 26:18). "Sins . . . wiped out" (Acts 3:19) is an appealing message. Being "justified from everything you could not be justified from by the law of Moses" (Acts 13:39) has an attractive ring.

Who, that is enslaved in trespasses and sins, does not rejoice to hear that Christ's "truth will set . . . free" (John 8:32)? Who, that lives in dark corners of despair, does not thrill to learn of a gospel that can "open . . . eyes and turn them from darkness to light" (Acts 26:18)? If you are of the world's lonely and homeless, are you not glad to hear heaven's message proclaimed "so that you also may have fellowship . . . with the Father and with his Son, Jesus Christ" (I John 1:3)? In the saving message of the Lord, He "preached peace" (Ephesians 2:17 cp. John 16:33). His spoken words were "life" (John 6:63). One is "born again . . . through the living and enduring word of God . . . the word that was preached to you" (I Peter 1:23,25). The consequence of preaching is that the reborn man "will never see death" (John 8:51), but rather enjoy "eternal life" (John 10:28).

Preaching can never become tiresome or outmoded, because man's needs have remained basically the same over the years. History is still being repeated, as converts continue to rise from baptismal waters to go on their way "rejoicing," and the evangelists keep going about "preaching the gospel in all the towns" (Acts 8:39-40 cp. verse 8).

The dynamic, creative, sin-destroying word makes whole all who receive it. The salvation it brings heals, defeats sin and gives life to each person who believes. The preacher is no huckster at a county fair promoting a product that matters very little. He is an ambassador on Christ's behalf, announcing reconciliation with God (II Corinthians 5:20). He is a physician of souls, offering the cure for man's basic problem of separation from his Creator. To God's church he does "speak tenderly . . . and proclaim . . . that her hard service has been complete, that her sin has been paid for" (Isaiah 40:2).

What a wonderful gospel that "will save both yourself and your hearers" (I Timothy 4:16)! "I commit you to God and to the words of his grace, which can build you up and give you an inheritance among all who are sanctified" (Acts 20:32). God's words of grace "turn man from wrongdoing and keep him from pride, to preserve his soul from the pit, his life from perishing" (Job 33:17-18). We preach a God of grace who "sent forth his word and healed" (Psalm 107:20). "The tongue of the wise brings healing" (Proverbs 18:21), so preach grace and bring life. True is the proverb that "the tongue that brings healing is a tree of life" (Proverbs 15:4 cp. 13:14).

THE REACH OF OUR PREACH

John the Baptist was a voice for God, who pointed to Jesus as "the Lamb of God" and testified, "this is the Son of God" (John 1:29-34). Note with interest the next line of Scripture: "When the two disciples heard him say this, they followed Jesus" (verse 35). Hearing the preacher, they followed Jesus. That is God's hope and intention in all preaching. Behind the preaching of man is the reaching of God. Sermons are Christ's way of reaching people. Preachers are his partners in the calling of the lost to himself.

As Matthew Simpson in 1879 wrote of God's co-worker the preacher, "His throne is the pulpit; he stands in Christ's stead; his message is the word of God; around him are immortal souls; the

Savior, unseen, is beside him; the Holy Spirit broods over the congregation; angels gaze upon the scene, and heaven and hell await the issue. What association, and what vast responsibility" (*Lectures on Preaching*, New York: Phillips and Hunt, p. 166.)

If you preach, you are an instrument of God. He is acting to convict, call and change the people He loves and for whom His Son died. There is a sense in which unless someone on earth will preach, God in heaven cannot reach the lost. We need to pray for God's contagious concern for people, so that we might preach with urgency. In the words of Rudolph Bultmann, true preaching is "the call of God through the mouth of man."

Jesus stated the purpose behind His incarnation in the words, "I have . . . come to call . . . sinners to repentance" (Luke 5:32; Matthew 9:13). The reach for souls continued as others felt "compelled to preach . . . to win as many as possible" (I Corinthians 9:16,19). The progress reports, that Luke records in Acts, tell "how the word of God spread; (6:7), "the church . . . grew in numbers" (9:31; 16:5; 19:20) and "the word of God continued to increase" (12:24), as its proponents "boldly and without hindrance . . . preached the kingdom of God and taught about the Lord Jesus Christ" (28:31).

You have heard the joyful sound, preaching saves. That is what the Bible says. Join David in the vow, "My mouth will speak in praise of the LORD" (Psalm 145:21 cp. 109:30). Make the Psalmist's prayer, your supplication for all preachers: "May the praise of God be in their mouths" (149:6). Why speak for the applause of men, when you can preach for the glory of God and man's salvation?

17

PREACHING EDIFIES

The same verse that calls on evangelists like Timothy to "Preach the Word," asks that it be done "with great patience and careful instruction" (II Timothy 4:2). There is the gospel that the people of the world need to know for their salvation and there are further truths that the saved of the church need to learn for their edification. The primary goal of preaching is to create a believing community where none exists and then to nurture and perfect that body of believers until they attain "the whole measure of the fullness of Christ" (Ephesians 4:13). The preacher is to be both evangelical and didactic. After he does "make disciples . . . baptizing them," he is then to start "teaching them" (Matthew 28:19-20).

Everyone who speaks in a Christian assembly, "speaks to men for their strengthening, encouragement and comfort" (I Corinthians 14:3). The KJV wording is "edification, and exhortation, and comfort." That makes the preacher's job description to build up, stir up and cheer up. The first of these is our present focus, for he who preaches "edifies the church" (14:4).

Note the similarity of sound and sense in the words edifice and edify. The Latin *aedification* is from the noun for house or temple (*aedes*) and the verb meaning to make or build (*ficare*). Each life in Christ is joined, as a living stone, to the other lives in him, constituting "God's building . . . God's temple" (I Corinthians 3:9, 16-17). That church needs to be edified or built up. The disciples of Christ continually gather to receive the instruction that the Christ of the disciples ever longs to give His followers.

Jesus, the one often called "Teacher," so edified an audience that both the individual or "the large crowd listened to him with delight" (Mark 12:37). Their question often became, "Where did this man get the wisdom?" (Matthew 13:54; Mark 6:2). As "the Queen of the South . . . came from the ends of the earth to listen to Solomon's wisdom," those who call Jesus Lord, gather to study at the feet of the one "greater than Solomon" (Matthew 12:42; Luke 11:31). The Old Testament record is true, "God gave Solomon wisdom and very great insight, and a breadth of understanding as measureless as the sand of the seashore" (I Kings 4:29). But, so is the New Testament affirmation that "the full riches of complete understanding" is in Christ where "are hidden all the treasures of wisdom and knowledge" (Colossians 2:2-3).

The modern preacher is the fulfillment of Christ's promise, "I am sending you prophets and wise men and teachers" (Matthew 23:34). These workers are "for believers" and "for the strengthening of the church . . . so that everyone may be instructed" (I Corinthians 14:22,26,31). The regular weekly talk, called the preacher's sermon, should be "only what is helpful for building others up according to their needs" and to "benefit those who listen" (Ephesians 4:29).

The church, as the body of Christ, listens to its preacher, as the voice of Christ.

EDIFYING SERMONS BUILD UP

A sermon in a Christian community is not to tickle ears but to inform minds. Once lives are founded on the rock foundation of the gospel, they need to be built up in understanding. That calls for steady sermonic diets of clarifying information. After a day of preaching, when "Jesus spoke the word" to the populace "as much as they could understand," He would then supplement His words with additional clarifying insights. The Bible reads, "But when he was alone with his own disciples, he explained everything" (Mark 4:33-34). If questions still remained and His disciples would inquire, "What does he mean . . . ? We don't understand what he is saying" (John 16:18), He would patiently keep exposing the truth.

All education comes very slowly and over much time. While there are cases of conversion, where in one night a pagan jailer can become a child of God (cp. Acts 16:22-34), there of necessity follows a life-time of growing into Christ-likeness. Impregnation takes a moment. Development from embryo to full manhood takes years of time. Paul and his associates understood "the commission God gave to present . . . the word of God in its fulness." Therefore they were "teaching everyone with all wisdom, so that (they) may present everyone perfect in Christ" (Colossians 2:25,28). He spent all his days laboring at a task that in this world can never be done completely.

It was the testimony of Saul of Tarsus that at "about noon . . . suddenly a bright light from heaven flashed around me" (Acts 22:6 cp. 26:13). Many a worshiper, after the Scripture exposition of an 11:00 A.M. Sunday service, has had a comparable experience at "about noon." Because of the helpful insights of the morning sermon, a clearer grasp of a Biblical passage radiates the sunshine of heaven into a life. One of preaching's purposes has been fulfilled. Vital information for Christian living has been given.

In every Jewish community the synagogue was a house for instruction. To every preacher the Christian congregation's meeting room is to be seen as a classroom, where Jesus' disciples have gathered to be taught. The members own the textbook — the Bible. They have read it, but when asked, "Do you understand what you are reading?" their answer is often that of the Ethiopian treasurer of the queen, "How can I . . . unless someone explains it to me?" (Acts 8:30-31). Happy is that congregation whose pulpit voice does not leave them mystified, but edified. The nature of good preaching is to reveal — to give insight — to interpret Scripture.

Parched souls are not helped by spiritual shepherds that "are clouds without rain" (Jude 12), failing the listener's expectation of refreshing words from the pulpit. "The fountain of wisdom is a bubbling brook" (Proverbs 18:4) and a "fountain of life" (Proverbs 13:14). Pray that God's Spirit gift you with "the message of wisdom" or "the message of knowledge" (I Corinthians 12:8). Paul thanked God for "the gift of God's grace . . . to preach . . . and to make plain" (Ephesians 3:7-9).

At what University does a speaker learn to communicate and "make plain" the ways of God? Solomon knew that "the LORD gives wisdom and from his mouth come knowledge and understanding" (Proverbs 2:6). David knew that it was God's revelation, which was "perfect . . . making wise the simple" and "giving light to the eyes" (Psalm 19:7-8). Seven earned Doctor's degrees do not guarantee that a preacher is prepared adequately to "feed (Jesus') lambs" or "sheep" (John 21:15,17). As "Ezra had devoted himself to the study and observance of the Law of the LORD, and to teaching its decrees and laws in Israel" (Ezra 7:10), the preacher must devote himself to studying, living and teaching the gospel of Christ. Know books, but especially the Book. Learn from teachers, but especially the Teacher. It is "God and . . . the word of his grace, which can build you up" (Acts

20:32) and build up the flock you feed.

EDIFYING SERMONS NAIL DOWN

If your converts are not to remain "infants, tossed back and forth by the waves, and blown here and there by every wind of teaching" (Ephesians 4:14) give attention to indoctrination. When strong winds of unsound doctrine blow like a gale across television screens and bookstore shelves, the babe in Christ is dependent on a teacher that will nail down the facts that eternally matter to him or her.

Indoctrination is neither a bad word nor a bad idea. *Doctrina* is the Latin word for teaching, for its root is the verb *docere* which means to teach. So, preacher, be a good doctor of the doctrine of Christ. It is astonishing how many persons "are turning to a different gospel — which is really no gospel at all" (Galatians 1:6-7).

Luke wanted Theophilus to "know the certainty of the things (he had) been taught" (Luke 1:4). The evangelist Timothy was sent as a fellow worker among congregations "to strengthen and encourage" believers in their faith. The preacher Epaphras from Colossae wanted his people to "stand firm in all the will of God, mature and fully assured" (Colossians 4:12).

How can the newly-baptized be saved from later being capsized by a false teacher? The convictions that brought the convert to Christ need to be confirmed. Tempting doubts need to be dispelled and troubling questions need to be answered. As a newly-planted tree may be saved from uprooting during the violent wind storm by the strong stake to which it is tied, a young church member can be rescued from being blown away by error because his wise minister of the Word has taken time to nail down the teachings that mattered. The apostle spoke of God being "able to establish you by . . . the proclamation of Jesus Christ" (Romans 16:25). "The words of the wise are like . . . firmly embedded nails" (Ecclesiastes 12:11).

The heart of the early church is revealed in the book of Acts, as you read of young churches being visited and revisited by preachers "strengthening the disciples and encouraging them to remain true to the faith" (14:22). "Strengthening the churches" (15:41), leaving them "strengthened in the faith" (16:5), was part and parcel of the task given the ministers of the Word. Has "strengthening all the disciples" (18:23) been the words written in your monthly minister's report of activities? Did you tell the "board" in that report how you spent time with a teacher and "explained to him the way of God more adequately" (18:26)?

The ability to think and reason is a distinguishing factor marking man as above the animals. God expects those made in His image to think. He wants His proclaimers to stimulate His people to use their minds. A sermon could well begin, "Come now, let us reason together" (Isaiah 1:18). It could well continue, "Reflect on what I am saying" (I Timothy 2:7). It might well review, "Don't you remember that when I was with you I used to tell you these things?" (II Thessalonians 2:5).

The sane, sensible, reasonable and rational religion of Christianity does not ask its followers to leave their brains at the door as they enter the church structure to worship. Moslems may take off their shoes as they enter a mosque, but the disciples of Christ put on their thinking caps. Jesus expects, over a period of time, for his followers to be "teachers." "Elementary teachings about Christ" (Hebrews 6:1 cp. 5:12) are the topics as we enter the school of Christ, but a teacher, who never raises his listener's level of learning beyond this first level, has cheated his students. Paul could say to his audiences, "You have been enriched" (I Corinthians 1:5). Regarding his "speaking," Paul wrote, "Everything we do, dear friends, is for your strengthening" (II Corinthians 12:19). He spent his days "defending and confirming the gospel" (Philippians 1:7). His daily schedule reads, "From morning till evening he explained and declared . . . the kingdom of God" (Acts 28:23).

Not to firmly fasten down a house's shingles could have the

consequence of losing the entire roof during the violent winds of winter. Not to cement well the saving truths in the minds of believers will have an even more costly loss. Join Peter in the resolution, "I will always remind you of these things, even though you know them and are firmly established in the truth you now have. I think it is right to refresh your memory" (II Peter 1:12-13). Repetition drives a truth home. The old, old story can be told in fresh and new ways, but it must be restated again and again lest we forget. It can still be said of the aging saint, who has been hearing sermons for half a century, "Instruct a wise man and he will be wiser still; teach a righteous man and he will add to his learning" (Proverbs 9:9).

Convictions are confirmed and beliefs are revitalized each Lord's day for those who do "not give up meeting together" (Hebrews 10:25). The evidence is in. When a shepherd feeds his sheep, those sheep do not become fed up with their shepherd.

EDIFYING SERMONS SMOOTH OUT

The carpenter's plane, rasp and sandpaper knock off the rough spots and smooth out the slivered boards until they are ready for painting. The preacher's lessons have the task not only of information and confirmation but of transformation. As surely as instruments of music need tuning, the Christian, as God's instrument, needs adjustment to the perfect standard. A mind informed, without a life transformed, leaves a believer deformed. Let the preacher remember that "rebuking, correcting and training in righteousness" (II Timothy 3:16) is the emery board required in preaching to get the desired finished product, which is a life like Christ's.

Since you are "transformed by the renewing of your mind" (Romans 12:2), the edifier must work with the mind so that it does "not conform any longer to the pattern of the world." A former demon-possessed man in the third pew before you, "sitting there, dressed and in his right mind" (Mark 5:15) is ample evidence of the transforming power of gospel preaching. If your homilies do not change lives, change the sermons.

EDIFYING SERMONS SHOW OFF

It is written long before the time of Christ, "The lips of a priest ought to preserve knowledge, and from his mouth men should seek instruction — because he is the messenger of the LORD Almighty. But you have turned from the way and by your teaching have caused many to stumble" (Malachi 2:7-8). It must be different today. He who lays the foundation for another's faith and builds on it with information, secures it with confirmation and works with it unto transformation, dare not fail to lack in personal demonstration. The builder of a house is always glad for the day, when the project is far enough along, that the doors can be opened and people can view the result of his labors. Show time has to come.

A good teacher in any discipline informs, instructs and demonstrates. The best teaching of the Christian walk is done by modeling. The requirement for preaching is not a PhD. The spokesman does not need to be a V.I.P. The first requisite is to be an example of the message preached. To preach prayer, love or self-giving with actions that drown out the words is futile. What Paul asked of Jewish teachers, he would inquire of the Christian instructors: "You, then, who teach others, do you not teach yourself? You who preach against stealing, do you steal? You who say that people should not commit adultery, do you commit adultery?" (Romans 2:21-22).

The proof of the pudding is in the eating. The value of the church is in the lives produced. If the way of life modeled by the leadership of the church is not of a higher order than that of the world, the pulpit should join Trappist monks in taking the vow of silence. Put up or shut up are the options. Jesus could say,

"Every day I was with you, teaching in the temple courts" (Mark 14:49). He could also affirm that every night and day, in Judea or in Galilee, He was teaching the same truths with His life that He was declaring with His lips. It is written of Him, "Everyone who heard him was amazed at his understanding and his answers" (Luke 2:47). I am more amazed at the attractive holiness of His life. That kind of preaching by demonstration is hard to contradict. When the Thessalonians were told, "You, yourselves, have been taught by God" (I Thessalonians 4:9), it is obvious that the lesson from heaven had come both through Paul's preaching and his example.

Is your example ample? You are well-advised to walk the talk before you talk the walk. To be a reflection of Jesus is the highest form of preaching. To tell of His perfections with flagrant imperfections in morals is to be a reflection on Christ. The vessel offering the water of life does not have to be golden, but it must be clean. Being Christian precedes preaching Christ.

18

PREACHING ENCOURAGES

Hear words spoken to an Old Testament preacher: "Comfort, comfort my people, says your God. Speak tenderly to Jerusalem" (Isaiah 40:1-2). Hear the prophetic words Jesus applied to His own preaching ministry: "The LORD has anointed me to preach good news. . . . He has sent me to bind up the broken hearted" (Isaiah 61:1). Hear the chronicler's words that explain God's reason for sending out preachers to Israel: "The LORD, the God of their fathers, sent word to them through his messengers again and again, because he had pity on his people" (II Chronicles 36:15).

Added together, these passages make clear that sermons are not only to save, inform and edify, they are to encourage. People, who have souls and intellects, also have feelings. The person in the pew may have found a place to park his car, but his gloom and guilt may still be with him. The lady with the new outfit may still not have had success in discarding some of her old confusion or her troubling fears. To the right and left may be families experiencing troubles and tasting failures. Will the sermon they are hearing leave them black and blue, or will it bring healing? Congregations have the authority to appeal to their preacher on human rights grounds, regarding sermons that lambaste. Ask with Job, "How long will you torment me and crush me with words?" (Job 19:2). It is written of "God's consolations" that they are "words spoken gently" (Job 15:11). The need of many hours is not for a lecture but for a lift. Feelings and emotions are crying for help. It is rational and reasonable to speak to hearts as well as to minds. It is wise for ministers of the gospel to have spent priority time in their parishioners' homes to uncover problems, as well as to have scheduled many hours in their pastoral studies to find answers to those needs.

Where one sermon turns on a light in the mind, another ought to offer a resting place for the weary. A technical idiom for the lesson of the day in the synagogue was "a message of encouragement for the people" (Acts 13:15). The full impact of the phrase is more clearly felt by comparing translations. Moffat translates, "any word of counsel." Weymouth words it, "anything encouraging." Goodspeed writes, "any appeal to make," The Twentieth Century New Testament reads, "any helpful words." It is written of Jesus and the crowd before him, "he had compassion on them" (Mark 6:34). The very next sentence begins with the word "so" and describes what His compassion for the people led Him to do. He had compassion, "so he began teaching them many things." Teaching grows out of the emotion of love and goes forth to bring comfort to the sad, refreshment to the weary and strength to the weak.

BE A BARNABAS – ENCOURAGE

The preacher, who traveled with Paul on the missionary journey to Cyprus and Galatia, was by "the apostles called Barnabas (which means Son of Encouragement)" (Acts 4:36). Barnabas is not a common name today, but encouragement is a common need. Be a Barnabas.

Jesus' parable of the sower shows His sharp focus of understanding about His audiences. He knew one kind of listener would be "the man who hears the word, but the worries of this life . . . choke it" (Matthew 13:22). Such worries must be dealt with or another fresh branch in Christ the vine will wither and die. It may be your very next exposition of the Scripture that changes some hearer's eternal future, "reviving the soul" (Psalm 19:7). To that listener your sermonic words in his ears may be the voice of Jesus rebuking the storm-center in his life with the command "Quiet! Be still" and the consequence may have followed that "the wind died down and it was completely calm" (Mark 4:39).

It is through "the encouragement of the Scriptures we . . . have hope" (Romans 15:4). In the Gospels the encouraging words of Jesus are heard telling us, "Do not let your hearts be troubled" (John 14:1), "do not worry" (Luke 12:22), "always pray and (do) not give up" (Luke 18:1). The Acts of the Apostles tell of preaching tours made to churches once and again "encouraging them to remain true" (14:22 cp. 16:40). Christ's men are found either "speaking many words of encouragement to the people" (20:2) or sending a letter that will make "the people . . . glad for its encouraging message" (15:31). The Epistles can be described as "word(s) of exhortation" (Hebrews 13:22). Paul's words in the storm at sea, echo throughout his letters to the churches, "Keep up your courage men" (Acts 27:25). He calls on Titus both to encourage (2:15) and to help find the right kind of elders that "can encourage others" (1:9). He orders Timothy to "preach" and "encourage" (II Timothy 4:2 cp. I Thessalonians 3:2). His own epistles not only bring encouragement to the readers but mobilize them to join together and "encourage each other with (his) words" (I Thessalonians 4:18 cp. 5:11).

Not everyone who starts a race finishes it. Not everyone who joins in a fight wins it. Not every student who enrolls in college graduates. We wish we could say that each person, who was given a baptismal certificate to mark the beginning of his or her Christian life, is going to remain faithful until death. But good preaching with its encouraging words will greatly increase the percentage.

BE AN ONESIMUS — HELP

Names sometimes are rich with meanings. Theophilus means lover of God. Philemon, like Philadelphia, has a Greek word for love as part of it and suggests friendship or brotherly love. A preacher who needs the trait of Barnabas as an encourager, also needs the quality of Onesimus, whose name means profitable or helpful.

The runaway slave of Philemon, who may have helped himself to some of his master's belongings and fled to distant Rome, was converted by Paul. The letter to Philemon suggests that conversion will make Onesimus better live up to his name. He will now be, by the help of Christ, Mister Helpful. Paul writes, "Formerly he was useless to you, but now he has become useful both to you and to me" (verse 11).

Most every congregation has need of messages from both a Barnabas and an Onesimus. Will there not be in any typical audience an ear needing encouragement and another seeking help? You likely have had someone greet you after the benediction, saying, "I was truly helped by your sermon this morning." Comments after Christ's works or words ran from "A great prophet has appeared among us" to "God has come to help his people" (Luke 7:16). "Were my words helpful?" can be to a preacher a good measuring scale by which to assay the value of sermonic words. The following proverb is packed with native wisdom honed over the centuries: "Pleasant words are a honeycomb, sweet to the soul and healing to the bones" (Proverbs 16:24). The words of Moses are labeled a "blessing" (Deuteronomy

33:1). All words bless that bring help to the weak, the weary or the wayward.

BE A CEPHAS – STRENGTHEN

The Master chose the name Peter, or Cephas, for His disciple Simon, for it suggested a quality He wanted in the big fisherman's life. These Greek and Hebrew words mean rock. Stability and strength are the words that this Christ-given appellation conjure up. Heaven has no room for spineless vacillators or quaking-kneed preachers. "The courage of Peter and John" led the Jerusalem Sanhedrin to conclude "that these men had been with Jesus" (Acts 4:13). That was the right connection to make, for in His presence disciples heard Him say, "Take courage! . . . Don't be afraid" (Mark 6:50).

Happy is the occupant of the pulpit who can claim, "The Sovereign LORD has given me an instructed tongue, to know the word that sustains the weary" (Isaiah 50:4). Blessed is the occupant of the pew who has been helped to "say of the LORD, 'He is my refuge and my fortress' " (Psalm 91:2). Rich are the memories of the evangelist-teacher who can be reminded, "Think how you have instructed many, how you have strengthened feeble hands. Your words have supported those who stumbled; you have strengthened faltering knees" (Job 4:3-4).

In a world of teetering morals and failing convictions, let the pulpits be towers of strength. "To make you strong" (Romans 1:11) was Paul's compelling drive to go to Rome. It ought to be the dynamic force compelling the preachers of a congregation to produce sermons of power. To each man of God, as he rises to speak, comes the admonition, "My son, be strong in the grace that is in Christ Jesus" (II Timothy 2:1). To "be strong in the Lord and in his mighty power" (Ephesians 6:10) is to be saved from weak sermons.

A "give-em-hell" sermon is better replaced by a "give-emhelp" message. Help comes to the weak with the strength only God can supply. "God . . . was at work in the ministry of Peter" (Galatians 2:8), but so will He be in yours.

BE A PARACLETE — COMFORT

The Holy Spirit is known as the "Comforter" (KJV), whom Christ sent to teach and testify (John 14:26; 15:26). This *paraclete* works in joint-endeavor with the witnessing church to comfort as well as convict. There is an art to the ministry of comforting. The friends of Job were worthy of a D– or an F grade, as the sufferer before them cried out, "I have heard many things like these; miserable comforters are you all! Will your long-winded speeches never end? What ails you that you keep on arguing?" Job himself believed, if the tables were turned and his friends were in pain and grief, he would get at least a B+, if not an A in consoling, for he claimed, "My mouth would encourage you; comfort from my lips would bring you relief" (Job 16:2-3,5).

Concerning death and dying, it is the Christian way not "to grieve like the rest of men, who have no hope" (I Thessalonians 4:13). These are "words" to encourage (4:18). But it is not alone the funeral sermon that is to bring comfort to the afflicted. When a young bread-winner has lost his job, or a young teen-ager has lost a friend, there is a need for comfort. People have fears. Feelings get ruffled. Broken hearts need mending and crushed hopes seek repair.

It is not Solomon alone who has learned in the difficult school of experience, that comfort is a world-wide boon. He wrote, "Like the coolness of snow at harvest time is a trustworthy messenger to those who send him; he refreshes the spirit of his masters" (Proverbs 25:13). It is not the preacher alone, who is to render this essential ministry. As Paul wrote, "(God) comforts us in all our troubles, so that we can comfort those in trouble with the comfort we ourselves have received from God" (II Corinthians

1:4).

Those who have heard Jesus' words, "Take care of my sheep" (John 21:16), have learned a part of their preaching assignment. Let them respond, "Listen, O heavens and I will speak; hear, O earth, the words of my mouth. Let my teaching fall like rain and my words descend like dew, like showers on new grass, like abundant rain on tender plants" (Deuteronomy 32:1-2). Let them "say these things . . . so that (Christ's disciples) may have the full measure of (Christ's) joy within them" (John 17:13). Harry Emerson Fosdick considered preaching to be personal counseling on a group scale. The words from the pulpit can cause light to shine in the darkness and joy to rise from the vale of tears.

Preach the Word! Preach the word of salvation. Proclaim the message that edifies. Herald the truth that heals. Speak forth the full gospel that meets the total needs of men.

19

PREACHING CHALLENGES

Wholehearted preaching includes preaching for a decision. "Heart" in Biblical usage includes the intellect, the emotions, the will and the conscience. The mind is to be addressed for it thinks (Proverbs 23:7; Acts 8:22) and ponders (Luke 2:19). The affections and feelings are to be communicated with for the heart loves (Matthew 22:37) and rejoices (Acts 2:26). Yet, to speak to the intellects and emotions of men and not their consciences and will is to do one's preaching half-heartedly. Peter's Pentecost sermon left his audience "cut to the heart" (Acts 2:37). Had their consciences not been pricked, their wills would not have been moved to action.

Is a salesman content to inform and amuse, but not to make the sale? It is the drive of a lawyer to win his case. It is the compelling urge of a quarterback to score a touchdown. The preacher who is one in fact and not only in name, works to gain a decision. A lecturer may count his mission completed, when certain facts make clear his topic. A preacher tests his sermons by the results of changed lives flowing from determined wills.

Yes, sermons inform. Yes, sermons inspire. But more, sermons call for decisions. If the hearer's imagination is kindled, his mind convinced, his emotions roused, but his will left dormant, there will be no lasting result. Jesus expects more than the empty phrase "Lord, Lord." He looks for the consequence or "fruit," where one "does the will of (his) Father who is in heaven" (Matthew 7:20-21). A sermon is weighed in the balance and found wanting that gets the listener to laugh or cry, but not to change direction. Let the explanation of a Scripture lead to its execution. More important than even the question, as to whether a Bible text was correctly explained, is whether its truth was carried into practice. James was a good leader in the early church advising his flock, "Do not merely listen to the word . . . . Do what it says" (James 1:22).

It is right that a message first enlighten the mind. Then let it disturb the conscience and energize the will. Preach with conviction. Call for decision at every sermon delivery. Speak to your hearers, both "leading them to a knowledge of the truth" (II Timothy 2:25 cp. I Timothy 2:4) and then to "obeying the truth" (I Peter 1:22). Sermons are destined for the scrap-heap of wasted time and energy that produce only pleasant feelings and relaxed minds.

I urge you, in this day of indifference, to preach with zeal. If you would learn about preaching from the Bible, hear the words of the great preacher Paul addressing elders from Ephesus, "Remember that for three years I never stopped warning each of you night and day with tears" (Acts 20:31). Is there ever a tear in your voice? Do you preach with all your might? Only that kind of preaching can rouse the indifferent to action. Peter's oral and written messages were "reminders to stimulate" (II Peter 3:1).

Dwight L. Moody (1837-1899) had the conviction that the best way to build a church was to build a fire in the pulpit. It is recorded as historical fact that he never spoke of the lost without tears in his eyes. He was no play-actor dramatizing the part of an evangelist. By the motives of God's love, the fact of future judgment and eternal hope of heaven, he moved many wills to make the right decision. Like the examples of preaching in the book of Acts, Moody understood a sermon as persuasive address. Truth was to be presented forcefully and directly to the consciences and will of men, as well as to their emotions and minds.

CHALLENGING SERMONS START SOME THINGS OUT

The preacher is to his congregation what a bus driver is to his bus. There are times that call for the church, like a vehicle, to start out, to slow down, to speed up or to steer right.

When Paul stood before Agrippa and Bernice in "the audience room with the high ranking officers and the leading men of the city" (Acts 26:23), God's apostle sought to be the ignition switch that might strike a spark in the heart of a Herod for Christ. At the end of the gospel testimony the king knew Paul's sermonic intent. He responded, "Do you think that in such a short time you can persuade me to be a Christian?" (Acts 26:28). Openly admitting his intent to "persuade," Paul replied, "Short time or long — I pray God that not only you but all who are listening to me today may become what I am" (verse 29).

John the Baptist was called to preach, so that "many of the people of Israel" would be brought "back to the Lord their God." Like a cable carrying heaven's igniting spark, the Baptizer sought "to turn the hearts of the fathers to their children and the disobedient to the wisdom of the righteous — to make ready a people prepared for the Lord" (Luke 1:16-17). To strike fire and launch lives toward Jesus, this forerunner told how the Christ would baptize with the Holy Spirit and with fire. He never lacked for words that "exhorted the people and preached the good news" (Luke 3:18).

What a spark plug was the fisherman from Capernaum that

gave the Sunday sermon at 9 A.M., Pentecost, 30 A.D. Clearly presenting Jesus as Lord and specifically telling how to come into covenant with God, Peter "with many other words . . . pleaded with them, 'Save yourselves from this corrupt generation' " (Acts 2:40). As many long ago "repented at the preaching of Jonah" (Matthew 12:41), many that day were motivated to act at the preaching of a "Simon son of Jonah" (Matthew 16:17).

"Proclaim this among the nations. . . . Rouse the warriors!" was the cry of God through His prophet Joel (3:9). "I suppose that even the whole world would not have room for the books that would be written" (John 21:25), if all life changes were recorded that were triggered by the words of a sermon. Families have been reunited, alcoholics have taken the pledge, youth have determined to enter full-time ministry in far-away lands, etc., etc., and the list goes on.

The gospel is the power of God. Its explosive power is freed by preaching. The divine message, in all its transforming dynamic, goes to work when the story is told. Unleash the powerful gospel. "The tongue . . . is a fire" (James 3:6). Modern choirs sing, "it only takes a spark to get a fire going." Ancient and modern spokesmen know it is true. Preachers across the centuries could be classified as "all you who light fires" (Isaiah 50:11). Speakers have effects upon their listeners. World-changing results can flow from speeches. If you want to start something good, preach the Word.

CHALLENGING SERMONS SLOW SOME THINGS DOWN

A good driver knows where the ignition switch is. He also knows where the brakes are. The man in the pulpit that needs to start one listener down the "highway . . . called the Way of Holiness" (Isaiah 35:8), needs to bring to a screeching halt another life that is headed full speed on "the road that leads to destruction" (Matthew 7:13).

The Word of God sets out brilliant red flares to warn of danger. Flashing amber lights or solid red stop signs are intended to save lives. The preacher, like the prophet Ezekiel, is under the order, "Son of man, I have made you a watchman for the house of Israel; so hear the word I speak and give them warning from me" (Ezekiel 3:17). It is written, "The LORD warned Israel and Judah through all his prophets and seers" (II Kings 17:13). It is recorded that He calls for the attention of His church in these days, adding spokesmen to be "rebuking, correcting and training in righteousness" (II Timothy 3:16). Those who "preach the Word" are to "correct (and) rebuke" (II Timothy 4:2). On some occasions it is fitting to "rebuke them sharply, so that they will be sound in the faith" (Titus 1:13). When it is needed, "rebuke with all authority" (Titus 2:15).

If the God of heaven "will strike the earth with the rod of his mouth (and) with the breath of his lips . . . will slay the wicked" (Isaiah 11:4), shall His faithful herald never speak, "Hear this word the LORD has spoken against you" (Amos 3:1)? If "God is light (and) in him is no darkness at all" (I John 1:5), is it honest preaching to allow sin to lurk in the dark recesses of human hearts unexposed? In the world of sin, will not the "voice from heaven say: 'Come out of her, my people, so that you will not share in her sins, so that you will not receive any of her plagues' " (Revelation 18:4)?

God speaks to His preachers, "Let the one who has my word speak it faithfully." He asks, "Is not my word like fire . . . and like a hammer that breaks a rock in pieces" (Jeremiah 23:28-29)? I add that God's word is also like a brake pedal. It needs to stop sinning-Christians before "they fall away . . . to their loss" (Hebrews 6:6). It needs to teach the wayward to pray, "Teach me what I cannot see (and) if I have done wrong, I will not do so again" (John 34:32). The preached word is that by which God's "servant (is) warned" (Psalm 19:11).

To some it may seem that the demands of the Old Testament and that of the New Testament like "two witnesses" and "two prophets (have) tormented those who live on the earth" (Revelation 11:3,10). But better to have tormented consciences now, leading to life-changing decisions, than endless torment in the future perdition from which there will be no escape. To have "repented at the preaching" (Matthew 12:41; Luke 11:32) is to have stopped going in the wrong direction and to have decided to turn about completely. The signs of "stop, look and listen" at the railway track are rearranged at the pulpit to "listen to God's word, look at your condition and stop before your life is wrecked beyond repair." Happy is the visiting unbeliever at an assembly who hears, not tongues he cannot understand but, rather, a clear message by which "he will be convinced . . . that he is a sinner and . . . the secrets of his heart . . . laid bare" (I Corinthians 14:24-25).

CHALLENGING SERMONS SPEED SOME THINGS UP

When it comes to following Christ, turn on the switch — get started. When it comes to living in sin and error, slam on the brakes — get stopped soon and completely. It is time to learn the lesson of the gas pedal. There are lives that stopped going pell-mell on the downhill route to emptiness and are in the right lane of the upward freeway heading toward L.A. (meaning Life Abundant). The trouble is not in direction but in speed. Their progress is so slow it is even slowing down the persons that are following behind. The preacher of the church, like the driver of the bus, needs to turn his sermon into an accelerator.

More accidents on the highway to heaven are caused by the slow movers than those who go like sixty. A preacher who sets some lives into motion the right direction, needs his sermons to encourage a greater movement forward. At the Red Sea God's message through Moses was, "Tell the Israelites to move on" (Exodus 14:15). Going in the right direction was a good start, but had they moved at a snail's pace toward freedom on the other side, the Exodus story would have had a likely different ending.

In Antioch, Iconium, Lystra and Derbe Paul turned on the ignition and the church was on the move. The rest of the history reads that from Derbe Paul "returned to Lystra, Iconium and Antioch, strengthening the disciples and encouraging them" (Acts 14:22). Same preacher, same gospel, but different purpose. Once things needed starting up. Now they need speeding up.

When Paul wrote of evangelists and teachers preparing "God's people for works of service" (Ephesians 4:12), he meant that to be for today's world not for tomorrow's eternity. The anguishing words, "by this time you ought to be teachers" (Hebrews 5:12), come from the sermon of one who hoped for his message to speed up the process. Another missionary proclaimed Christ with the ultimate goal to "present everyone perfect in Christ" (Colossians 1:28-29). Such a target would take a lifetime. Yet, that was no excuse for measuring progress by inches, where God's help makes possible movement in miles.

You are heading for Christlikeness? Good! Never be turned around or simply parked by the side of the road. But what about increasing your speed of progress? "The hour has come for you to wake up . . . the night is nearly over; the day is almost here" (Romans 13:11). "Redeem the time" (Ephesians 5:16 KJV). Step on the gas. The message is to be of such importance that the people are to "go quickly and tell his disciples" (Matthew 28:7). There are messages of such power that the hearers are motivated neither to crawl nor amble, but to start running. "Philip ran" (Acts 8:30) and the gospel reached Ethiopia.

CHALLENGING SERMONS STEER SOME THINGS RIGHT

No person should try to be all things to all men and no sermon would succeed to accomplish all homiletical goals at any one time. No pilot can take off, speed up, slow down and land in one maneuver. "There is a time for everything . . . a time to tear down and time to build" (Ecclesiastes 3:1,3). There is a time for a particular message to neither start one practice nor stop another, but only to steer a life right, to give it direction, to guide it "in the paths of righteousness for his name's sake" (Psalm 23:3).

The pastor heart informs the flock, "I will instruct you and teach you in the way you should go; I will counsel you and watch over you" (Psalm 32:8). The sheep respond to the caring shepherd, "Teach me, and I will be quiet; show me where I have been wrong" (Job 6:24). Who of those who follow Jesus would not gladly "accept instruction from his mouth and lay up his words in (their) heart" (Job 22:22)?

Steering the car, piloting the ship or guiding the life is an important thing to do. As to that maneuver of a minister called preaching, its purpose is "to turn man from wrongdoing and keep him from pride, to preserve his soul from the pit, his life from perishing" (Job 33:17-18). "The word of God . . . judges the thoughts and attitudes of the heart" (Hebrews 4:12). Let the searching, guiding, directing word be "heard . . . seen . . . (and) put into practice" (Philippians 4:9). Don't allow the preaching of the way of the cross, so clearly mapped in ancient Scripture, to be replaced by modern weathervanes content only to record the way the momentary winds are blowing.

Let the preacher head his sermon toward a charted destination: Either a soul to be saved, a life to be guided, a passage to be clarified, a heart to be comforted or an action to be accomplished. He will be one "who speaks . . . for the honor of the one who sent him" (John 7:18). His audience then becomes a people "glorifying and praising God for all the things they (have) heard" (Luke 2:20). P.T. Forsyth, in his book *Positive Preaching and the Modern Mind*, spoke of preaching as "the organized Hallelujah of an ordered community."[1] If you set out to do "whatever you do . . . in word . . . in the name of the Lord Jesus, giving

---

1. (London: Independent Press, 1907), p. 66.

thanks to God the Father" (Colossians 3:17), it may one day be written of you as it was of John the Baptist's father: "Immediately his mouth was opened and his tongue was loosed, and he began to speak, praising God" (Luke 1:64).

Part Five
THE METHOD
(THE HERE'S HOW OF PREACHING)

20

HOW TO BEGIN

Public enemy number one to the minister of a congregation is not knowing how to prepare and deliver a sermon. There is no task more important in the written or unwritten job description of the preacher than the creating of a meaningful message and presenting it effectively. If the Levites were in the temple service to offer only "a lamb without blemish or defect" (I Peter 1:19), the messenger of the gospel ought to offer sermons from his pulpit that have a spotless quality about them.

There is no act a minister of the Word does with more regularity in public assemblies than to preach. There is no expectation a congreagation has of its spokesman greater than their longing for hearing a clear message from God. They wish he would make house calls. They hope he can administer the program. But they insist they want sermons that lift, lead and bring learning. Let the preacher recall the ordination vows that certainly give priority to "preach the Word" and likely only speak in whispered voice if ever, "run the show."

Where ought one to turn for a course in homiletical method? There are many helpful books in sermon structure, but none more full of assistance than the New Testament itself. It has long been recognized by many as the best of all books on what to preach. It needs to be seen also as an excellent guide on how to preach. A careful reading of the sermons in the Bible can turn a pulpit-dwarf into a mighty gospel-giant. Why be content to remain a speaker whose message is comparable to a drama to be viewed on a six inch black and white television set, when with effort the same story can come across more clearly in twenty-four inch color pictures. Admittedly the story is the same, but effort on your part can make the reception easier to enjoy by a larger number of viewers.

The methodological questions of sermonizing begin by asking how to start a message. You likely have heard a sermon-builder, who like the tower-builder in Jesus' parable "began to build and was not able to finish" (Luke 14:30). The art of concluding a sermon is of high necessity, but it is of slightly less importance than the skill of beginning well.

Is it trite to say that the purpose of an introduction is to introduce? The introduction ought to be simple, not complex; clear, not confusing; brief, yet not abrupt. As a frequent flyer, I testify to the joy of the take-off that gets the plane off the ground and headed for its destination. The congregation — your passengers — breathe a sigh of relief once the message is launched and on its way.

Frequent writers compare a speech's introduction to the vestibule or the porch of a house. A good architect does not want his portico to attract too much attention to itself. His desire is for it to blend in with the major structure and lead one's eyes to the oneness and beauty of the whole. An out-of-proportion porch, or a way-too-long introduction, will not please the eye or the ear of the carpenters from either Nazareth or from your town. It is only logical to ask why there would be sizeable porches on midget houses.

The introductions only ought to be of sufficient length to accomplish their purpose, which is to orient the hearers to the theme. You recognize that the word "Orient" means to face East. Looking East, we see the sun rise and the day get started. The orientation an introduction brings is to attract the hearer's attention, arouse his interest in the theme and secure his good-will, so that the ideas discussed may gain consideration.

WIN EARS

"A curse on him who is lax in doing the LORD's work!" (Jeremiah 48:10). Such a curse will never fall on the diligent preacher. He has used his time efficiently to find his theme and to ponder his text. He may have labored long to find a title that was inclusive, adequate, true to both text and topic, and attractive in appeal to the imagination. He now, with diligence, seeks his opening sentence.

The most important minute of a thirty-minute message is the first sixty seconds. That brief time period may fate either the hearing or the rejecting of the entire message. High on the list of the homiletician's ten commandments is the imperative, "Thou shalt not kill your lesson with a poor opening sentence." Work for an ear-grabbing introduction.

Achtung! Whatever the words you choose, they are the call for "attention!" Before Alexander spoke to the mob in Ephesus "he motioned for silence." Failing in his effort "the city clerk quieted the crowd" before he attempted to address them (Acts 19:33,35). When Paul spoke to the Jewish mob after his Jerusalem arrest, the text reads, "Paul stood on the steps and motioned to the crowd. When they were all silent, he (spoke) to them in Aramaic" (Acts 21:40). To begin to deliver the burden of your message before you get the attention of an audience is like talking into your telephone before the party at the other end of the line has picked up his receiver. Somewhere I heard a meaningful Russian proverb that went something like this: "It is the same with people as with mules: whoever would hold them must get a very good grip on their ears!"

A similar humorous truth comes out of Ireland, where it is reported that a cookbook was found with each step in preparing rabbit stew spelled out in detail. Step one read, "Catch your rabbit." Step one in speaking is "Catch their attention." For you to speak and unburden your soul is an important part of the communication process. The other part is for the auditors to get these spoken words heard. The hard, slow, difficult hours of sermon preparation will have been spent for naught, if the hearer's ears are closed.

Jesus used the beatitudes as the on-ramp for His Sermon on the Mount (Matthew 5:2-10). Peter marshalled the minds before him with explanation of the Pentecost miracle the people had just experienced. With that the first sermon of the church age was launched successfully (Acts 2:14-21). Paul was off and running on Mar's Hill, offering to introduce the philosophers to the "Unknown God" Athenians worshiped (Acts 17:22-23). The strategy in each case was to begin where the listeners were and lead them to where they should be. Paul's opening remark to the Greeks was not belligerent in denunciation, slamming closed the door to their ears. He rather opened the gate of those ears by the compliment, "Men of Athens! I see that in every way you are very religious" (Acts 17:22-23). Likewise his opening words to Roman Jews out of Christ began, "My brothers" (Acts 28:17).

It is good to memorize your well-designed opening words. This way you avoid wandering around for a trail to take toward the sermon's objective. Where is that group of hearers that doesn't appreciate a speaker that will not waste even one meandering minute? Everyone likes a leader that is going some place and invites others to come along. One time begin with a striking quotation. Another occasion start with a dramatic description. Still again directly state your purpose or describe a problem to which you will give God's answer. Let the methods vary for the diner can tire of exactly the same menu day after day no matter how healthful or well-prepared the food.

In the rhetorician Cicero's three lessons for an introduction, the arousing of interest heads the list. Every preacher has a distinctive personality. Each congregation has a different make up. But each speech-occasion gets off to a good start with a short, gripping, intriguing opening line.

WIN MINDS

He who fishes for men may bait his hook with an opening question. It may be more than accidental that a question mark has almost the appearance of a fish-hook (?). A well-phrased question may be just the lure to get a listener to nibble at the attractive subject until caught for the rest of the hour as an interested listener. In other words, the introduction can suggest the question to which the sermon is to be the answer or it can point to the need which the message is to solve.

Many of Jesus' lessons were introduced by the Gospel writer's phrase, "The Lord answered him" (Luke 13:18) or "Jesus asked" (Luke 17:17). It has been estimated that of the 125 recorded incidents of Jesus communicating with people, over half of the time he was responding to something they asked or said. We might say He preached in conversational style. He responded to objections, answered questions and followed the interests of the people. The apostolic sermon of Acts 2 rose from the questions, "Are not all these men who are speaking Galileans? Then how is it that each of us hears them in his own native language" (verses 7-8). That of Acts 3 commenced with the queries, "Why does this surprise you? Why do you stare at us as if by our own power or godliness we had made this man walk?" (verse 12). That of Acts 4 began as answer to the asking, "By what power or what name did you do this?" (verse 7). Toward the end of the history book by

Luke, sermons were introduced by the short phrase, "Paul replied" (Acts 24:10).

The sooner a hearer realizes that he has a personal stake in the message to be brought, the quicker he will pick up his ears in a learning state. To perceive that the text of centuries ago has God's personal message for the problem of today is to move from ho-hum to hallelujah. Harry Emerson Fosdick never lacked for filled pews to which he could speak, for the populace discovered his sermons to be problem solving in character and pertinent in need. His congregation did not feel he had spent the week thinking about theological themes, but thinking about them and the hard life they faced. Job held the same caring stance with the people around him, describing the mouth-to-ear relationship of heart-to-heart words: "Men listened to me expectantly, waiting in silence for my counsel. After I had spoken, they spoke no more; my words fell gently on their ears. They waited for me as for showers and drank in my words as the spring rain" (Job 29:21-23).

A sermon leaving the station without the interest of the hearers on board was compared by John Edgar Park to a preacher playing "a pleasant game of sacred solitaire."[1] To avoid talking only to one's self and to get the listener aboard, the introduction's purpose is to arouse interest in the subject. It is to start down the track from the local station of the hearer's present knowledge to the final destination of further wisdom on the theme.

The proposition stated is announcing where the sermon is headed and is the invitation "All aboard!" The wording of the proposition must be reworded until it is exact, even when it is not openly declared at the beginning of the message but reserved for later as was Peter's in Acts 2 (verse 36). It is one terse sentence what the sermon is about — but more of that in the next chapter.

---

1. *The Miracle of Preaching* (New York: The Macmillan Co., 1936), p. 7.

To kindle interest a sermon introduction may contain the proposition and may also bring in the sermon's text. Jesus worked from the text of Isaiah 61 in His Nazareth message (Luke 4:16-19). Paul worked from "the Law and the Prophets" in the Antioch synagogue (Acts 13:15). The texts read in Nazareth and Antioch were well-worn passages, but the speaker's charisma created confidence in the audience that something fresh and new was about to be said on the subjects heard many times before.

A wise builder of sermons will be well on his way to the body of his message by the first paragraph or two. Moving from an opening sentence of captivating power, the speaker is whetting the hearer's appetite for the spiritual meal about to be served. Nothing can derail the forward movement of the message, unless a hostility become wedged between hearer and speaker.

WIN HEARTS

People are not likely to accept a man's thoughts, if they reject the man. Medium and message are closely linked. I must be accepted before anything I say will be received. That leads to the conclusion that an introduction must do more than attract attention and develop interest. It must create a warm, receptive atmosphere.

In the beginning of an oration, audience and speaker begin to think together and feel together. There needs to be both intelligence reception and heart reception. The listener, who has a favorable feeling toward the man at the podium, will give the lesson he speaks responsive consideration. To shut out the man is to keep out the message.

To have been in the homes of the congregation is to have been allowed, in most cases, entrance into their hearts. Audiences must know, without your saying so, that you love to preach. They also know, beyond your denying, whether you love those to whom you preach. To lack the latter is to turn preaching to hearts into lecturing to minds. The ever repeated observation, that home-going preachers produce church-going congregations, would be hard to deny. My experience is that the introduction's objective to secure favor and create good-will is most easily obtained before the introduction begins. Greet the people one by one as they gather. Give them a warm smile, a kindly word and a warm handclasp and the speech's need for a favorable hearing will already be accomplished.

One gains the right to speak by being right with the people. Apathy and hostility are seldom known enemies to be defeated by the preacher's introduction, when he has shown recent concern for his flock. Knowing the shepherd as a listener, the sheep are alert to his voice when he speaks. Loving the shepherd, their ears do not hear a cold lecture nor a formal address, but rather a familiar and welcomed voice. Notice how the Bible speaks of Jesus relating to the crowds that followed Him. It says, "He welcomed them and spoke to them" (Luke 9:11). Why follow Christ's step two and miss step one?

By the time the few minutes of introduction are over, the listeners know what menu lies ahead. Is it to be a hot-dog with mustard thrown together for a quick gulping down, or a delightfully readied feast to be quietly consumed and gratefully remembered? The introduction precedes the sermonic main course, like the table-setting and decor appear before the food comes to the table, but anyone can tell what to expect. A careful introduction promises good things to come.

In delivery, introductions come first, but in preparation, they may come last. When the product to be introduced is finished, it may be the right time to decide how best to word the introduction. Precious gifts ought not be hidden in cheap wrappers.

21

HOW TO UNIFY

"Ready. On your mark. Get set. Go!" Those are meaningful words to one who knows where he is heading, but confusing orders to a person with no sense of destination. "Ready. Aim. Fire!" are commands that make sense only to a rifleman, who has a chosen target before him. The preacher's target or goal in a given sermon is called the proposition of the message.

There is a similarity and yet a distinct difference between hunters and Fourth of July celebrants. The guns of the huntsman and the firecrackers of the patriots alike make noise when they are fired off. The former see their game fall, when their weapon is fired with good aim. The latter have only the joy of sight and sound with neither the intention nor the result of hitting a mark. Woe to that preacher who fires off a sermon, filling the air with sound, but lacking a specific target. He needs the intention of hitting a particular objective and bringing something back home.

The proposition of a sermon is the aim of the message in a

single sentence. That sentence needs to be worked over until it bears the marks of unity and clarity. It ought not to be phrased as a question, suggesting doubt or uncertainty, but as a positive declaration of what the sermon affirms. It is to be a complete sentence in concise form. Where the title of the sermon has given it a name, the proposition gives it direction. It functions as an invitation to the audience to follow the train of thought to its destination. It announces the theme and becomes the nucleus around which the speech will be organized. Every message, that will leave a forceful impact on a hearer, flows from the integrating center called the proposition. That proposition saves the sermon from disunity in content and misdirection in movement.

When you page through a Bible, what do 5:20, 2:36 or 5:13 have in common? They are not the New Testament airport arrival times, but sermon propositions. Matthew 5:20, Acts 2:36 and I John 5:13 are the single sentences in messages by Jesus, Peter and John that map out the direction of their sermons. "Unless your righteousness surpasses that of Pharisees and the teachers of the law, you will certainly not enter the kingdom of heaven" is the incisive, suggestive, unifying sentence around which all the rest of the Sermon on the Mount rotates. "Let all Israel be assured of this: God has made this Jesus, whom you crucified, both Lord and Christ" is the case Pentecost's message sets out to prove. "I wrote these things to you who believe in the name of the Son of God so that you may know that you have eternal life" is the proposition of the written homily which is I John.

AID TO THE MEMORY

When a congregation departs from a service with people wondering what the preacher was driving at, it is very likely the case that the minister himself was not sure. But, when the man of God has thoughtfully honed the gist of his sermon into a single statement, he will remember what he intends to say and his church will go home recalling what he has said.

The value of the proposition can not be overstated. It aids the memory of both speaker and hearer. Shotgun sermons, that hurl out diverse thoughts that bounce in many directions, only confuse. Observation on any tennis court will demonstrate that, when you toss two balls, one at a time, to the server, he will catch them both. Now throw him both balls at once and notice that nine to one he will not catch either. What is the conclusion? A sermon ought to be presenting one main thought. Rambling speeches, like reeling drunks, will not go straight to their mark. There is strength in a united congregation and there is power in a unified message. The result of a sermonic proposition is a cohesive message that goes like an arrow to its intended goal.

Unrelated religious comments over a thirty minute period, do not deserve the title "sermon." Children, whom you would expect to enjoy any circus, might rather be confused in a seven ring circus with so much going on that they really do not see anything. "One thing I do" (Philippians 3:13) is goal enough for any given sermon.

Keep your central idea brief. This will solve the problem of sermon organization, for once the proposition is framed the outline that is to establish it will flow naturally from it. A long sentence will be harder for both preacher and people to remember. Long, longer and longest mean fuzzy, fuzzier and fuzziest. Be concrete, terse, precise. Don't be general, abstract, encyclopedic.

AID TO THE MATERIAL

"All Scripture is God-breathed and is useful for teaching" (II Timothy 3:16). But, please, not all at one time. Most lucid illustrations are man-made and also useful for teaching. But, useful and profitable stories at one particular time may not be appropriate to a given group at another time. The many Scriptures, quotations or stories that flood the mind, while the preacher works on his message in the study, ought not all be used. The proposition — the sermon in a nutshell — helps determine what available sermonic material ought to be allowed to enter the particular message.

Controlling the sermon's conceptual development, the proposition determines what keeps the message on course and what would be apt to send it on an unnecessary side excursion. The last portion of the last chapter of the Bible's last book warns against adding anything to what had been given, or taking away anything from what had been written. The sermonic warning is for the preacher to be true to his propositional sentence throughout the entire message. He is to let it speak clearly, while adding nothing extraneous nor subtracting something basic. Few words in perfect focus are preferable to many words of hocus-pocus. Sweep the sermon of all peripheral items. You have no time for them. Like racers heading for the finish line, "let us throw off everything that hinders . . . and let us run with perseverance the race marked out for us" (Hebrews 12:1).

The preacher should not hesitate in using pruning shears. Lop off elements that do not relate. Shear away what is incongruous with the purpose of the hour. Cut back lengthy stories where succinct illustrations better keep the ship headed directly toward harbor. Have a point. Get to the point. "How good and pleasant it is when brothers live together in unity!" (Psalm 133:1). And how good and pleasant it is, when sermon parts work together in harmony. Christ is the magnetic force that holds the church together in oneness. The proposition is the sun around which our sermonic planets rotate to make a cosmos and prevent a chaos. Any material created for the sermon should clearly fit, making a universe of harmony for the ear and not a multiverse of ideas confusing the mind. The three peas in the pod of the proposition are purpose, precision and pertinence.

AID TO THE MOVEMENT

How does one get from Jerusalem to Jericho or from introduction to conclusion? The proposition helps map the road. Only a fool will wander first to Bethlehem, then to Gaza, next to Ashdod and finally to Bethel, if the point of arrival was to be Jericho. The preacher with an acceptable I.Q. follows the compass of his proposition and sets out in as straight a line as possible. He moves from where the congregational caravan is to the destination he hopes them to reach.

To go everywhere preaching the gospel in a single sermon is to be exposed as a travel-guide who has neither studied the map or charted his course. The persons in an average audience do not wish to be treated as casual tourists with time to kill for multiple side trips. They entrust themselves to a leader who has announced the destination and knows how to get there. From your hotel window, or from a bench by the bus-stop, become a people-watcher. Notice in the mass of persons before you the man who steps right out, heads in a definite direction and acts like he knows exactly where he wants to go. Then pray that the sermon proposition you have worded with care will aid you to keep your message moving toward its stated objective.

No matter how many major divisions a sermon has, it in fact has but one point, as expressed in the propositional statement. The smallest child can remember one point, while the oldest adult will have trouble with many. Convey a central truth, not a confusing smatter of ideas. One writer compares some sermons he had heard to a lemon meringue pie, saying "they splatter over everything, but hit nothing very hard."[1] Check your last sermon. Was it like a man walking toward his village, or was it more like a dog running back and forth and all around? If it was like the man

---

1. Haddon W. Robinson, *Biblical Preaching: The Development and Delivery of Expository Messages* (Grand Rapids, Michigan: Baker Book House), p. 107.

headed home, give thanks. If it was more like the dog, repent.

Before you give birth to a sermon, visualize your prospective congregation. Individualize their needs. Settle on the text and topic that can minister to those needs. As the Spirit of God hovered over the earth that was formless and empty at creation (Genesis 1:1), ponder for hours over your people and your Bible until an idea is conceived. Write the sermonic idea in a precise, clear sentence, revealing the purpose you have in mind. Let it incubate over the days. Allow it to develop slowly. The time will come, as certain as birth follows begetting, that a sermon will be born that would make a parent proud. The development will be without major complications, once the pregnant possibilities of the proposition get implanted in the homiletician's mind.

The preacher is not in need of a bag of tricks. His success is not dependent upon a book of sermon starters nor a file of instant illustrations. His one basic requirement for the saving of his sermonic soul is a proposition to direct and formulate the movement of his message.

AID TO THE MEASUREMENT

Upon the completion of a sermon's private formation and public delivery, how shall it be measured? Is it a total success or a partial failure? The proposition, which was stated as a promise to the audience of things to come, now becomes the standard by which the message must be tested. Did the proposition do what it promised? Did it heal? Did it exhort or admonish? Did it confirm or edify?

Students of the New Testament know that every epistle was written out of a pastoral concern and worded to meet the condition of a specific congregation. It is not too much to expect that New Testament sermons, rising out of pastoral concern and directed to particular needs in a given community, be tested for results. The question before delivery was to be, "Why am I giving this particular message and what am I hoping to accomplish?" The check-point after delivery becomes, "Did I hit the bull's eye or miss my objective by a country mile?" Worse than a mimeographed letter of generalities to be stuffed in the screen door of every house where Mr. Everybody and Anybody live, is the unspecific sermon dumped on the gathered crowd with no particular end in view. Count the number of persons in the audience and multiply it by the number of minutes the message took. You then have a mathematical insight into the number of wasted man-hours the unfaithful steward's message took.

If the people Jesus touched were made whole, pray for His touch to your sermons. As a carpenter in Nazareth, He measured as He built and built what He measured. With His assistance and through your propositions, your messages will be healthier and more wholesome. Because of His assistance and by your propositions, those messages will reveal "good measure, pressed down, shaken together and running over" (Luke 6:38).

22

HOW TO STRUCTURE

From the first days of the church, its apostolic leaders had concern for propriety in the worship assemblies. Paul's guiding principle was that "everything should be done in a fitting and orderly way" (I Corinthians 14:40). Let the polar star be followed by the preacher, as well as the other participants in the community's gatherings for praise, prayer and proclamation. The message of the messenger should meet the description of a "fitting and orderly" presentation.

The God who structured our beautiful universe is best served by a spokesman who can bring cosmos out of chaos. The relationship of the word cosmetics to the term cosmos is not accidental. Any woman with a desire to be beautiful has an interest in giving an orderly arrangement to her appearance. Any preacher, with a desire to make the truth he presents more attractive to his audience, spends good time considering the structure he will use.

As the proposition is the entire sermon in its most condensed form, the outline becomes the unfolding of the message in attractive packaging. Even breakfast cereal won't sell well without thought given to the packaging question. Once the designer of a sermon decides what needs to be said (the proposition), he is ready for the problem, "Now, how do I best say this?" (the outline).

The principles of outline construction include a call for unity, order, movement and originality. When the proposition has been chosen, as the pivot around which the sermon will orbit, the hard work of message development begins. There are no easy fixes. There is no escape route for he who would preach. The basic idea, at first but a jumbled mass of thoughts, must now be prayed over and pondered over until the hodge-podge begins to suggest form. The sermonic baby soon to be born comes through the essential, long and often painful struggle in the study. After the idea is first conceived, there follows gestation, labor and only finally delivery. But each time joy will follow the hard struggle and all will be proven worthwhile. There, at last, before the creative speaker lies an outline that brings an undeniable sense of pride. Every part of the structure reflects coordination, relevance and clarity. It is now time to "write down the revelation and make it plain in tablets so that a herald may run with it" (Habakkuk 2:2).

LET THERE BE ORDER AND CLARITY

What a contrast can be heard from the pulpits of church A and church B. In one, the sermons are ever "meaningless talk" (I Timothy 1:6). In the other, every speaker "will make the teaching about God our Savior attractive" (Titus 2:10). In the latter, the structure is so clear the preacher could remember what he was going to say, if he lost his notes. And better still, the audience could go home recalling what the minister had said. In church A, no outline basket was provided the congregation so each member could carry home the lesson. If ideas are not put together with the easy to grasp hand-holds of a well-structured outline, the chances of catching the central idea are about as good as the people in the pews catching a greased pig.

As sure as there is a potential oak tree in every acorn, there is an outline latent in every proposition. Only time can bring forth the structure. For the sake of the audience, who has neither the time nor the inclination to find it, the preacher on their behalf must spend the hours to first discover and then offer it. A sermon with no logical or psychological sequence of thought will not go down in history. It will not even make it to the vestibule.

Good sermons are made of good parts. A healthy body is a healthy body because each part of that body is strong. Structure is essential to the body of a sermon. A fuzzy thinker becomes a slip-shod speaker. A clear reasoner works with ideas and words until his outline becomes solid pegs that will carry the weight of the message all the way home.

That an oral presentation must be instantaneously understood by the hearers is evident, when a moment's thought is given to it. The reader of a text book, when he is confused by what was written, has a text before him to reread and review for clarity. That opportunity evades a listener. For the hearer to misunderstand leaves a gap in understanding, as confusing as it would be if the instructions for filling out State or Federal taxes were only heard once and not available for eye perusal.

Since the glorious gospel we proclaim is worthy of the highest expression we can give it, work with your outline as an iron worker fires and hammers his metal until the form is just right. As "all things work together for good to them that love God" (Romans 8:28 KJV), let all divisions of the sermon work together for good to those who love preaching. Like any artist, the more you work at sermon building the better skilled you become at the art. As one learns to sing by singing and to paint by painting, one learns to shape outlines by shaping outlines.

Symmetry will not allow the different sections of an orchestra to be playing a waltz, a march and a tango at one and the same time. Neither will it allow the three or four major points of a sermon's structure to be expressed in sentences that do not correspond in nature. Stand back and look at your proposed outline. Are the sentences balanced? If, like Alexander Maclaren, you plan to feed your congregation with a three-pronged fork, be sure each tine in your outline is of equal length and shape. Standing before the mirror of truth, an athlete would rather see his measurements at 45-32-40 than 30-57-20. A healthy chest, slim waist and moderate thighs leaves a better impression than a sunken chest, obese mid-section and weak legs. I long have found value in chart sermons, blackboard designs or printed outlines in that, at a glance, the balance is seen and the proposition comes clear. Before all eyes is the epitome of the message. The proposition is revealed and the plan for its establishment is uncovered. The fortunate congregation that often before had passed by the text and its truth, suddenly is made aware that that scripture was loaded. But it took the preacher to pull the trigger.

LET THERE BE UNITY AND SIMPLICITY

If order and clarity are brothers, unity and simplicity are sisters belonging to the same family. Order and clarity call for the points of an outline to be parallel, of equal importance, in balanced symmetry and in no way an overlap. Each point that develops the proposition is to be harmonious with it and in clear relationship with the other divisions or parts. Unity and simplicity seek to develop the proposition — period! They want no more nor less to be accomplished. A store window crammed with all kinds of items for sale speak for the cheapness of "the five and dime" market. How different is the store featuring a fur coat or a man's dress suit!

There is value in simplicity. There is worth in featuring one eternal truth in a message and avoiding the clutter of so many ideas that the beauty of a single saving truth is demeaned by the mass of things around it. The "one thing I do" (Philippians 3:13) in a given sermon is more impressive on a mind than a multitude of other things poured simultaneously into the funnel of the mind. The argument of Paul against the misuse of the tongue gift at Corinth is cogent regarding the mass of unrelated thoughts strung on the thirty minute string called a sermon. He preferred the speaking of "five intelligible words" over an unintelligible "ten thousand words" (I Corinthians 14:19).

To make the oral product of the sermon sayable, it must have the quality of oneness and it must be expressed in simplicity. Complexity is not in a healthy diet for the feeding of the sheep. When there are simple ideas expressed in simple terms, the sermon will be one and the hearers won. Whatever the weather on the outside of the building, pray for clear sunshine at the pulpit with no trace of fog.

LET THERE BE MOVEMENT AND PROGRESS

If the sermon outline has a certain number of points establishing the proposition, the question of balance and symmetry is only one inquiry to be asked. Another has to do with which should be first and which last. Homileticians are not taking their congregations for a ride upon a merry-go-round with people getting off at the same spot they got on. The sermon is supposed to move listeners from the point where they are found to the place they ought to be. A good sermon is a congregational journey. The preacher's words are not but a few nicely scattered remarks. They are a charted course leading purposefully, steadily and progressively toward a chosen destination. The determined purpose has called for regular progress and unbroken movement toward the expressed goal of the proposition.

To have no recognizable purpose is to keep from measuring any real progress from the first of the message toward the last. In serving a gospel feast from the pulpit, it is prudent to save the best wine until the last (cp John 2:10). Grain production like sermon production is in steps. The experienced farmer knows it is "first the stalk, then the head, then the full kernel in the head" (Mark 4:28). The experienced preacher realizes the sermon must of necessity move from the kindling of imagination to the convincing of the mind to the stirring of the emotions to the challenging of the will. Some decisive action contemplated from the first is to be completed at the last. Conviction and decision result from a sermon with movement. Confusion and bewilderment are the non-results where a message lacks logical and psychological direction.

When the preacher struggles in the preparation of his message, he needs to be sure his outline is structurally sound, coherently clear and orderly in progression. The finished product will often be a long time coming. But, when the sermon bed is watered with tears of struggle and the perspiration of toil, the message will sprout and blossom. Out of textual investigation will spring forth interpretation. And out of sound interpretation will grow practical application.

Charles W. Koller makes the insightful comparison of the modern preacher crafting a sermon and a primitive Indian shaping his arrow. He stresses the importance of the shaft being straight, lest it wobble in flight; the feathers being correct, lest the thrust be slowed down and the point being sharp, lest it not penetrate.[1] James T. Cleland's parallel is that of a diamond cutter who first chisels the stone from the rock, next cuts and polishes it to reveal its glory and finally places it in the setting of a ring.[2]

LET THERE BE ORIGINALITY AND VARIETY

In the days long past, "God spoke . . . through the pro-

1. *Sermons Preached without Notes* (Grand Rapids, Michigan: Baker Book House, 1964), p. 41.

2. *Preaching to be Understood* (Nashville: Abingdon Press, 1965), p. 79.

phets . . . in various ways" (Hebrews 1:1). Elihu pointed this out to Job, saying, "God does speak — now one way, now another" (Job 33:14). The Old and New Testaments are rich in truths and wealthy in suggestive forms for the packaging of those truths. Variety has been named the spice of life. The same old truth in the same old way loses its inviting tang. To walk the exact same route Sunday after Sunday to the sermon's destination can not be called an exciting experience. But let the preacher, as guide, take the listeners by a new and different scenic walk each time and they will wait in anticipation for the next week's stroll through the Scripture. The element of suspense is added when it is not a foregone conclusion which way the speaker will be going with the topic of the day.

The call for variety has a cost to it. The price is hard effort and added hours, but the satisfaction in both pulpit and pew is worth it. Mediocre messages are a dime a dozen and never worth the dime. Beyond price are those sermons that may have cost the preacher an hour of preparation for each minute of delivery. Blessed is that minister of the Word who labors long with his text until it comes alive in him. Then it may come alive for his people. When a parishioner goes to the post office to get his mail, or to the church to receive his sermon, there is a higher level of excitement when the package is marked priority, first-class, rather than fourth-class, book rate. The cheaper option may save a few cents, but the costlier choice has its much higher rewards.

" 'The abomination that causes desolation,' spoken of through the prophet Daniel" (Matthew 24:15), was not a reference to the abomination of a preacher using the canned outlines from a sermon book purchased Saturday night at the religious book store. Yet it is abominable to deliver another's message without first making it your own. Luke records the failure of some Jewish exorcists, who used the very words Paul had uttered, but they did not have the apostle's results (Acts 19:13-16). Copying another's paragraphs is not equivalent to capturing another's power.

You are to be more than the dummy for a ventriloquist. You are to be more than the mouthpiece for the outline provided by some book of sermons. The truth of a text must pierce your own heart before it can pierce that of another. Brood over the Scripture that gave the author of the sermon book his message until the Author of the Sacred Text gives you yours. Sleep on it. "The LORD . . . giveth his beloved sleep" (Psalm 127:1-2). More than that, he gives to his beloved preachers while they sleep. Creative ideas will rise out of the subconscious for the sermon builder who falls asleep on his bed brooding over his coming message.

Halford E. Luccock spoke of the Jericho sermon, where a preacher in implicit faith marched around the outside of a subject seven times making a loud noise expecting that to bring the walls falling down. It will never happen that way. But walls will fall and conquests will be made by modern Joshuas of the pulpit who go to battle well-prepared and with God on their side. Order and clarity, unity and simplicity, movement and progress, originality and variety make steadfast allies in the battle for the mind.

23

HOW TO ESTABLISH

The preaching in the Bible, both New Testament and Old, expected a response. Since an action on the part of the people was called for, the messenger spoke with conviction and reasoned with persuasion. In Acts they explained (2:14), witnessed (2:32), warned (2:40), persuaded (5:40; 18:4,13; 26:28), proved (9:22; 17:3; 18:28), debated (9:29), answered (13:46), reasoned (17:2,17; 18:4,19), disputed (17:18), made defense (19:33; 25:8; 26:1), testified (23:11), and convinced (28:23). Apostolic teaching was not only prophetic, didactic, evangelistic and therapeutic, it was apologetic. As the God of Isaiah invited the listeners, "Come now, let us reason together" (1:18), the God and Father of Jesus must have been pleased when the incarnate Son was "heard . . . debating" and giving both Pharisees and Sadducees "a good answer" (Mark 12:28).

A unifying proposition, developed in a well structured outline, still needs to be presented in a convincing manner. The case made must carry the mind before it will move the will. Never hesitate to appeal to the highest faculty of the human soul — the right of choice. False religions may argue with the sword. True religion respects the nature of man and persuades with gentle but powerfully convincing argument. Domineering over another's will is not the Christian way. Calling for the consideration of the testimony of Apostles, Prophets and good logic is the Christ-like route.

PROVE THE POINT

As you "contend for the faith that was once for all entrusted to the saints" (Jude 3), you will need wisdom from above. To reach the mind of man with the message from the mind of God, the reasonableness of Christianity will need to be made evident. May it be later written of you, as it was of Solomon long ago, "God gave Solomon wisdom and very great insight, and a breadth of understanding as measureless as the sand on the seashore" (I Kings 4:29).

Jesus' parable of the sower speaks of some that would hear "the message about the kingdom and . . . not understand it" (Matthew 13:19), while others would (13:23). After telling his stories, we find Jesus leaving the crowd, entering a house and responding to the disciples' appeal, "Explain to us the parable" (13:36). If the goal is not blind acceptance but convinced hearts, the case must be made line upon line until the intellect is persuaded. "For whatever is hidden is meant to be disclosed, and whatever is concealed is meant to be brought out into the open . . . (each is to) consider carefully" what is heard (Mark 4:22-24).

Creatures made in the image of God will not be convicted "with empty notions . . . useless words" or "speeches that have no value" (Job 15:2-3). God himself called the speeches of Job and his friends, "words without knowledge" (38:2 cp. 35:16). All followers of Jesus, and especially His preachers, ought "always (to) be prepared to give an answer to everyone who asks . . . the reason for the hope that (they) have" (I Peter 3:15). If "a Pharisee named Gamaliel, a teacher of the law" can have it recorded that "his speech persuaded them" (Acts 5:34,40), ought not a Christian by your name, as a teacher of the gospel, be able to speak persuasively? If Stephen, a deacon from the Jerusalem congregation, faced in debate "members of the synagogue of the Freedmen" and argued so effectively that "they could not stand up against his wisdom or the Spirit by which he spoke" (Acts 6:9-10), is it unreasonable to expect you to teach effectively by the same wisdom and Spirit?

It is written of the missionary-minded Paul that he, having entered a synagogue, "reasoned with them from the Scriptures, explaining and proving that the Christ had to suffer and rise from the dead" (Acts 17:2-3). After reasoning, explaining and proving came results. "Some . . . were persuaded and joined" (Acts 17:2-4). Are you getting additions? Are you expecting conversions? Are you preparing sermons of persuasive power? Are you taking the time to build a strong case that will carry the day? Hear the words of the wise to the wise lest they be otherwise: "Do you see a man who speaks in haste? There is more hope for a fool than for him" (Proverbs 29:20).

Preachers live in the hope that "through patience a ruler can be persuaded" (Proverbs 25:15). Paul targeted Felix and his wife Drusilla and "spoke about faith in Jesus Christ" (Acts 24:24). He aimed at winning Festus, Agrippa and Bernice, making his defense and that of his gospel before them. He appealed, "What I am saying is true and reasonable" (Acts 26:25). Agrippa felt the persuasion being applied to make him a Christian (26:28).

"The heart of the righteous weighs its answers" (Proverbs 15:28). You can be sure Paul weighed every word he spoke. He could have begun any message with the words of Job, "Listen to my words; let your ears take in what I say. . . . I have prepared my case" (Job 13:17-18). Yet, even though he often labored "from morning to evening (as) he explained . . . declared . . . and tried to convince . . . (only) some were convinced by what he said, but others would not believe" (Acts 28:23-24). There will always be the "who-so-ever-wills" and the "who-so-ever-won'ts." The preacher's task is not to be always successful, but ever faithful at proving his point.

People seldom make important decisions without another's help. You can help others to make the most vital of all decisions by the patient showing why one course is right and ought to be taken, and another is bad and should be rejected. Forcefully and directly speak to the conscience and call for the will to act. But also mind the mind, for it must first be persuaded. For this reason Paul "reasoned in the synagogue with the Jews and God-fearing Greeks, as well as in the market place day by day with those who happened to be there" (Acts 17:17). For the same reason you must reason, explaining and defending the faith. Prove your case!

APPROVE THE PROCLAMATION

Saying "Amen" (I Corinthians 14:16) to a prayer or a preachment, is to give approval to a request or a testimony. "The words of the wise . . . their collected sayings (are) like firmly embedded nails" (Ecclesiastes 12:1). The word of approval to a teaching from another source is putting in another nail to support the idea being presented.

When the apostles set out to prove their proposition that Jesus was "Lord and Christ" (Acts 2:36), they would bear their witness to Jesus' resurrection and then bring in the approving testimony of the Scriptures. James followed Peter's case before the Jerusalem Conference, with the supportive testimony, "The words of the prophets are in agreement with this" (Acts 15:15). "Every matter must be established by the testimony of two or three witnesses." That was true in the apostolic period (II Corinthians 13:1) and in the earlier Mosaic times (Deuteronomy 19:15). Recognizing the need for another voice of agreement,

Christ argued, "I am one who testifies for myself; my other witness is the one who sent me — the Father" (John 8:18).

A letter, aimed at removing ignorance with information and sadness with good news, makes the case for resurrection not only by the teaching of an apostle but also by "the Lord's own word" (I Thessalonians 4:13-15). A sermon, targeted at getting Ephesian elders at their pastoring tasks, calls for Paul's encouraging words to be supplemented by "the words of the Lord Jesus himself" (Acts 20:35). If the Lord saw wisdom in sending out workers "two by two" (Luke 10:1), I can see value in sending out ideas the same way. It has been said that great authorities are great arguments. To allow the "Amen" to be heard to a sermon idea from a prophet, apostle or Christ the Lord gives the approval needed to sway the hearer.

Behind preaching lies conviction. What is being preached is not the novelty of a single mind. It is the long-held beliefs of the Lord's church across the centuries from Pentecost to the Parousia. There is a "yesterday and today and forever" (Hebrews 13:8) dimension to the unchanging gospel. To find Moses and Mary, Paul and Priscilla, David and Dorcas or ancient prophets and modern preachers speaking "the same thing" (I Corinthians 1:10 KJV), has accumulative, convincing power. To find on the first day of the church all twelve apostles on their feet, voicing through Peter their united testimony, had the winning outcome that Acts 2 records. To the apostolic affirmation of the Big Fisherman was added the "verily" of the others: "We are all witnesses to the fact" (verse 32).

The preacher, in establishing the reliability of his proposition, helps prove his point by pointing his audience to the approval of other voices who addressed the same issue and drew the same conclusion.

REPROVE THE PERVERSION

The orators of history, that have initiated liberty, civilization and progress, have not only been strong in proving their case. They have held up the weakness and ineffectiveness of alternate positions. The Biblical orator among the prophets of Israel and the apostles of the church, likewise approved what was true and reproved what was in error. To reprove is to prove or establish a point again. You establish the truth again by destroying its opposition. Prejudices have to be removed. Objections need to be overcome. Disagreements and questions require fair and honest treatment. They will not just go away. Doubts vanish in the arena of dialogue.

As the Scripture itself is for "rebuking and correcting" (II Timothy 3:16), so is the sermon. Wherever the pure gospel has gone, perversions of it have followed in as many forms as Joseph's coat had colors. "Expose them" (Ephesians 5:11) is the Divine order to those who uphold the light. Titus is to see that elders "hold firmly to the trustworthy message . . . and refute those who oppose it" (Titus 1:9). Paul knew he was "put here for the defense of the gospel" (Philippians 1:16). Error and truth cannot co-exist. One or the other must die out.

The heart of an honest disputant cries out with Job, "Teach me, and I will be quiet; show me where I have been wrong" (Job 6:24). "Foolish and stupid arguments" (II Timothy 2:23) are to be exposed for what they are. "Meaningless talk" by teachers who "do not know what they are talking about or what they so confidently affirm" (I Timothy 1:6-7), needs to be shown to be but meaningless. If we do not our sheep will stray. "So-called deep secrets" (Revelation 2:24) deserve to be known for the shallowness they really possess. "Fine sounding arguments" (Colossians 2:4) ought to receive the rays of truth, revealing what they actually are.

There is a place for affirmation and also a place for denial. Those who heard Jesus teach were "amazed at his understanding and his answers" (Luke 2:47 cp. 20:26). Dealing with many mistaken notions, it is written that "Jesus answered" (Luke 13:2,15,23) those wrong ideas. He refuted error until "no one dared to ask him any more questions" (Luke 20:40). His disciples, when confronted by an amazing and perplexing question like, "What does this mean?" responded with the helpful, "Let me explain this to you; listen carefully to what I say" (Acts 2:12,14).

When false prophets "fill you with false hopes . . . (and) speak visions from their own minds, not from the mouth of the LORD" (Jeremiah 23:16), what defense do the righteous have? Is there an "apt reply . . . a timely word" (Proverbs 15:23)? Has not the Lord been "teaching you true and reliable words, so that you can give sound answers" (Proverbs 22:21)? God's men "debated" (Acts 9:29) and "answered . . . boldly" (Acts 13:46). They "reasoned" (Acts 18:19) and "vigorously refuted the Jews in public debate" (Acts 18:28). They could say to their opponents, as Job did to his, "Nothing is left of your answers but falsehood" (Job 21:34). No other option lies open to the one who enters the preaching ministry than to equip himself so that he can reprove gospel perversions and prove gospel points.

IMPROVE THE PREACHER

Prove, approve, reprove and improve are not plays on words but pleas to Word proclaimers. The best evidence of the gospel's power is a changed life — a living demonstration. Prove a case with words and disprove it by life is an unforgivable inconsistency. "To add to your faith virtue" and to possess this quality "in increasing measure . . . will keep you from being ineffective and unproductive" (II Peter 1:5,8).

The effectiveness of Paul in preaching and living increased over time. Luke writes, "Saul grew more and more powerful and baffled the Jews living in Damascus by proving that Jesus is the Christ" (Acts 9:22). As to "righteousness, peace and joy in the Holy Spirit . . . anyone who serves God in this way is pleasing to God and approved by men" (Romans 14:17-18). "Approve what God's will is" (Romans 12:2) by your actions. "As servants of God . . . commend (yourselves) in every way" (II Corinthians 6:4). "Test the sincerity of your love" (II Corinthians 8:8). Any lawyer can find a loophole in your argument, if he doesn't want to believe. But it is exceedingly hard to explain away a transformed life. Work at improving your sermons, but especially at improving your life. "Let your light shine before men, that they may see your good deeds and praise your Father in heaven" (Matthew 5:16). According to the Master Teacher, that is the way it works.

24

HOW TO ILLUSTRATE

George E. Sweazey renders the verdict that "a sermon without illustrations is like a television program with the picture tube turned off."[1] Are illustrations that essential to effective preaching? Concerning the Master Teacher, Matthew writes, "Jesus spoke all these things to the crowd in parables; he did not say anything to them without using a parable" and the tax collector considers that fact a fulfillment of the prophecy "I will open my mouth in parables" (Matthew 13:34-35 cp. Psalm 78:2). Jesus' best known sermon, the Sermon on the Mount, is from beginning to end picturesque language at its best.

We need to be reminded that Jesus was a Jew, not a Greek — a rabbi, not a philosopher. He believed the Good News He brought to the world would reach a larger audience, if clothed in

---

1. *Preaching the Good News* (Englewood Cliffs, New Jersey: Prentice-Hall Inc., 1976), p. 193

picture stories rather than abstract analysis. Over ninety-five percent of the people can visualize a well-told story, but less than five percent can understand abstract explanations, however true they may be. Good shepherds feed sheep close to the ground. Great scientists bless the world with lofty equations, but common people benefit by the end-product without any grasp of the process by which the mind of these Einsteins came to their conclusions.

Logical arguments may soon be forgotten. Analogous stories will long be recalled. Illustrations paint enduring pictures in the mind. Our word "illustration" comes from the Latin "*illustrare*," meaning "to light up." As an Arab proverb puts it, "He is the best speaker who can turn the ear into an eye."

Keep your listeners in mind. Not all of them will be scholars, able to follow each turn of your argument. Most of them — scholars included — will see with appreciation and clarity any picture you paint with words.

WHY USE THEM?

Why should a preacher use illustrations? That very question was asked of Jesus. His disciples put the inquiry, "Why do you speak to the people in parables?" His puzzling reply was, "The knowledge of the secrets of the kingdom of heaven has been given to you, but not to them. Whoever has will be given more, and he will have an abundance. Whoever does not have, even what he has will be taken from him. This is why I speak to them in parables" (Matthew 13:10-13 cp. Mark 4:10-12; Luke 8:9-11). Christ seems to be saying that his teaching, like a broadcasting station, will send out the message of God's kingdom, but the hearers, like receiving sets, must bring receptive hearts to the process. Otherwise materialism will work like static and worldliness will cause such interference that God's message will not get through. Those with humble, teachable, receptive hearts will be enriched more and more by Jesus' parables. The hardened, rejecting, spiritual "have nots" will not be possessors, because they have no desire to accept what Jesus is offering. They will continue to sink deeper in their religious confusion.

To those who hunger for truth and thirst for knowledge, illustrations open doors of understanding. The disciples, hungry for further insight and understanding, would ponder over Jesus' stories throughout the day and then, later in the house, would seek the further knowledge that the earlier parable had stimulated. They would request, "Explain to us the parable" (Matthew 13:36). Mark says that "with many similar parables Jesus spoke the word to them, as much as they could understand . . . but when he was alone with his own disciples, he explained everything" (Mark 4:33-34).

Illustrations gain attention and assist retention. Many a person identifies with listeners who remember a story in the sermon long after the rest of the message has faded from the memory. That means a good illustration will not only help the truth of a sermon to be understood, it will help it longer to be remembered. If you are lifted by a stirring hymn, you enjoy hearing it sung again and again. If your children have purchased a recording of one of the top ten popular songs, chances are they didn't play it but once and then lay it aside never to be heard again. A parable, like that of the Prodigal Son or the Good Samaritan, never seems to lose its freshness in the retelling.

The power of an illustration is not spent fully when it gains the attention, aids the memory or enlightens the understanding. The analogy or example, likely, will enhance the truth under discussion and make it more attractive as well. A bare idea, clothed in the majestic garb of a story, may begin to show the splendor and glory of the concept and impress the hearer of the importance of pursuing the line of thought that is being advocated. Any jeweler knows that to hold some gem on a black velvet cloth under a brilliant spot light will show to the prospective buyer the magnificence of the jewel. Let the gospel herald use illustrations that turn on the light and expose the beauty of Christ and His teaching.

Yesterday, God "spoke to the prophets . . . and told parables through them" (Hosea 12:10). When the "last days" began, He spoke "to us by his Son" (Hebrews 1:1), who "told . . . many things in parables" (Matthew 13:3). According to Mark's Gospel, "Jesus . . . spoke . . . in parables" (3:23; 12:1) and "taught . . . many things by parables" (4:2). Matthew's account often lists one story after another with the simple opening line, "Jesus told them another parable" (13:24,31; 21:33) or, "He told them still another parable" (13:33). A group of stories might end, "When Jesus had finished these parables, he moved on from there" (13:53); or, a new list of parables might begin, "Jesus spoke to them again in parables" (22:1). Luke's Gospel initiates analogy after analogy with the words, "He told them this parable" (5:36; 8:4; 12:16; 13:6; 15:3; 18:9; 20:9).

Each story stirred some emotions and pricked some consciences. It is written, "When the chief priests and the Pharisees heard Jesus' parables (of the Two Sons and the Tenants), they knew he was talking about them" (Matthew 21:45; Mark 12:12; Luke 20:19). When Nathan related to David the story of the rich man with large numbers of sheep killing the one and only little ewe lamb of a poor man, the king saw the injustice of the incident before the verdict fell, "You are the man!" (I Samuel 12:1-7). Stories have ways to pull us mentally and emotionally into the drama and thus accomplish an essential work in preaching. Persuasive speech must reach mind, emotion, conscience and will. The interest-capturing, truth-clarifying, mind-challenging illustration heads straight for the heart. It is never just a story for the story's sake. It is a bridge to transport the hearer to a charted destination. Notice how your Bible reads: "Then Jesus told his disciples a parable to show them that they should always pray and not give up" (Luke 18:1). The parable was a road not the destination. Or, listen again to the Scripture: "To some who were confident of their own righteousness and looked down on everybody else, Jesus told this parable (of the Pharisee and the Tax Collector)" (Luke 18:9). The bull's eye was humility. The story was the arrow, bringing the mind quickly to the issue.

To the credit of a well-honed and carefully-chosen story, it becomes a channel for the preservation of important truth. No wonder Asaph begged, "O my people, hear my teaching; listen to the words of my mouth. I will open my mouth in parables, I will utter things hidden from of old — things we have heard and known, things our fathers have told us" (Psalm 78:1-3).

WHERE FIND THEM?

Economic advisers want to help their clients make investments that will produce good dividends and avoid losses. Homiletic advisers, for the same reasons, ought to caution embryo preachers against putting big money into promising volumes of sermon illustrations. These "treasuries" of anecdotes for the pulpit contain pages of fool's gold for every single paragraph of rich ore. The large volumes, in which I early invested heavily, did not become the rich resource for which I had hoped. Finding my study shelves filled with what was often "wretched, pitiful, poor, blind and naked," I was ready for the Master Teacher's words, "I counsel you to buy from me gold refined in the fire, so that you (and your preaching) can become rich" (Revelation 3:17-18).

Show me a child who does not wait longingly for a father to tell him or her a bedtime story. Preachers need to remember that the term "children of God" has significance to the man in the pulpit, who is preparing to talk with the persons that will be before him.

Learn from Jesus. Take a lesson from Rabbis. They illuminated, illustrated and instructed with parables. The Greek παραβολή is equivalent to the Hebrew *mashal*. The words speak of placing things side by side for comparison. The Synoptic Gospels are said to preserve thirty-nine parables by Jesus. Some scholars put the number as high as fifty-nine and others as low as twenty-seven; depending on how inclusively you apply the term.

To a Rabbi a *mashal* could be a (1) "proverb" (Luke 4:23), (2) a maxim such as "Everyone who exalts himself will be humbled, and he who humbles himself will be exalted" (Luke 14:11), (3) a riddle, such as "Nothing outside a man can make him 'unclean' by going into him. Rather, it is what comes out of a man that makes him 'unclean' " (Mark 7:15,17), (4) a simile, such as "The kingdom of heaven is like yeast that a woman took and mixed into a large amount of flour until it worked all through the dough" (Matthew 13:33), (5) a metaphor, such as, "You are the light of the world" (Matthew 5:14), and the list goes on. Examples, figures of speech, sayings, etc. can become grist in a Rabbi's mill.

Jesus spoke in figurative language about narrow gates and broad roads (Matthew 7:13), sheep's clothing (Matthew 7:15) and throwing pearls to pigs (Matthew 7:6). He used allegories occasionally comparing His Messiahship to that of a good shepherd (John 10:1-18) or his relationship with the disciples as that of vine to branches (John 15:1-11). His proverbs will never be forgotten, as He admonished, "Give to Caesar what is Caesar's and to God what is God's" (Mark 12:17), "Everyone who exalts himself will be humbled, and he who humbles himself will be exalted" (Luke 14:11), or "The Sabbath was made for man, not man for the Sabbath" (Mark 2:27).

The Lord is most famous for the parables, more narrowly defined as earthly stories containing heavenly meanings. Some of these compared God's love to that of a waiting Father for a prodigal son (Luke 15:11-32), while others contrasted God's willingness to provide our needs with an unconcerned judge who only reluctantly gives in to the pestering cries of a needy widow (Luke 18:1-8). We might term Jesus a folk theologian, who took the profundities of heaven and simplified them for the people of earth. The preacher, who wants to follow in Jesus' footsteps, ought to pray for the gift of interpretation (I Corinthians 12:10), so that he can translate the foreign language of theologians and communicate it by simple stories to the common mind. One value of a story told in conversational style is that attention goes up while defenses go down.

Jesus added additional strength to His parables by pointing to scenes for the hearer's eyes to behold, as He told His story for their ears. Centuries earlier Ahijah the prophet, when addressing Jeroboam, "took hold of the new cloak he was wearing and tore it into twelve pieces" (I Kings 11:30). This became the object lesson by which the prophet explained how and why God would divide the tribes. Years later Paul the apostle, when speaking to Elders from the Ephesian church, held out his calloused hands for all to see, calling out, "These hands of mine have supplied my own needs and the needs of my companions" (Acts 20:34). The admonition to work hard for the kingdom had strengthened appeal, when what the eye could see gave "amen" to the words being spoken. It was Jesus' style to use a scene the hearer's vision could behold to increase the lasting effect of his words. "See how the lilies of the field grow," He said in His Sermon on the Mount (Matthew 6:28). By the lake He began His parables of the kingdom, "A farmer went out to sow his seed" (Matthew 13:3). The chances are high that the audience, standing on the shore, could see a farmer doing exactly that. The Master could find sermons in Roman coins (Matthew 22:19-21), dirty dishes (Matthew 23:25-26) or white-washed tombs (Matthew 23:27-28). If you have eyes to see eternal truths in the common things of time, you too will find illustrations in patched hand-me-downs (Matthew 9:16) or misplaced money (Luke 15:8-10).

The place Christ turned for illustrations was not to a volume in the corner book store. He found His stories in everyday life. Imagination is an asset. Observation is an ally. The Lord talked about children playing (Matthew 11:17), neighbors borrowing food (Luke 11:5) and women house cleaning (Luke 15:8). When it comes to life's illustrations, "the fields . . . are ripe for harvest" (John 4:35).

In dealing with life, where your people live, watch the traffic signals. There is always a green light to speak, reporting "in detail what God (has) done . . . through (your) ministry" (Acts 21:19). Only be careful to hide behind the cross and not hide the Christ with the pronouns "I," "me" or "my." Let Paul's words to his listeners be your words to your hearers, "Before your very eyes Jesus Christ was clearly portrayed" (Galatians 3:1). Observe the flashing amber light or the solid red stop sign, when it comes to letting last week's counseling become next Sunday's illustration. Remember the wisdom of Solomon's guide-line, "Do not betray another man's confidence, or he who hears it may shame you and you will never lose your bad reputation" (Proverbs 25:9-10). The audience should be spared from personal embarrassment by all the bright sayings of your children or constant reference to your last holy-land visit. They would rather hear what God has done than what you have experienced.

To the question, "Where can I find illustrations for my sermon?" we find the answer in life today and in the historic records of life in the past. Jesus drew heavily on the history of Jewish people. The great religious festivals like Passover, Pentecost or Tabernacles became springboards for His message. When His countrymen were recalling God's guidance through the wilderness, His leading by the pillar of fire or His providing water from the rock in the desert, He pointed to Himself as the shepherd (John 10:14), the light of the world (John 8:12) and satisfying drink for the thirsty (John 7:37).

"The law of Moses, the Prophets and the Psalms" (Luke 24:44) were not only filled with verbal and picture prophecies about Him, they also overflowed with heroic tales worth retelling. The New Covenant preacher has an inexhaustible supply of sermon illustrations in his Bible, both Old and New Testaments. Much of the Book of books is narrative. Who has not been inspired to courage by recalling how youthful David met the giant Goliath for his countrymen or remembering the three Hebrew youth who refused to bow before the image of King Nebuchadnezzar? Better stories have yet to be invented than the Biblical account of Elijah facing singlehandedly the 450 prophets of Baal on Mount Carmel or some dozens of other records from either Israel's past, the church's missionary outreach or the Lord's battles with evil from His baptism to His cross. Bible stories have a strong hold on the human heart. They were put there by Divine inspiration for parents, teachers and preachers to use. Read them, ponder them, feel them and tell them in a thrilling way. Make the then and there of the text become the here and now of God's present action. Thou shalt not treat the book of the ages as a cadaver to be dissected by a critic who acts in cold indifference. Rather thou shalt relive the story with a devout heart and a sensitive imagination.

The book of Nature and the book of Revelation have the same Author. That fact suggests the preacher can find a host of illustrations in the Bible before him and the world around him. Jesus talked of "the birds of the air" and "the lilies of the field" (Matthew 6:26,28). He noticed that sheep know their shepherd's voice and do not follow strangers and "used this figure of speech" (John 10:4-6) in His teaching. Paul's sermons included the evidence of God's "kindness by giving . . . rain from heaven and crops in their seasons" (Acts 14:17). The hymn-book of Israel sang, "The heavens declare the glory of God; the skies proclaim the work of his hands" (Psalm 19:1). The wisdom literature of the Old Testament points to nature as an illustrative mine loaded with rich ore. Job spoke, "Ask the animals, and they will tell you; or speak to the earth, and it will teach you, or let the fish of the sea inform you" (Job 12:7-8).

There is no science, no history or no literature that is wanting in illustrative material for preaching. Read widely, for all great preachers are also great readers. Observe carefully, for the wonders of God are everywhere. Worship personally, for second-hand knowledge of God can never substitute for "I know whom I have believed, and I am convinced" (II Timothy 1:12). Absorb the Bible like a blotter or a sponge. Know its truths and make its phraseology your own.

It is no accident that the Master Teacher often quoted from the hymns of His people. The hymn book of any generation can be called "the holiest thoughts of the holiest men at their holiest moments." It is good apostolic advice to "speak to one another with psalms, hymns and spiritual songs" (Ephesians 5:19) and to "teach and admonish" (Colossians 3:16) with these poetic words. To quote hymns is Biblical. It is written of the lawgiver, "Moses recited the words of this song from beginning to end in the hearing of the whole assembly of Israel" (Deuteronomy 31:30), and then follows forty-three verses of inspiring song.

It is legitimate to love the old songs of the faith and to like to hear the familiar terms of the believing community. It makes you know you belong to the faith of one's fathers. It is likewise right to create new hymns, praying with David, "put a new song in my mouth, a hymn of praise to our God" (Psalm 40:3). It ought not only be Solomon concerning whom it can be written, "He spoke three thousand proverbs and his songs numbered a thousand and five" (I Kings 4:32). All styles of literature can be resources for sermons — "Proverbs" (Proverbs 1:1), "riddles" (Psalm 49:4) and the writing of "poets" (Numbers 21:27). If Paul can quote from the great literature of pagan poets like Epimenides and Aratus (Acts 17:27-28; Titus 1:12), you can too.

In searching for the source of illustration for a Bible preacher, we have pointed to music and literature, science and history, holy days and holidays. Let us not leave out current events. If Jesus could call attention to a recent tragedy about "the Galileans whose blood Pilate had mixed with their sacrifices" or concerning "eighteen who died when the tower of Siloam fell on them" (Luke 13:1-5), your morning's newspaper can make ancient truths as modern as this week's calendar.

The joke column and comic strip of the tabloid, however, are to be used with extreme caution. Yes, there is humor in the Bible. But, learn post-haste that while humor is a value, silliness is a vice. Humor communicates. Humor, *per se*, can relieve tension, break the ice, make an audience more responsive and more ready to listen. It can create bonds of understanding between the person in the pulpit and the people in the pew. But, jokes at the beginning signal that the message may not be serious and wisecracks at the end derail the burden of the message. You don't improve Peter's sermon on Pentecost by inserting a Smothers brothers routine. You might possibly insert George Burns, Jack Benny or Bob Hope light-heartedness in your message and have parishioners chuckling all Sunday afternoon as they play nine holes of golf. Yet, the question remains as to how many you started toward the baptistry or led further down the road to holiness.

HOW TEST THEM?

"A worthy woman who can find?" (Proverbs 31:10). The same can be asked of a sermon illustration. It must be worthy. A sermon is a serious venture. It can not be enhanced by what is cheap. Take a "reed like a measuring rod and . . . measure the temple of God and the altar" (Revelation 11:1) and, while you're at it, lay the tape measure on your prospective illustrations. If wise gardeners prune their vines and sage bankers weigh their gold, let wise sermon builders only use quality material in their homiletical endeavors. Take a good look at the illustration. Is it cogent? Is it pertinent to the point of the sermon? Does it belong in the message at all, and if so, is it being put in the right place?

Next to relevancy is the concern for brevity. As a rule, shorter is better. Someone said, "An illustration can open its big mouth and swallow up the whole sermon." Just as street lights are to illumine the road and are not put on the posts with the purpose of drawing attention to themselves, so are analogies to make clear the truth and that is their single mission. Just as a window requires a solid wall, an illustration presupposes a truth to be illustrated.

If shorter is better, so also is fewer best. James Daane observes that "a sermon is not a shish-kabob skewer, alternating biblical meat with interesting anecdotes.[2] Quality takes precedence over quantity. Whether a string of anecdotes is a sign of dotage or the hallmark of a novice may be debatable, but in no case is it recommended. No story is to be added as an ornament. Each illustration is to be an integral structural part of the message. Resist the temptation to use an illustration simply because you like it. If it does not fit the purpose, save it for another day and another sermon. As a good editor, only write *stet* by the vital, the valid and the varied.

People can empathize with a traveler getting mugged (Luke 10:29-37). They can feel for a wedding hostess, when a guest arrives in outlandish and unfitting attire (Matthew 22:14). Affluent folk from the suburbs can identify when a man's prosperity calls for expanding one's holdings (Luke 12:16-21). Learn from the teacher from Nazareth who used parables by the dozens and metaphors by the score. If Jesus can use sixty-five metaphors in His one sermon recorded in Matthew 5-7 and one hundred sixty four in His teaching preserved in the Synoptics, His heralds will be wise to store up tools of the same kind.

---

2. *Preaching with Confidence* (Grand Rapids: William B. Eerdmans Publishing Co., 1980), p. 75.

25

HOW TO SPEAK

Eli advised Samuel to say, "Speak, LORD, for your servant is listening" (I Samuel 3:9). My counsel to preachers is to say, "Speak and do it effectively, servant, for your Lord is listening."

It is time for me to make a confession. In the training of preachers, if given a choice between teaching New Testament or Homiletics, I will opt for giving Bible content as against working for effective speech delivery. But this is only to argue that gospel content has priority over good packaging. An effective speaker with heresy for a message is all the more dangerous. I have attended debates where truth was left languishing, because the advocate of error was polished in his art at swaying the audience, while the proponent of truth could not effectively present his case. This leads to the obvious conclusion that, while a preacher's doctrine must be sound, his skill at delivery, even though second in importance, is tremendously vital nevertheless.

The great missionary Paul confessed to his converts, "I did

not come with eloquence or superior wisdom as I proclaimed to you the testimony about God. . . . my message and my preaching were not with wise and persuasive words" (I Corinthians 2:1,4). Some in the community at Corinth agreed completely, retorting, "In person he is unimpressive and his speaking amounts to nothing" (II Corinthians 10:10). To which the apostle only replied, "I may not be a trained speaker, but I do have knowledge" (II Corinthians 11:6).

So that the message be prime and its power not be attributed to the oratory of a professional, Christ often chose for His advocates day-workers over rabbis. Even in Old Testament times, He chose Moses in spite of Moses' protest, "O Lord, I have never been eloquent . . . I am slow of speech and tongue" (Exodus 4:10). Then, as now, God's answer remains the same to those He calls: "I will help you speak" (Exodus 4:12,15).

Do you in insecurity cry out, "I speak with faltering lips" (Exodus 6:12,30)? Then join the club. But hear the words of hope given an earlier member of the prophetic band: "See, this (live coal) has touched your lips. . . . Go and tell" (Isaiah 6:7,9). To the testimony of Isaiah is added the witness of Jeremiah: "The LORD reached out his hand and touched my mouth" (Jeremiah 1:9). Your experience can be similar to that of Daniel, who confessed, "I was speechless. Then one who looked like a man touched my lips, and I opened my mouth and began to speak" (Daniel 10:15-16).

The New Testament Gospels tell how some persons brought to Jesus "could hardly talk and they begged him to place his hand on (them)" (Mark 7:32). The good news at the end of that old story will be the same in your case. At the touch of Jesus, "he began to speak plainly," so the populace "kept talking about it" and concluded, "He even makes . . . the dumb speak" (Mark 7:35-37).

If the one of whom it is written, "No one ever spoke the way this man does" (John 7:46), be your tutor for what to say and how to say it, the experience of Zacharias will be yours. Luke's early words about John the Baptist's father were, "he . . . remained unable to speak" (1:22). But that was not the end of the account. That record closed, "His mouth was opened and his tongue was loosed, and he began to speak" (1:64). The one with a message to tell, who feels he "is possessed by a spirit that has robbed him of speech" (Mark 9:17), I recommend you have a good talk with your Doctor, the Great Physician.

Paul did not quit and there are left behind records where he was considered, "the chief speaker" (Acts 14:12) and his words were acknowledged to be spoken "so effectively that a great number of Jews and Gentiles believed" (Acts 14:1). The great apostle had the foresight to ask his congregations for prayer support. His request was, "Pray . . . for me, that whenever I open my mouth, words may be given me so that I will fearlessly make known the mystery of the gospel. . . . Pray that I may declare it fearlessly, as I should" (Ephesians 6:19-20). Every speaker's prayer, as he rises to address audiences large or small, ought to be, "May the words of my mouth and the meditations of my heart be pleasing in your sight, O LORD, my Rock and my Redeemer" (Psalm 19:14).

Did you know the Bible describes the experience of one calling for help with the words, "my throat is parched" (Psalm 69:3)? Are you aware of the Messianic Psalm that tells of a sad condition, when the speaker relates, "my tongue sticks to the roof of my mouth" (22:15)? I point to these texts in Heaven's book, to assure you that God knows the occasional problems that plague a speaker. But, I want to turn your eyes to other passages that offer encouraging help in the art of communication. God wants all young Timothies to "set an example . . . in speech" (I Timothy 4:12). He desires every preacher to join David in the vow, "I have resolved that my mouth will not sin" (Psalm 17:3) and "I will put a muzzle on my mouth" (Psalm 39:1). He hopes to hear each speaker pray, "Set a guard over my mouth, O LORD; keep watch over the door of my lips" (Psalm 141:3).

A good text-book for beginning speech or preliminary

homiletics is Proverbs. Be reminded that "the tongue has the power of life and death" (18:21) and that "a word fitly spoken is like apples of gold in settings of silver" (25:11). Learn, before you start speaking publicly, that "reckless words pierce like a sword" (12:18) and that a rule never to be broken reads, "Let another praise you, and not your own mouth; someone else, and not your own lips" (27:2). The guarantee that comes with Solomon's curse in communication is that "He who guards his mouth and his tongue keeps himself from calamity" (21:23).

Take advanced homiletics from the little Jew from Tarsus, who warned against "smooth talk and flattery" (Romans 16:18 cp. I Thessalonians 2:5) and insisted, "Do not let any unwholesome talk come out of your mouths, but only what is helpful for building others up . . . that it may benefit those who listen" (Ephesians 4:29). Paul insisted that gospel preachers "be eager" to speak (I Corinthians 14:1,39). It is the nature of Christianity to share the story of Christ and to do so with excitement. Why should a world-changing story suffer from a damp firecracker delivery?

Music buffs recognize that the words of the opera are important, but so is the music! Preachers ought to know that the message is vital, but so is its delivery! Ornate style is inconceivable to the apostles. However, when they spoke, people were "persuaded" (Acts 17:4; II Corinthians 5:11) and "cut to the heart" (Acts 2:37), for the Christ they preached was as present in the spoken word as He earlier had been in human flesh. In the Bible records, where Jesus or His apostles spoke, things are said that should help us in our search for the way to speak most effectively.

LET YOUR WHOLE BODY SPEAK

Whether Jesus "stood up to read" (Luke 4:16), "was standing . . . with the people crowding around him and listening" or had "sat down" to teach (Luke 5:1,3), His whole being was communicating the burden of His lesson. Audiences began to sense the urgency of the disciples, as they "stood up in the meeting of the Areopagus" (Acts 17:22), or "sat down . . . to speak to the women . . . gathered" by the river (Acts 16:13). Most times they rose to their feet and spoke out like heralds of vital news (Acts 2:14; 13:16; 22:30; 27:21 cp. 1:15; 15:7; 25:18). But at every time they radiated "courage" (Acts 4:13) and manifested "boldness" (Acts 4:29,31), until the words "fearlessly" (Acts 9:27) and "boldly" (Acts 13:46; 14:3; 18:26; 28:31) became the adverbs and "more and more powerful" (Acts 9:22) became the adjective description.

To preach, as did Christ and His men, is to speak with "deep conviction" (I Thessalonians 1:5). In those days, audiences were "astonished at (the) teaching" (Matthew 22:33; Acts 9:21) and the "authority" that it carried (Matthew 7:29; Mark 1:22; Luke 4:32 cp. Matthew 21:23; Mark 1:27; Luke 4:36). In our time, it is astonishing how such a message as the gospel can be told with so little ardor in some quarters. There is a passion that befits the telling of Jesus' passion. He who preaches the Word is to "be urgent in season and out of season" (II Timothy 4:2 KJV). He is to feel "compelled to preach" (I Corinthians 9:16). He is to sense that he "cannot help speaking" (Acts 4:20). He is to confess with Jeremiah, "His word is in my heart like a burning fire, shut up in my bones. I am weary of holding it in; indeed I cannot" (Jeremiah 20:9).

The Christian message is not to be delivered, as if nothing is at stake. The sermons of the Bible might well have been printed in capital letters, rather than in lower case, for they were persuasive because of their passion. William Jennings Bryan is quoted to have said, "Eloquence may be defined as the speech of one who knows what he is talking about, and means what he says. It is thought on fire." He who uttered, "I had to be in my Father's house" (Luke 2:49) and "we must do the work of him who sent me" (John 9:4), is poorly served by persons unmoved by the truth that "now is the day of salvation" (II Corinthians 6:2).

A yawning church led by a tired minister is deaf to the call of God. Maybe you noticed that when you yawn the inner chamber of your ear is closed and for a moment you are deaf to all sound. "Zeal" was a distinctive mark of God's messiah (John 2:17). If Jesus can be "deeply moved" (John 11:38), "troubled in spirit" (John 13:21) and unashamed to weep (John 11:35), His spokesmen do not have to be stoic and unemotional. Let urgency be restored to preaching. Jesus had not lost faith in His Bible's authority. He had full confidence in its truth and the urgency of its message. It showed in His eyes and radiated from His whole being, as He rose to speak, not quoting authorities, but teaching as "one who had authority" (Matthew 7:29).

Take the pledge "to speak the word of God more courageously and fearlessly" (Philippians 1:14). Vow, "I will extol the LORD with all my heart" (Psalm 111:1). Work at preaching with unbroken eye-contact.

Admitting the discipline of written sermons and being aware that the New Testament is heavy with letters written to churches, some of which can be labeled homilies, I still challenge you to labor at preaching without a manuscript. Yes, in the Nazareth Synagogue Jesus read His text. But, no, He did not then talk to the assembly with His eyes meticulously glued to notes.

Face to face encounter is to be preferred over talking to a clock on the back wall, scanning a manuscript on the back of your mind or reading the printed notes on the pulpit before you. The less paper before you and the less reading from any paper in front of you, the less barrier there will be in communication with the flock. It is hard to believe that Jesus would have been speechless without His folio, or that Peter on Pentecost and Paul before Felix could not have made it through their messages without constant breaking of eye contact with the persons before them.

The people before you need to sense that you are genuinely interested in them. To look them in the face helps your concern to come through. They recognize more readily that you are talking to them personally. In a conversation with a friend you do not read your remarks.

Someone suggested that a written sermon is like a pressed flower in that much of the color, fragrance and substance has disappeared. I do not deny the beauty of a well-read manuscript. I only encourage the better way. I do not suggest that it is easy, but I do insist that you can do it and do it well. The memory, like any muscle of your body, only needs to be developed. The "I-thou" relationship between pulpit and pew is heightened when the preacher is looking at people rather than papers. "Go and tell" has a better ring to it than "Write and read." The half-way house of effective reading is not reached by many who prefer the printed manuscripts. Eugene Smith, at a World Methodist Conference, compared making a speech with a manuscript to courting a girl through a picket fence. He quipped, "Everything said can be heard, but there is not much contact."

Can you remember the movement of your message without the crutch? Do you expect the people who hear you to recall any of it after the benediction? Work on the sermon until you are full of it, for eloquence flows out of saturation with a theme. Only when the truth conquers you, can it capture the audience. Spurgeon told his students, "Sin cannot be taken out of men, as Eve was taken out of Adam, while they are fast asleep."[1] He was pleading for preaching with one's whole being and not just the voice. Sweezey on the same point called attention to the futility of a blacksmith pounding on cold iron. He pleaded that a preacher recognize the need to raise his hearer's "emotional temperature," so that the "shaping" of character can take place.[2] I feel that all of our being will be involved in our messages, when we consider our situation to be comparable to that of a medic at the scene of a critical accident. It is not time for sharing coffee and light dessert or switching ties more color-coordinated with the patient's suit.

---

1. *Spurgeon's Lectures to His Students* (Grand Rapids, Michigan: Zondervan, 1945), p. 103.

2. *Ibid*, p. 194.

Twenty minutes might be all the time one has for turning potential death to hope of life.

Does a neighbor use notes to announce that your house is on fire? Writing has its place in preparation, as you struggle for how to say something with transparent clarity, picturesque wording and vigorous force. But, if you would speak as the Bible preachers, rise to preach from a heart aflame. The comparatively modern practice of preaching from a manuscript can not be traced back to Christ and His apostles. In no way does preaching from a manuscript spell "sin." But, in some ways learning to speak without one may help you to spell "success."

LET YOUR ENTIRE AUDIENCE HEAR

The buzz word today among embryo preachers is "conversational style" and among developing teachers is "group dynamics." I buy the value of two-way communication or feedback for maximum learning. I recognize that several of Jesus' sermons were preceded by or followed by conversation. I admit that dialogue is an ideal way for small group learning. But I insist that preaching meets a need unmet any other way. The church, to say nothing of the world, needs to be motivated and not just taught.

If you like a sermon to be a nice intimate chat between you and the man in the pulpit, I can understand. But, I pick up from the Bible that it is appropriate for a minister of the Word to visualize himself as a herald sent to proclaim the message ordered by his king. In this latter concept the hearer is more apt to be motivated to act, having listened to an urgent message from his Lord.

What says the Scripture? What were Christ's instructions? "What I tell you in the dark, speak in the daylight; what is whispered in your ear proclaim from the housetops" (Matthew 10:27; Luke 12:3). How did the twelve disciples preach? "Peter stood up with the Eleven, raised his voice and addressed the crowd" (Acts 2:14). "With great power the apostles continued to testify" (Acts 4:33).

If a preacher is to have an intellect and use it and, if he is to have a heart and show it, could it not be expected that he have a voice and develop it? Why, in a Gothic building shaped to resemble a bowling alley where a large percentage of the audience can only see the preacher with difficulty, should the message go partially unheard? Wherever Jesus spoke, in the temple or in a boat, it was "in the hearing of the people" (Luke 7:1). All spoke of Him as "powerful in word" (Luke 24:19). This does not mean He always "cried out in a loud voice" or "a loud cry" (Luke 15:34,37). Yet, it certainly suggests that what He spoke could be heard. In Revelation the voice of the Risen Christ was described by John as "a loud voice like a trumpet" (1:10; 4:1) and "like the sound of rushing waters" (1:15). In the Apocalypse, when heaven's angels spoke, it was "in a loud voice" (8:13 cp. 10:1).

The Old Testament bears testimony to God's communicating with His people in sufficient volume to be heard by all. A speaker did not mumble, he "opened his mouth" (Job 3:1; Ezekiel 33:22). Deuteronomy tells how "the LORD proclaimed in a loud voice to (Israel's) whole assembly" (5:22). Nehemiah records that Ezra read the Law to the entire assembly and he did it "aloud from day break till noon" (8:3). To Nehemiah it was important that all the reading be "aloud in the hearing of the people" (13:1). Daniel knew it was fitting for the word of a "herald (to be) loudly proclaimed" (3:4). Isaiah knew the time would come when "the LORD (would) cause men to hear his majestic voice" (30:30). He foresaw the day of Christ, rejoicing that "in that day the deaf (would) hear" (29:18 cp. 42:18). He knew his prophetic mission to be under the order: "You who bring good tidings to Jerusalem, lift up your voice with a shout, lift it up, do not be afraid" (40:9 cp. 52:8; 58:1; 62:1).

All will agree that "the quiet words of the wise are more to be heeded than the shouts of a ruler of fools" (Ecclesiastes 9:17). But, will you not also agree that a well-prepared message from

God's word ought not be missed, because it has been spoken too softly to be heard beyond row seven? "The voice of the LORD is powerful; the voice of the LORD is majestic" (Psalm 29:4). Shall that of His spokesman be weak, like a wimp? Hear God's order, "Let your voice be heard" (Jeremiah 22:20). Listen to God's promise, "I will make my words in your mouth a fire" (Jeremiah 5:14). In God's domain there is a place for "shouts of joy and victory (to) resound" (Psalm 118:15 cp. 71:23). If "Wisdom calls aloud . . . raises her voice . . . cries out . . . (and) makes her speech" (Proverbs 1:20-21 cp. 8:1), do not be afraid to be heard, as if only a whisper is fitting in the church building. Let all the people hear without strain and do it without the auditors feeling you are speaking with difficulty. Project, but do not strain.

LET EVERY WORD BE CLEAR

The person with a hearing aid will be the first to tell you that volume is not as important in understanding communication as enunciation. Articulation is of number one importance. Good diction makes a whisper understood better than a shout.

Jesus had little good to say for the "careless word" (Matthew 12:36 cp. Isaiah 58:13). The "idle word" (KJV) does not do its work. It does not accomplish its purpose of communication. How blessed is the speaker who with discipline can move from the state, where he "could hardly talk" to the new condition, where he "speak(s) plainly" (Mark 7:32,35).

As a novice in a few foreign languages, I can discern a message in print more easily than what I hear orally. Distinct pronunciation helps immensely. If "your speech will mumble" (Isaiah 29:4), who will understand? "Obscure speech" and the "incomprehensible tongue" (Isaiah 33:10) must be exchanged for what is "fluent and clear" (Isaiah 32:4). Hear the injunction to set "forth the truth plainly" (II Corinthians 4:2). Consider Paul's appeal for "intelligible words to instruct others" (I Corinthians 14:19). He writes at length: "How will anyone know what tune is being played unless there is a distinction in the notes? Again, if a trumpet does not sound a clear call, who will get ready for battle? So it is with you. Unless you speak intelligible words with your tongue, how will anyone know what you are saying? You will just be speaking into the air. . . . If then I do not grasp the meaning of what someone is saying, I am a foreigner to the speaker" (I Corinthians 14:7-11).

From one end of the Bible to the other, there is the consciousness that no edification happens unless words are understood. Eliakim, Shebna and Joah requested the field commander to "please speak . . . in Aramaic, since we understand it" (II Kings 18:26; Isaiah 36:11). Xerxes sent out his dispatches to each province in "its own script and . . . language" (Esther 1:22; 3:12). Asaph and Israel were only confused when they "heard a language . . . they did not understand" (Psalm 81:5). Paul captured the ears of the Jerusalem crowd and they fell silent, as he spoke to them in "Aramaic" (Acts 21:40). The very special gift of "other tongues" (Acts 2:4), granted to the missionaries of the first century, enabled them as unschooled Galileans to speak in the hearer's "own language . . . (his) own native . . . tongue" (Acts 2:6-11). This Holy Spirit-given tool of communication endowed some Christians with "the ability to speak in different kinds of tongues" and others with the ability to handle the "interpretation of tongues" (I Corinthians 12:10).

Apply this fact that God wants clear communication from his spokesmen. Let any "who speaks . . . pray that he may interpret what he says." Woe to the poor hearer, who "does not know what you are saying" (I Corinthians 14:13,16). A modern application of this ancient principle calls for clear enunciation, but also for using terminology that is not foreign to the people before you.

The fact that the Holy Spirit chose κοινή Greek, rather than the Classical, for the New Testament should catch our attention. Κοινή is the language of the common man. Avoid big-word-itis. Put theological jargon in the isolation ward. Christ did not send you "to preach the gospel . . . with words of human wisdom." (I Corinthians 1:17). Choose the vernacular over the classical, the short over the long, the specific over the general and the picturesque over the abstract. In preaching, "by your words you will be acquitted, and by your words you will be condemned" (Matthew 12:37). In sermons we look for faith, hope and clarity. Shallow puddles are often muddy. Deep pools are often clear. The deep things of God need more the familiar words of the market place than the code language of the scholars.

Haddon W. Robinson warns against the preacher developing "a stained-glass voice."[3] You can lift up your eyes either to the mountains or the stars through clear glass and clear words. Fred Craddock, in his distinctive way, bemoans that "the church had no retirement program for old words that fought well at Nicaea, Chalcedon and Augsburg."[4]

What does the Bible say about the words we speak? Words can be "hard to understand" (II Peter 3:16). Some conversation can be but "meaningless talk" (I Timothy 1:6). Certain religious leaders, like "mediums and spiritualists . . . (only) whisper and mutter" (Isaiah 8:19). Proverbial wisdom reminds us that "when words are many, sin is not absent" (10:19), that the man is to be avoided "who talks too much" (20:19), and that "a man of knowledge uses words with restraint" (17:27), letting his "heart guide his mouth" (16:23). Why be a person "of obscure speech and difficult language, whose words you cannot understand" (Ezekiel 3:6)?

Only one who looked at his sermon as a filibuster to kill time, would rest content with a people asking, "What is this babble trying to say?" (Acts 17:18). Happier is the spokesman who has read the book named "The Preacher" or Ecclesiastes. There he could learn that there is both "a time to be silent and a time to

---

3. *Biblical Preaching: The Development and Delivery of Expository Messages* (Grand Rapids, Michigan: Baker Book House, 1980), p. 18.

4. *As One with Authority* (Nashville: Abingdon, 1979), p.7.

speak" (3:7). There he could glean that you are not to "be quick with your mouth" (5:2) for "many words are meaningless" (5:7) and it too often follows that "the more the words, the less the meaning" (6:11). We conclude that, if Solomon "the Teacher searched to find just the right words" (12:10), the modern counterpart is commended to spend priority time in a similar pursuit. For why should either quality ideas or good people clad themselves in untidy garb that cover their nobility? Elegant truth about God blends with the eloquent telling of that truth. The saving word "is in your mouth" (Romans 10:8). Different moods and meanings are conveyed by the variable uses of your voice. Why talk "like a child" (I Corinthians 13:11), when with effort you can mature until your message can be "clearly portrayed" (Galatians 3:1)

LET YOUR TOTAL ATTITUDE BE LOVE

Do not just be loud is the Pauline counsel. For "a resoundng gong or a clanging cymbal" rates a "one," where the tone of love scores a "ten." Crude language, raging tirades and loud shouts are poor packaging for a gospel of grace. "Speaking the truth in love" (Ephesians 4:15) is to sound more like Jesus. His hearers were "amazed at the gracious words that came from his lips" (Luke 4:22). Paul's people became accustomed to the fact that even his warnings by "night and day (were) with tears" (Acts 20:31 cp. Psalm 126:6). To the early disciples a sermon that goes forth from the mouth into the ear was to originate in the heart.

When the speaker is giving himself to his listeners, they sense it. The apostle to the Gentiles served God with his "whole heart," as he preached "the gospel of his Son" (Romans 1:9). His felt obligation made him "eager to preach" (Romans 1:14-15). He sought "to win as many as possible" (I Corinthians 9:19).

Driven by the love of God for humanity, Paul's every conversation was "full of grace, seasoned with salt" (Colossians 4:6). There were "no no's" for the preacher of the cross. There were to be no "empty, boastful words" (II Peter 2:18) or "arrogant" terms (Psalm 94:4). "To pronounce a curse" (Psalm 109:17) was never in place. "Tongues as sharp as a serpent's" (Psalm 140:3), ill befitted the representative of God. There could be no "complaining or arguing" (Philippians 2:14). "The tongue of the crafty" (Job 15:5) and "words of wickedness" (Job 27:4) were never to be heard, for they cut "like a sharpened razor" (Psalm 52:2) or a "drawn sword" (Psalm 55:21). "The Lord's servant must not quarrel . . . (but) gently instruct" (II Timothy 3:24-25). Among the List of "no's" or "nevers" will always be placed "obscenity, foolish talk or coarse joking" (Ephesians 5:4), along with "corrupt talk" (Proverbs 4:24), "flattering lips" (Psalm 12:2-3), "slander" (Psalm 15:3) "evil" and "lies" Psalm 34:13; 78:36). But above the "No-no's," hear the "know-knows." Know your message. Know your people. Know that gentleness is not a handicap and genuine love is not a weakness. "A gentle answer turns away wrath" (Proverbs 15:1). "A gentle tongue can break a bone" (Proverbs 25:15). "Pleasant words are a honeycomb, sweet to the soul and healing to the bones" (Proverbs 16:24). "He . . . whose speech is gracious will have the king for his friend" (Proverbs 22:11). Know that "pleasant words promote instruction" (Proverbs 16:21). Know that "men sent from God . . . speak with sincerity" (II Corinthians 2:17).

When you can tell your people, "You have a place in our hearts that we would live or die with you" (II Corinthians 7:3), they will listen to every word. Such love considers the other person's feelings (cp. I Corinthians 9:22). Such love never ignores a problem, insults a listener or puts down a brother. Let it be said of you that you "Preach Christ . . . out of good will . . . in love" (Philippians 1:15). Heart-to-heart and eye-to-eye is the effective way to build rapport.

LET YOUR COMPLETE STYLE BE VARIED

David could not fight in Saul's armor, and you are not meant to act like a clone of your favorite preacher. It is also good to not even make all your sermons after the same pattern. Variety has much to commend it. A great pitcher in the big leagues has more than one way he hurls the ball.

It is just as Scriptural to speak "with great fervor" (Acts 18:25) as with a "hushed voice" (Job 4:16). It is equally Biblical to "express devotion . . . with a beautiful voice" (Ezekiel 33:32), as to refute "vigorously" (Acts 18:28). At one time "discussions" (Acts 19:9) are in order. At another occasion, "talking until midnight" and then "until daylight" (Acts 20:7,11) can pass muster. But never should a speech be as "tasteless (as) food eaten without salt" (Job 6:6).

Variety in pace is good. To ever speak in low gear will put the people to sleep. To always go like a house afire — gas pedal to the floor board — will tire the listeners out. Variety in pitch makes the story more true to life and easier to listen to. Variety in tone is a help. You cannot express exasperation, elation or sadness in a monotone voice.

George Bernard Shaw understood that there were "fifty ways of saying Yes and five hundred of saying No, but only one way of writing them down."[5] All actors, speakers or reader of literature need to put themselves into their story so that pitch, rate and tone make the telling of it real to life. The "sweet" voice of a lover (Song of Solomon 2:14) ought not sound like the "long-winded speeches" of Job's comforters (Job 16:3). The "praise" on David's lips (Psalm 34:1) has a different sound, than the "charming" speech of a proficient liar (Proverbs 26:25). He who "speaks in haste" (Proverbs 29:20) or has a mouth that "gushes evil" (Proverbs 15:28), ought not to be heard as the same voice that speaks "peaceably" (Psalm 35:20). Make the Bible live. Play all the parts in the Divine drama until the then and there of Sacred history becomes the here and now of your people.

---

5. *Semeia 39* (Decatur, Georgia: Scholar's Press, 1987), p. 70.

26

HOW TO GESTURE

There have been many hours spent in debate as to whether the singing of the early church was accompanied by instruments. The Eastern and Western branches of the Catholic church, the Lutheran and Calvinistic wings of the Protestant Reformation and the Christian churches and churches of Christ in the Restoration tradition hold different views. But there need be no dispute as to whether the ancient vocal preaching was accompanied with gestures of the body.

The history by Luke preserves the record that "standing up, Paul motioned with his hand" (Acts 13:16), as he began the sermon at Pisidian Antioch. On another occasion in Jerusalem, while standing "on the steps . . . (he) motioned to the crowd" (Acts 21:40). While in Caesarea, this time before King Agrippa, "Paul motioned with his hand and began his defense" (Acts 26:1). It is no stretch of the imagination to suspect that Paul's hands were held out for all the Ephesian elders to see when he reasoned, "You yourselves know that these hands of mine have supplied my own needs and the needs of my companions" (Acts 20:34). It is only natural that all speakers, including Alexander in Ephesus, "motioned for silence in order to make a defense (or speech) before the people" (Acts 19:33).

Personified Wisdom in Solomon's Proverbs "makes her speech," but regrets that "no one gave heed when (she) stretched out her hand" (1:21,24). In Ezekiel's message against Jerusalem and the sanctuary, the "Sovereign LORD (declared) 'So prophesy, son of man, and strike your hands' " (21:2,14). Such an instruction is modest by comparison to the order to enact the siege of Jerusalem, as described in Ezekiel's chapter 4. There drama and symbol, requiring iron pans, battering rams, ropes, bread and even cow manure, was used to get across God's message. Jeremiah used a clay jar, as God instructed: "Then break the jar while those who go with you are watching, and say to them, 'This is what the LORD Almighty says: I will smash this nation and this city as the potter's jar is smashed and cannot be repaired" (Jeremiah 19:10). The New Testament prophet Agabus used Paul's belt for a visual demonstration, regarding Paul's awaiting fate in Jerusalem (Acts 21:11).

The Random House Dictionary of the English Language gives two definitions of a gesture. It calls it any "movement of the body, head, arms, hands, or face that is expressive of an idea, opinion, emotion, etc." It also defines a gesture as "any action or proceeding intended for effect or as a formality." The illustration of the second definition is "a gesture of friendship."[1] Under either definition, it is clear that communication is both vocal and visual. Eyes, hands, voice and the whole person preaches. Body movements express attitudes that may confirm or contradict each other. You do not announce that you "love the brotherhood of believers" (I Peter 2:17), with fists clenched and face scowling.

---

1. Jess Stein, Editor in Chief (New York: Random House, 1966), p. 594.

GESTURES AS ACTIONS FOR EFFECT

To watch East Indian dances or those of the South Seas is to learn that gestures are as expressive as words. Hands, legs, bodies and heads move to tell a story. Modern deaf choirs "sign" their hymns and bring tears to an audience's eyes, for the hearers are grasped by the gospel expressed without words, as each member of the group talks with his or her hands.

Not all actions, intended for effect, are positive. Solomon warned against "a scoundrel and villain . . . who works with his eye, signals with his feet and motions with his fingers, (while at the same time) plots evil with deceit in his heart" (Proverbs 6:12-14). I have wondered if some of my classmates, who took up pipe-smoking in seminary or who let their hair grow ever longer than before, were not breaking from the traditions of their past. They seemed by their practices to be saying that their higher learning had freed them from the ignorance still held by the unfortunate common people of the church who lacked their new-found enlightenment. This is to say that consciously or unconsciously, actions speak as loud as, if not louder than, words. A clerical robe can say, if one is not careful, "I am different from you." A raised pulpit can imply, if one is not cautious, "I am above you." Given the practicalities of being seen and heard, convey your oneness with the people before you. Let them sense that you are sharing with them and not talking down to them.

Jesus' gestures of friendship left that correct impression. He cared. When "he called a little child and had him stand among them" (Matthew 18:2), or when He received the "little children brought to (him) for him to place his hands on them and pray for them" (Matthew 19:13), it was communicated that He cared for children. When He "took (the ruler's dead) girl by the hand" (Matthew 9:25), it became evident He cared for grieving parents. Touching a blind man's eyes (Mark 8:25), or putting His fingers into a deaf man's ears (Mark 7:33), showed His concern for the ailing. The unheard of love that brought Him to actually touch a leper (Matthew 8:3) or shield an adultress from stoning (John 8:1-11), left no one in doubt that His love was more than empty words.

A Pilate might wash his hands of Jesus and want no responsibility for what happens to Him (Matthew 27:24), but a follower of the Savior is ready to wash the feet and serve any lowly disciple (John 13:1-17). A genuine voice for Christ not only speaks His word from the pulpit, but greets them at the curb, calls upon them in their homes and has an open door for them at his study so that the message of his sermon and the actions of his life harmonize rather than conflict.

The goose step of Hitler's troops was fitting the ways of the Third Reich. The blessing of the people (Luke 24:50 cp. Leviticus 9:22) and the greeting of "one another with a holy kiss" (Romans 16:16) or "a hearty handshake" (Phillips) are actions appropriate to the ways of Christ's kingdom. Holding an open Bible in one's hand (Revelation 10:2), rightly focuses attention away from self and to God's message. Holding out one's hands in invitation to the people (Romans 10:21), or clapping one's hands in expression of the joy that goes with the gospel (Psalm 47:1 cp. Ezekiel 25:6), or lifting them up in prayer to point the congregation toward heaven (I Timothy 2:8), or even laying them upon workers being set aside for special acts of ministry (Acts 6:6; I Timothy 4:14; II Timothy 1:6), are actions that confirm the teachings of Scripture. As the visible actions of the Lord's Supper and water baptism accent the message of the pulpit, so ought each gesture express the truths being taught.

"Any action or proceeding intended for effect or as a formality" (Random House) ought to do what is intended and not undo what is said. The content of the sermon will determine what action there ought to be, if any. They cannot be programed or manipulated. They must be natural and arise from within. The body and its parts are to be the responsive instruments of the mind. Movement can hold attention or constant movement can detract. One's body may scatter an audience's thought, like a cute baby or a mischievous child. Or, that body may add weight to the argument or forcefulness to the appeal. As a driver's hand-signals inform other drivers of his intention to stop or to turn, let your hands not confuse but only clarify.

GESTURES AS EXPRESSIONS OF THOUGHTS AND FEELINGS

Study the uninhibited expressions of little children and compare them to the often stoic inaction of the adult. It may be that "unless you change and become like little children" (Matthew 18:3) in your freedom of gesture, you may inhibit the contagion of your message. Allow your zeal for the kingdom to show. Why read a Scripture aflame with passion in an icy voice that chills the listener? Why preach a momentous message devoid of enthusiasm?

Your posture, as you stand, and your walk, as you move to the podium, express the real you. A slouched torso will command no respect, while a stance of confidence will add authority to what you say. "As Paul discoursed on righteousness, self-control and the judgment to come" (Acts 24:25), it was Felix, the listener, and not Paul, the speaker, that trembled. A nervous preacher licking his lips and overly conscious of his hands, will beget an audience as tense as he is. The habits of unease, like constantly adjusting one's glasses, blinking one's eyes or spitting in one's hanky, must be overcome. Yet the victory over fears is overcome by being so prepared in the content of your message that you lose yourself in the expression of the truth that just has to be told.

Bad habits of gesture that express feelings, more easily overcome than nervousness, are those of carelessness. Yes, facial expressions do communicate happiness with a smile, assurance with a nod and sadness with a tear or a frown. But that same face, if it needs a shave, expresses disrespect and lack of interest. Dirty shirts, crooked ties and unkempt clothes can keep the gospel from getting through. Equally distracting are gaudy ties or elegant suits that call so much attention to themselves that people see them, when they ought to "see Jesus" (John 12:21).

Your message is too important to let anything interfere with it, least of all your dress or your movements. Why endanger the communication of the saving gospel by wearing an unbuttoned shirt to the navel or a pierced ear, if it closes the mind of the people over fifty years of age? Why wear diamond rings on every finger or park a limousine-like car in your driveway if it makes the poor feel your motives are mercenary? There is no way to silence it. Money talks. Dress talks. Actions talk. Make sure they say what you want them to say. Possibly the more you join Paul who "knelt down with all of (the elders) and prayed" (Acts 20:36), the more the kneeling posture will portray the needed humble attitude that befits every messenger of Christ.

27

HOW TO CONCLUDE

Sermons are like highways with both on-ramps and off-ramps — introductions and conclusions. Preachers are like aircraft pilots, needing to be expert at both taking off and landing their planes. Too many speakers do not know how to get started and too few know how to quit effectively. It is an idle question as to which question is the most important — that of starting right or that of stopping well. To not get the audience's attentive interest at the beginning is to speak the message in vain. But, to not bring the listener to act on the Biblical teaching presented is to have wasted their time, your time and God's time.

Any book on speaking or preaching calls for the conclusion to be brief, serious, congruous and confrontational. The one who has developed and delivered the message must have envisioned what he would like to see happen now that the burden of the speech has been delivered. The conclusion is the time to make that clear to each listener. A lawyer pleads for the desired verdict.

A doctor concludes his diagnosis with a specific remedy prescribed. An orchestra conducter leads into the grand finale wanting the audience to be lifted to their feet. A teacher, whose lesson is on joy, wants to have produced it and not only discussed it. A preacher, whose message is on Jesus the Savior, wants men of free-will to decide for Christ and not only to have heard some interesting facts about Him.

To test one's conclusion we do well to make specific inquiries regarding four areas. (1) The closing sentence: Was it concise? unmistakable? striking? carefully prepared? (2) Relevance: Was it true to the theme? the title? the text? (3) Purpose: Did it accomplish the goal of the proposition? the movement of the outline? (4) Style: Was it climactic? motivating? decisive?

The Old Testament preacher concluded his written sermon, Ecclesiastes, with the words, "Now all has been heard; here is the conclusion of the matter: Fear God and keep his commandments, for this is the whole duty of man" (12:13). The Gospel records in several places end a message by Jesus with the words, "When Jesus had finished saying all these things" (Matthew 26:1 cp. 7:25; 11:1; 13:53; 19:1; Luke 7:1; John 12:36). Luke's exciting history of the expansion of Christianity from Jerusalem, capital of Judaism, to Rome, capital of the world empire, draws toward its final victory shout, noting that the audience "began to leave after Paul had made his final statement" (Acts 28:25). These Biblical texts simply remind us that God's spokesmen were not only cognizant of the body of their messages but they also knew it would be necessary at some point to "have finished their testimony" (Revelation 11:7).

FINALLY, BROTHERS

Scrolls run out of space, as speakers run out of time, so ink or voice is drawn to the words, "Finally, brothers" (II Corinthians 13:11). The observation, that all good things must come to an end, could well have been said of even the finest sermons.

I know that the highly respected Karl Barth wrote, "One does not give glory to God with an eye on the clock."[1] Yet, I have a nagging in my soul that preachers would do well to watch the fidgety hands of their people, if not the hands of the clock on the back wall. When the congregation is heard whispering that their minister of the Word missed several good opportunities to quit, it is time for the speaker to become a listener. Too many to be ignored are the jokes that a wise preacher should stand up, speak up and shut up. The humorist Will Rogers got many a laugh by referring to the Chinese preacher On Too Long.

Take a critical look at your ego, if you are having trouble with your terminal facilities. I have known of speakers at national conventions, who after early written instructions to keep their messages to twenty-five minutes, exceeded their time not by a few minutes but by more than doubling their allotted time. The Bible that says there is "a time to speak," also cries out there is "a time to be silent" (Ecclesiastes 3:7). Professional entertainers know that it is wisdom and good business to quit with the audience wanting more. The professional chef of a quality restaurant would be fired if he overcooked every steak order that requested it to be medium-rare. The professional woodworker is aware that continual hammering on the nails will not improve the final product, but will rather split the board.

Surely it is better for the congregation to say to its spokesman, "I could listen to you for hours," than to sigh with Job, "Will your long-winded speeches never end" (Job 16:3). If a Holy Spirit-inspired and Christ-appointed apostle took what King Agrippa considered "a short time" (Acts 26:28) to make his case for Jesus, why do we think that the more voluble is the more valuable. If the highly respected lawyer for the Jews, named Tertullus, has the wisdom to address Felix with the words, "But in

---

1. *The Preaching of the Gospel* (Philadelphia: The Westminster Press, 1963), p. 78.

order not to weary you further, I would request that you be kind enough to hear us briefly" (Acts 24:4), why should the people of this world be "more shrewd . . . than the people of the light" (Luke 16:8)?

Make your sermons half as long but twice as good. Make them remembered for their depth more than their length. The only happy ending some sermons and plays have is that everyone is glad when they are finally over. The longer the hours of diligent preparation, the fewer need be the minutes of effective delivery. What General Douglas MacArthur said of old soldiers ought never to be fitting words to describe old or new sermons. His remembered words were "They never die, they just fade away." My musical ears shudder at the new music played by the radio disk jockeys. A song never actually ends any more but only gradually fades out.

An introduction that can't get started is like a car with a dead battery. But a conclusion that can't get stopped is like a car with brakes that do not function. The second instance can be more dangerous than the first. There is a starting time. There is a concluding time. If you spend money keeping your car in working order, spend time tuning up your homiletical skills.

CLEARLY, BROTHERS

When John the Baptist ended his sermons about the Messiah to come, the listeners were asking, "What should we do then?" (Luke 3:10). When Peter and the apostles finished their testimony regarding the Christ who had come, the people "were cut to the heart and said to Peter and the other apostles, 'Brothers, what shall we do?' " (Acts 2:37). When you conclude your messages, your hearers ought to be seeking clear words as to what you want them to feel, to understand, or believe, or do.

What certain action do you seek? When Jesus proclaimed the

good news that the kingdom of God was near, He did not leave His audience asking, "So what?" He gave out the specifics sought, answering, "Repent and believe the good news!" (Mark 1:15). When His message compared the kingdom of God to a great banquet, He issued in His conclusion the clear invitation, "Come, for everything is now ready" (Luke 14:17).

Even though a teacher's task may be fulfilled when his pupils understand, a preacher's job may not be concluded. Upon knowing, the believer is to be called upon "to obey everything (Christ) commanded" (Matthew 28:20). Preach, knowing what you want to happen and expecting it to happen. Conclude, securing the decisive action you contemplated from the outset. End, leaving the impression that you expect specific response and you anticipate it soon.

Your sermonic proposition was your sermon in a sentence. Your development established its truth. Your conclusion is the call for action — the appeal for decision — the clarification of the options. As Moses brought his message from the Eternal into contact with time, let your spotlight show the way: "See, I am setting before you today a blessing and a curse — the blessing if you obey the commands of the LORD your God that I am giving you today; the curse if you disobey the commands of the LORD your God and turn from the way that I command you today by following other gods, which you have not known" (Deuteronomy 1:26-28).

Lethargy in the pew demands the sounding of "a clear call" (I Corinthians 14:8). The instruction of what to do must not be lost in the fog bank of confusing religious talk. Today when evangelists tell the uninitiated to let Jesus into their hearts, there may be but a misty notion of what is supposed to happen. Better is the way clearly charted by the apostles, who spoke "as the Spirit enabled them," that believers in Christ were to "repent and be baptized" (Acts 2:4,38). That heaven-given answer to the questioning soul is emphatic, direct and unmuddied by a religious jargon unknown in Bible times.

DECISIVELY, BROTHERS

If we use the term preaching in harmony with the Bible's definition of the word, it will always conclude with an appeal — an invitation. Scriptural proclamation is not introducing a concept to be embraced but a person to be followed. The preacher's ministry is a commitment to the message of reconciliation. He sees himself as an "ambassador" of the God who makes his "appeal" through preaching. He is not afraid to "implore . . . on Christ's behalf" (II Corinthians 5:20).

True preaching must be fervent. It pleads, "Listen to my appeal" (II Corinthians 13:11). Its content is not morally neutral truths, but the confrontation of Christ with men demanding decision. A sermon's concluding time is clarifying time and commitment time. The end of preaching is persuasion. Everything preceding has been but the means to this desired end. Men need to hear the gospel and then to be urged to accept that gospel. The body of the message should be interesting, but the invitation that concludes must also be challenging. In the conclusion the audience is to hear Christ's knock at the door and His invitation, "Come to me" (Revelation 3:20; Matthew 11:28).

Good preaching becomes great preaching when God's entreaty is felt. Decisions are the fruit of proclamation. In the conversion accounts in Acts, preaching is seen to be the proclamation of the gladness, followed by God's appeal. It is the news about what Christ has done, ending with His call for response. It is the relating of Jesus' atoning death and justifying resurrection, demanding an answer of "yes" or "no" from each hearer. On day one of the church, Peter "warned them; and he pleaded with them, 'Save yourselves from this corrupt generation' " (2:40). The sermon by Peter in the next chapter presents Christ with the warning, "Anyone who does not listen to him will be completely cut off from among his people" (3:23). It matters not if the proclaimer is Stephen (7:51) or Paul (13:40; 17:31), the promise and warning is issued and the response is asked. The result is usually the same: "Some were convinced by what he said, but others would not believe" (28:24).

First time converts were pointed to baptism as the place to enter covenant with Christ (Acts 2:38; 22:16). Renewed vows to follow more closely and serve more faithfully found expression in prayer (Acts 8:22) and at the table where there was "the breaking of bread" with Christ and His people (Acts 2:42; 20:7).

The conclusion can be called the most imporant part of the sermon. It is there the message's main point is made to stick and the audience is summoned to a verdict. All the talking of a salesman is for naught, if he fails to get a signature on the bottom line. When thinking about a sermon length, remember there will likely be further opportunities to speak. But when dealing with the message's concluding appeal, preach as if you may never have a chance to reach some of those hearers again. The hearer must see his options as heaven or hell, promise or peril, salvation or condemnation (Mark 16:16). The speaker must be convinced that the persons before him are really eternally lost or graciously redeemed.

Compare your conclusion to that of Moses: "This day I call heaven and earth as witnesses against you that I have set before you life and death, blessings and curses. Now choose life, so that you and your children may live and that you may love the LORD your God, listen to his voice, and hold fast to him" (Deuteronomy 30:19-20). Measure your appeal to that of Joshua: "Choose for yourselves this day whom you will serve, whether the gods of your forefathers served beyond the River, or the gods of the Amorites, in whose land you are living. But as for me and my household, we will serve the LORD" (Joshua 24:15).

An audience may say "stop confronting us" (Isaiah 30:11), but an apostle writes, "These are things you are to teach and urge on them" (I Timothy 6:2). A modern church may allow a soft organ background to the minister's moralistic "tut-tut" to community evil, but Biblical preaching sounds a clarion call for repentance, saying, "Today, if you hear his voice, do not harden your hearts" (Hebrews 3:7,15). Don M. Aycott reminds his readers that John R. Bisagino began his chapter on giving an invitation with the words, "You can't hatch eggs in a refrigerator."[2] The appeals in the Scripture are based on promise (Numbers 10:29-32), hope (Luke 23:42), reason (Isaiah 1:18), love (II Corinthians 5:14), curiosity (John 1:46), obedience (Acts 5:29) and even fear (Acts 4:25). But in every appeal of any kind there is fervor. There may be recapitulation (II Peter 3:1) to corroborate and confirm what was said, but there must always be the making of a timeless truth very timely. The secret is to take the "then" of an ancient text and make it live "now" in the present context.

---

2. *Herald to a New Age* (Elgin, Illinois: Brethren Press, 1985), p. 225.

Part Six
THE MEETINGS
(THE HERE'S WHERE AND WHEN OF PREACHING)

28

WHERE TO PREACH

There is only one word to define where preaching is to be done. That single word is the Bible word "everywhere." The Gospels tell us that Jesus' disciples before His crucifixion "set out and went from village to village, preaching the gospel . . . everywhere" (Luke 9:6) and again after Christ's death "went out and preached everywhere" (Mark 16:20). The book of Acts carries the account that "they that were scattered abroad (by persecution) went every where preaching the word" (Acts 8:4 KJV) and the Epistles bear witness to apostles affirming that they "teach everywhere" (I Corinthians 4:17).

The final order Jesus gave His followers, before He ascended to heaven, was to "go into all the world and preach the good news" (Mark 16:15) and to let the apostolic witness be heard "in Jerusalem, and in all Judea and Samaria, and to the ends of the earth" (Acts 1:8 cp. Luke 24:47). Prior to that assignment, Christ's teaching included predictions that His gospel would be "preached throughout the world" (Mark 14:9). His countrymen raised the question, "Will he go . . . teach the Greeks?" (John 7:35). His own voice told of receiving His message from the Father and asserted, "What I have heard from him I tell the world" (John 8:27). He spoke of having other sheep yet to be called by His voice (John 10:16). The historical records of the apostles and the early church fulfilling the great and final commission, read like a success story in world conquest. The complaint of the Jewish Sanhedrin was, "You have filled Jerusalem with your teaching" (Acts 5:28). The "Samaritan villages" (Acts 8:25) and "all the towns until . . . Caesarea" heard gospel preaching (Acts 8:40). Soon believers were speaking "to Greeks also, telling them the good news about the Lord Jesus" (Acts 11:20). Luke's account in Acts uses terms like "the whole region" (13:49), "the province of Asia" (16:6) or "place to place" (18:23). He tells of workers going to both major "cities . . . and to the surrounding country, where they continued to preach the good news" (14:6-7,21). His records gladly reflect the gospel word reaching "Gentile" ears, like his own (15:7; 18:6).

The Damascus Road call of Paul to be Christ's apostle to the Gentiles, carried the assignment to be a "witness to all men" (Acts 22:15). The Pauline epistles echo the Divine order to preach everywhere. The early Galatian letter reflects the apostle's concept of his job description. He wrote, "God . . . called me . . . so that I might preach him among the Gentiles" (1:16). He knew beyond any doubt that he "had been given the task of preaching the gospel to the Gentiles, just as Peter had been given the task of preaching the gospel to the Jews" (2:7). The late Pastoral Epistles keep the church aware that Jesus is to be "preached among the nations" (I Timothy 3:16). The Prison Epistles rejoice that "the gospel . . . has been proclaimed to every creature under heaven" (Colossians 1:23) and the weighty doctrinal masterpiece of Romans relates how Paul is "eager to preach the gospel also . . . to Rome" (1:15). Until "all the earth" and "the ends of the world" (10:18) were reached, Paul would hold to his "ambition to preach the gospel where Christ was not known" (15:20). The evangelistic success of this former opponent of Christianity can be laid at the feet of his conviction that he was "to be a minister of Christ Jesus to the Gentiles with the priestly duty of proclaiming the gospel of God" (15:16). In Johanine phraseology, the "where" to preach question is answered by the words, "the eternal gospel" is to be proclaimed "to those who live on the earth — to every nation, tribe, language and people" (Revelation 14:6 cp. 10:11).

Even Old Testament prophets were to spread their messages to distant points. Jeremiah was to be heard in "Jerusalem" (2:2; 4:15; 44:26), "north" (3:12) as far as "Dan" (4:15), south beyond "Judah" (4:5; 5:20; 7:2) to "Egypt" (44:26; 46:14) and west "in distant coastlands" (31:10). When Jeremiah went out to reach Jews everywhere, he wanted the populace as a whole informed, so he spoke "to all the people, including the women" (44:24). Ezekiel was called to "preach against the south" (20:46), "prophesy to the mountains" (36:1) "to (dead) bones" (37:4), "to Gog" (38:14; 39:1) and to "the house of Israel" (40:4). Hosea brought God's message to "Israelites" (4:1). Joel sought to inform their "elders . . . children . . . and their children to the next generation" (1:2-3). Amos had words to be heard from "Ashdod and . . . Egypt" (3:9) to "the house of Israel" (5:4), including the "cows of Bashan on Mount Samaria" (4:1). Jonah was to preach against "the great city of Nineveh" (1:2; 3:1; 4:11). Micah spoke to the metropolitan center, with the words, "Listen! The LORD is calling to the city" (6:9) and he addressed the world, "Hear, O peoples, all of you, listen, O earth and all who are in it" (1:2). It was Micah who predicted, "The law will go out from Zion, the word of the LORD from Jerusalem" (4:2) and it was Habakkuk who foresaw the day when "the earth will be filled with the knowledge of the glory of the LORD, as the waters cover the sea" (2:14).

When New Testament days dawned, where was the Christian gospel preached? Church buildings, so evident now, were unheard of then. The saving message was to be heard in the Holy City of Jerusalem, the wicked city of Corinth, the eternal city of Rome and potential ghost towns of tomorrow that were but tiny villages then. The Bible makes it clear that the message meant for everyone was to be told everywhere. Homes to hilltops, boats to chariots, jail cells to castle stairs, market areas to schoolrooms made excellent pulpits for the everlasting gospel. Congregations the size of "almost the whole city" (Acts 13:44), or only a single person (Acts 8:35), constituted an audience worthy of a preacher's best. The message is what mattered, not the facility. So, "day by day, in the temple courts and from house to house, they (the apostles) never stopped teaching and proclaiming the good news that Jesus is the Christ" (Acts 5:32).

SYNAGOGUES AND TEMPLES

Let something be said for preaching to a gathered congregation. It takes little more effort to teach a few hundred than a mere handful of ten. Such a gathered religious community is psychologically ready to listen to a religious discourse. Jesus is often portrayed as travelling "throughout Galilee, teaching in their synagogues, preaching the good news of the kingdom" (Matthew 4:23; 9:35; 13:54; Mark 1:21,39; 6:2; Luke 4:15,28; 13:10; John 6:59). He not only spoke in the synagogues of Galilee, but those of Judea (Luke 4:44). Following his Master's example, Paul upon conversion, "at once . . . began to preach in the synagogues" (Acts 9:20). He followed that practice on his first missionary journey (Acts 13:5), and continued it until it could be called "his custom (to go) into the synagogue, and on . . . Sabbath days" reason from the Scriptures, proving Jesus as the Christ (17:2,17 cp. 18:4,19).

The synagogues may have arisen from Ezekiel's addresses to God's people during the Babylonian captivity. Away from their temple in Jerusalem, the Jews still gathered and did so in the prophet's house (Ezekiel 8:1; 20:1-3 cp. Jeremiah 39:8). The custom of expounding on the portion of Scripture being read possibly arose after the exile. Ezra read the Law to assembled people and the Levites instructed the people. The book of Nehemiah says, "They read from the Book of the Law of God, making it clear and giving the meaning so that the people could understand what was being read" (8:8). In the Christian era speaking followed the reading of a pericope from the Law and Prophets (Luke 4:14-22; Acts 13:14-15). In over a thousand synagogues the estimated four to seven million Jews of the diaspora heard preaching as a regular feature of their Sabbath synagogue service. Many of the populace would not know Hebrew, so a translation into the Aramaic vernacular followed. This explanation or "word of exhortation" (Hebrews 13:22) was often the application of what had been read to the gathered community. The expounded text of the written word made it a contemporary lesson for the present hour.

The church is wise to learn that, while one to one sharing of the faith is always in order, nothing can replace the power of an oral proclamation to a gathered community. In many pagan religions shrines meet the needs for individuals who come one by one to worship. In the revealed religions of Judaism and Christianity, the people in covenant with God meet "together" (Hebrews 10:25) for instruction and have people designated as "rabbis" or "teachers."

Christ, who shared in the weekly gatherings of the local community, also took advantage of the annual festal-gatherings of Israel at the temple in Jerusalem. The family unit was God's design for propagating the faith (Deuteronomy 6:7-9) and the extended family manifested itself in the local synagogue and the national temple. He, today, who only knows the warm fellowship and instructive possibililties of one small group, but has never built the strong ties with God's bigger family at regional, national or international assemblies, has robbed himself of enriching opportunities.

Consider the implications of Christ-likeness. "He went into the synagogue, as was his custom" (Luke 4:16). It is often written of Him that He "entered the temple courts, and . . . was teaching" (Matthew 21:23; Mark 12:35; 14:49; Luke 19:47; 20:1; John 7:28; 8:2,20). Jesus said of Himself, "I always taught in synagogues or at the temple, where all the Jews came together" (John 18:20). Angels directed His apostles to likewise "stand in the temple courts . . . and tell the people the full message of this new life" (Acts 5:20). This command they happily obeyed "day after day, in the temple courts . . . proclaiming the good news that Jesus is the Christ" (Acts 5:42).

One safe conclusion to draw is that preaching to gathered congregations has a Biblical example and evident power. "Paul and Barnabas went as usual into the Jewish synagogue . . . (and) spoke so effectively that a great number of Jews and Gentiles believed" (Acts 14:1). Souls mature best in a living community.

HOMES AND STREETS

Be it ever so humble, there is no place like a home for preaching. "For two whole years Paul stayed there in his own rented house and welcomed all who came to see him. Boldly and without hindrance he preached the kingdom of God and taught about the Lord Jesus Christ" (Acts 28:30-31). Earlier in Corinth, when Paul left the synagogue, he "went next door to the house of Titius Justus . . . and many of the Corinthians who heard him believed and were baptized" (Acts 18:7-8). A "house to house" (Acts 5:42; 20:20) ministry can be very productive. Sheep "do not recognize a stranger's voice" (John 10:5). A pastor in the homes of his people, or a people in the home of their shepherd, get to know each other on a personal level. It was "while Jesus was having dinner at Matthew's house, many tax collectors and 'sinners' " (Matthew 9:10) had opportunity to hear Jesus speak and become drawn to Him.

When Jesus set free the demon-possessed, He told the delivered person where to start his ministry. He gave the guidance, "Return home and tell how much God has done for you" (Luke 8:39). Mary, the mother of John Mark, had often opened her home for Jesus' disciples. Its upper room, according to tradition, became the holy place where the Lord's Supper was instituted and the comforting sermon of Christ to His disciples was heard (Acts 12:12; John 14-16). "The apostles' teaching and . . . fellowship . . . the breaking of bread and . . . prayer" often took place "in their homes" (Acts 2:42,46). "The church that meets in your home" (Philemon 2) could be words addressed to Philemon, Priscilla and Aquila (Romans 16:5), Nympha (Colossians 4:15), and many unnamed others.

Cornelius invited Peter to his house so that he could hear the gospel preached (Acts 10:22). The believers in Troas heard Paul preach "in the upstairs room where (they) were meeting" for the breaking of bread (Acts 20:7-8). Whether it be the Philippian Jailer's "house" (Acts 16:32), "Lydia's house where they met" (Acts 16:40) or your house, there the old, old story can be retold.

As everyone is to hear the call of God, everywhere is a likely place for that hearing. Paul might be found speaking for his Lord in a home, a synagogue or "in the market place day by day with those who happened to be there" (Acts 17:17). It mattered not to him if the listeners were religious Jews from the holy city or pagan philosophers "in the meeting of the Areopagus" (Acts 17:22). If the opportunity was preaching, he would be "making the most of every opportunity" (Ephesians 5:16). If "wisdom calls aloud in the street (and) . . . raises her voice in the public squares" (Proverbs 1:20), can "Christ Jesus, who has become for us wisdom from God" (I Corinthians 1:30), not be heard in public places where masses gather?

In the theater at Ephesus "Paul wanted to appear before the crowd" (Acts 19:30). To "the mob (in Jerusalem that) was so great he had to be carried by the soldiers . . . Paul stood on the steps (of the castle of Antonia) . . . motioned to the crowd" and gave his testimony (Acts 21:35,40). Peter brought the gospel to "all the people . . . (that) came running to them in the place called Solomon's Colonnade" (Acts 3:11). We remember Jesus speaking to individuals like the woman at the well (John 4), but we are reminded that He often addressed "the crowd" (Matthew 12:46), as He spoke "publicly" (Luke 20:26; John 7:26). In His ministry "Jesus traveled about from one town and village to another, proclaiming the good news of the kingdom of God" (Luke 8:1; 9:6; 4:43).

It is Christian to be concerned for "even larger numbers" (Acts 28:23). It is pleasing to God when "the good news is preached to the poor" (Luke 7:22), for there are such numbers of them. It is wise to combine feasting and talking, for so many meals are eaten in a lifetime and so many friends can be won with a word (Luke 15:2). It is the knock of opportunity for commuters to see in either the long ride to work or the short flight to grandma's, a wonderful occasion to talk shop. Your "chariot" may fly thousands of feet higher than the Ethiopian Eunuch's or many miles an hour faster, but the seatbelt will hold in place that potential child of God as today's Philip tells "the good news about Jesus" (Acts 8:29,35). It is invitation time to heaven's banquet. "Go quickly into the streets and alleys of the town. . . . Go out to the roads and country lanes" (Luke 14:21,23).

OPEN SKIES AND CLOSED PRISONS

Our Master taught as often in the open air as He did in a building's enclosure. He spoke life-changing words by an ancient well at Sychar (John 4:5-6). He delivered truths that will never pass away from "a mountainside" in Galilee (Matthew 5:1) and "the Mount of Olives" in Jerusalem (Matthew 24:3). "On another occasion Jesus began to teach by the lake," where the enormous crowd forced Him to make "a boat" His pulpit (Mark 4:1; Luke

5:1-3; Matthew 13:2).

John the Baptist, Jesus' forerunner, was "a voice . . . calling in the desert" (Matthew 3:3; Mark 1:3). He found the Jordan River a fitting setting for His "preaching a baptism of repentance for the forgiveness of sins" (Mark 1:4-5). The evangelistic team of Paul, Silas, Timothy and Luke "went outside the city gate (of Philippi) to the river . . . (where they) sat down and began to speak to the women who had gathered there" (Acts 16:13). A bump on a log or a seat in a boat — no matter — as you go "make disciples" (Matthew 28:19).

It came as no surprise to the apostle Paul that preaching "Christ crucified" (I Corinthians 1:22) could mean the gospel heralds might know frequent imprisonment (II Corinthians 11:23). He wrote New Testament epistles from his prison cell in Rome and turned his years of house arrest into opportunities to teach and preach Christ (Acts 28:30-31). Onesimus, the runaway slave of Philemon, is but one testimony to the positive results that can come from preaching in prisons (Philemon 10). "Those who belong to Caesar's household" (Philippians 4:22) can testify as well that, while a preacher may suffer "to the point of being chained like a criminal . . . God's word is not chained" (II Timothy 2:9).

Preparing His disciples for the hard road ahead as proclaimers of the cross, Jesus foretold that they would be "handed over to the local councils and flogged in the synagogues." But the good news was that the preachers could then "stand before governors and kings as a witness to them" (Mark 13:9; Luke 21:12-13). Paul was glad to have experienced "the fellowship of sharing in his sufferings" (Philippians 3:10), for this meant he could witness to the Jerusalem rabble (Acts 22), the Jewish Sanhedrin (Acts 23) and government leaders like Felix (Acts 24), Festus (Acts 25) and Agrippa (Acts 26).

A missionary's prayer is always that the "area of activity . . . will greatly expand, so that (he) can preach the gospel in regions beyond" (II Corinthians 10:15-16). His drive is to make Christ "known among the nations . . . known to all the world" (Isaiah 12:4-5; 34:1; 66:19; cp. Psalm 9:11). With "the ends of the earth" (Isaiah 62:11), the "islands" of the sea and the "distant nations" (Isaiah 49:1) all to be covered, the order is out, "Go, swift messengers" (Isaiah 18:2). Use "the lecture hall of Tyrannus" (Acts 19:9), the academic center of Athens (Acts 17:22), the palace halls of kings (Acts 25:23) or the execution block for martyrs (Acts 7:58), but "Preach the Word . . . in season and out of season" (II Timothy 4:2), in synagogue and out of synagogue, indoors and out of doors. Even when governments command spokesmen "not to speak or teach at all in the name of Jesus" (Acts 4:18), He "who holds the key of David . . . (will place) before you an open door that no one can shut" (Revelation 3:7-8).

29

WHEN TO PREACH

"There is a time for everything, and a season for every activity under heaven . . . a time to be silent and a time to speak" (Ecclesiastes 3:1,7 cp. 3:17). Solomon tells us "there is a proper time" (8:6), but is not long on specifics as to the best days or hours for preaching. Is there a marked calendar we can buy, or a special clock we can order, that will chime at the most opportune hours for preaching?

Time of day seemed no barrier to Jesus. The Gospels tell that, when Jesus was in Jerusalem for some feast, "all the people came early in the morning to hear him at the temple" (Luke 21:38). The marginal gloss in John's Gospel reports that it was "at dawn (when Jesus) . . . appeared again in the temple courts, where all the people gathered around him, and he sat down to teach them" (8:2). But, before we conclude He was an early-morning person, we recall His wonderful teaching to the Samaritan woman at Jacob's well "about the sixth hour" (John

4:6) or His unforgettable message on the new birth to Nicodemus who "came to Jesus at night" (John 3:2). Each Lord's Day at the time of communion the words ring out, "The Lord Jesus, on the night he was betrayed, took bread." Our minds flood with the scene of the Last Supper in the upper room and we visualize the disciple hearing their Master give the message to those around the table that is preserved in John 13-16.

To His disciples, likewise, no hours of day or night seemed inappropriate for preaching. The first apostolic sermon preserved in the book of Acts begins, "Fellow Jews. . . . It's only nine in the morning" (2:14-15). The second message is timed "at three in the afternoon" (3:1). Yet, later in Luke's historic account, a Philippian jailor is prepared for a sermon on how to be saved by hearing "about midnight Paul and Silas . . . praying and singing hymns to God," with God joining in with His amen by means of an earthquake (16:25-26,33). Some of the Scriptural passages speak of earlier hours and some later. One text tells of angels releasing apostles "during the night," ordering them to preach. That passage relates that "at daybreak they entered the temple courts, as they had been told, and began to teach the people" (5:19-21). Other verses say that Paul "kept on talking until midnight" (20:7). And, that is not the end of the story. After the fatal fall of Eutychus from the third story window, his miraculous restoration is followed by the apostle "talking until daylight" (20:11).

The conclusion to which Bible study forces one is that on many occasions Jesus was to be found "every day . . . teaching in the temple courts" (Mark 14:49; Luke 19:47; 21:37). His disciples, likewise, not only "never stopped teaching and proclaiming . . . day after day" (Acts 5:42; 17:17), they did so "night and day" (Acts 20:31). Even when Paul's ministry was limited by being kept under Roman guard, he is reported "from morning till evening (to have) explained and declared . . . the kingdom of God" (Acts 28:23).

The Bible is serious about preaching both "in season and out of season" (II Timothy 4:2). It means it when it admonishes, "make the most of every opportunity" (Colossians 4:5; Ephesians 5:16; cp. Galatians 6:10). It intends for a preacher not to take his tasks lightly but to "be diligent in these matters; (giving himself) wholly to them" (I Timothy 4:15). If a man of poor health named John Wesley could in his ministry travel over 250,000 miles, preaching more than 40,000 sermons — an average of fifteen per week — how can God accept the complaint of a robust youth, who finds it next to impossible to work out a night sermon for Sunday, when he is expected to do a morning message as well?

PREACH WHENEVER CHURCH-BELLS RING

At times Jesus spoke to very large crowds "of many thousands . . . gathered, so that they were trampling on one another" (Luke 12:1 cp. 5:1). On other occasions His gems of wisdom were shared with but a single individual (John 4:27). But a pattern can be seen developing as He would be there teaching on every day the synagogue assembled. The most influential single service a rabbi could address was held on the Sabbath. So we read of our Lord: "On a Sabbath Jesus was teaching in one of the synagogues" (Luke 13:10) or "When the Sabbath came, he began to teach in the synagogue" (Mark 6:2). To enter the synagogue on the Sabbath day to read and teach was said to be "his custom" (Luke 4:16).

It makes sense for a preacher to take advantage of that certain day and hour when the scattered flock of God comes together. What an opportunity to do at that one time and place what would take many hours in multiple homes to accomplish. When an apostle of Christ purposed to win Jews for Jesus, he would meet with them on their day of assembly to address them. The evangelistic plan was so effective that Luke writes, "On the next Sabbath almost the whole city gathered to hear the word of the Lord" (Acts 13:44). He calls it Paul's "custom . . . (to go) into the synagogue, and on Sabbath days" to proclaim Christ (Acts 17:2-3). When serving as missionary to Jews he would do this "every Sabbath" (Acts 18:4). On other occasions we find that Paul "met with the church and taught great numbers of people" (Acts 11:26). These Christian assemblies were gatherings for "the apostles' teaching and . . . the breaking of bread" (Acts 2:42). They appear to have been held on the memorial day of Christ's resurrection. At least one record says, "On the first day of the week we came together to break bread (and) Paul spoke to the people" (Acts 20:7 cp. I Corinthians 16:2).

When word and sacrament combine, there is simultaneously preaching for eye and for ear. Sacred actions with sacred objects joined to sacred hours and sacred words make an indelible impression. When bread and cup "proclaim the Lord's death until he comes" (I Corinthians 11:26) and "the first day of the week" proclaims His resurrection, the full gospel is seen as the preacher adds his human voice to the divine testimony. The sacrament without the sermon is mute, but with it it is mighty. When baptism and supper and sermon join forces "there are three that testify: the Spirit, the water and the blood; and the three are in agreement" (I John 5:7). Each Sunday at the table sight, sound, taste, touch, aroma and action all join to preach that Jesus is the Lord.

PREACH WHENEVER FESTAL-TRUMPETS SOUND

As Israel had the Sabbath day and the church has the Lord's day, is there afforded for the New Covenant period teaching opportunities like "a religious festival (or) a New Moon celebration" (Colossians 2:16)? The Old Testament calendar, in addition to the weekly Sabbath, had room for the annual feasts of Passover, Firstfruits, Pentecost, Trumpets and Tabernacles plus the fast of the Day of Atonement (Leviticus 23). Jesus took advantage of these festal days to bring His message to the pilgrims gathered in Jerusalem. He also observed community celebrations that grew up after the time of Moses, such as the Festival of Lights (Hanukkah). When the minds of His countrymen were recalling their great past of divine deliverance, Jesus was making the typological applications to His own ministry (cp. especially John). Study the life of Christ and discover that on the weekly Sabbaths Jesus made His way to a synagogue and that on the occasion of historic festivals He made His way to Jerusalem and its temple (John 2:23; 7:2,14,37; 13:1).

In the present day, when gospel preachers know that the Easter and Christmas festivals developed long after New Testament times, should they oppose, ignore or take advantage of the general community's festive mood? Men that are free in Christ can do what they deem best for the kingdom's goals. If these winter and spring festivities bring bigger numbers of people together than usual, it presents an occasion for the larger group to hear the preaching that saves. No season is a poor season to hear of the wonder that God's grace brought the incarnation event or that His amazing love and power has created hope for human hearts in the raising of His crucified Son from the grave.

One small word of caution here. On those occasions, when your church is apt to have the greatest numbers of prospective Christians within the walls of its meeting-place, do not muff the opportunity by eliminating gospel preaching. Let choirs sing. Let children live out the drama of Jesus' birth. But, let these once-a-year audiences hear preaching. Let them know what a normal service would be like. Good stewardship of time — good management of the hour — can allow for the preaching that the Bible calls "the power of God" that saves (I Corinthians 1:18,21). Two less songs by the choir and one less skit by the children allows a sage preacher the time needed to proclaim the gospel with power. Great sermons do not need to be great in length but they do need to be heard. When the audiences are large, let the preacher vow, "I will proclaim righteousness in the great assembly; I do not seal my lips" (Psalm 40:9). Remember how prophets were commanded, "Speak to all the people in the towns . . . who come to worship" (Jeremiah 26:2). Recall how often the Bible raises consciousness for the entire community to hear the proclamation. In Exodus it tells of Moses addressing "the whole Israelite community" (35:1,4,20), as does Leviticus (8:5; 19:2) and Deuteronomy (5:22; 29:2; 31:1). That is the way the historical records read (I Kings 8:14,55), with Joshua amplifying that, when he says "whole assembly of Israel, (he is) including the women and children, and the aliens who lived among them" (8:35 cp. Nehemiah 8:2).

If a Christian minister of the Word can use his freedom to teach on the virgin birth, when community activities open the door for such a lesson; and, if an evangelist has the liberty to herald evidences of Christ's resurrection, when the mood of the populace allows for it; does the option of preaching on themes suggested by other holidays and holy days ever make sense? Once in a while, a preacher may find that following the high points of a good lectionary or a church calendar can help him bring a well-rounded view of biblical truth and keep him from riding his hobbies. It could have the same benefit as preaching through a Bible book or section, such as Colossians or the Sermon on the Mount.

PREACH WHENEVER GOLDEN OPPORTUNITIES KNOCK

Men of God are always looking for a chance to teach and listening for a preaching opportunity to knock at their door. Peter, the one chosen by Christ to preach the first full-gospel sermon for Jewish ears and again, later for Gentile ears, gives the advice, "Always be prepared to give an answer to everyone who asks you to give the reason for the hope that you have" (I Peter 3:15).

He and the other original disciples of Christ knew that such occasions would arise unexpectedly. Jesus had prepared them for these opportunities by His words, "They will lay hands on you and persecute you. They will deliver you to synagogues and prisons, and you will be brought before kings and governors. . . . This will result in your being witnesses to them" (Luke 21:12-13). Imagine the joy of the missionaries to Cyprus, when "Sergius Paulus the proconsul, an intelligent man, sent for Barnabas and Saul because he wanted to hear the word of God" (Acts 13:7). What an opportunity! The winning of a leader can open further doors of evangelism to those under his influence. Imagine the excitement in Paul's heart when the commander of Roman troops, Claudius Lysius, "ordered the chief priests and all the Sanhedrin to assemble (and) . . . he brought Paul and had him stand before them" (Acts 22:30). What an opportunity! What a captive audience!

The pen of Luke recalls how in Caesarea "Paul was called in" before Felix, Ananias and elders from Jerusalem and "the governor motioned for him to speak" (Acts 24:1,10). "Several days later Felix came with his wife Druscilla, who was a Jewess. He sent for Paul and listened to him as he spoke about faith in Christ Jesus" (Acts 24:24). What opportunities! The doors kept opening as King Agrippa, discussing Paul with Porcius Festus, concluded, "I would like to hear the man myself" (Acts 25:22). Before such an audience, the invitation came to Paul, "You have permission to speak" (Acts 26:1). At every opportunity offered, Paul was ready. When others did not make the preaching occasions for him, Paul was capable of making his own. Upon reaching Rome, he wasted no time. "Three days later he called together the leaders of the Jews" and, when they came, their invitation was "we want to hear what your views are" (Acts 28:17,22).

When opportunity knocked in Iconium, "Paul and Barnabas spent considerable time there" (Acts 14:3). In Corinth the door remained open "for a year and a half . . . (for) teaching them the word of God" (Acts 18:11). In Ephesus it was "for three years" (Acts 20:31). Every preacher's prayer ought to be "that the message of the Lord may spread rapidly" (II Thessalonians 3:1) and then the gospel "be fitly proclaimed and all the Gentiles . . . hear it" (II Timothy 4:17). Make that your daily plea to God and don't be surprised when the answer comes and doors open in unexpected places for you. Get ready, get on your mark, get set, so when those doors open, you can go.

Part Seven
THE MODELS
(THE HERE'S AN EXAMPLE OF PREACHING)

30

FROM THE GOSPELS: A SERMON BY JESUS

To hear good messages prods a preacher to prepare and deliver good messages. To make a study of historic sermons is an excellent way to discover ways to improve one's own sermons in both content and presentation. It pays us to remember that the New Testament was written by preachers. It contains several sermons by giants in communication from John the Baptist to Jesus and from Peter to Paul. It is addressed to the Christian community, every member of which became a follower of Jesus by responding to the gospel that was heard from some proclaimer's lips.

Is it surprising to hear New Testament scholars calling the Gospels "sermons?" Is it interesting to learn that the abbreviated gospel sermons in Acts follow the similar points made in the Gospel of Mark as C.H. Dodd has pointed out? No wonder Willi Marxen calls the Markan Gospel *predict* or preaching. Is it stimulating to find five of Jesus' sermons scattered throughout

Matthew's Gospel, in which the tax-collector is presenting Jesus as the new law-giver and deliverer replacing Moses who had been behind the five books of the Jewish Torah? It was as if the New Israel of the church needed the guidance that a Christian Pentateuch could bring.

Keep reminding yourselves that the Gospel of Mark was written to be read out loud in the public assembly, rather than in silence and in private. That Gospel, beginning with the preaching of John (Mark 1:1-4) and concluding with the church being sent out to preach (16:15), tells of Jesus preaching (1:14-15,38); but, even more, it is, itself, preaching about Christ — His life, crucifixion and resurrection. The clearly noticeable eye-witness quality of this sermon is best explained by the tradition preserved in the historical records by Eusebius, where Papias attributes the testimony in Mark to Peter. At the martyrdom of Peter in the days of Nero, Mark is said to have written down the testimony of the Big Fisherman, whom he so often had heard.

Read aloud the sermons of Peter in their shortened form in Acts 2, 3 and 10. Then scan-read Mark's gospel to see if you are not convinced that you are hearing in Mark the same gospel facts and promises that you heard in Acts. Are not these truths being brought in similar progression? If you are convinced, you may begin to join those scholars, who speak of all the Gospels, especially Mark, as expanded kerygma, or passion narratives with extended introductions. I say read the Gospel of Mark aloud, for even when a person was alone in Bible days, the Scriptures were read aloud (cp. Acts 8:30 where "Philip . . . heard the man reading Isaiah the prophet"). The medium of Scriptures, like that of symphonies and operas, is sound. They may be preserved in printed form, but they each were composed to be heard. Let me arbitrarily select one of Jesus' sermons from Matthew for construction analysis.

It is a joy to hear Jesus' sermon in Luke 15 defining the purpose of His ministry as seeking the lost. That story-telling message can never be forgotten, as Christ tells of lost sheep (15:3-7), lost valuables (15:8-10) and lost sons (15:11-32). He is illustrating how important people are to God. It is an inspiration to sit in on the message recorded in John, that was delivered in the upper room, as the Savior built up the disciples' faith (John 14), love (John 15) and hope (John 16). It is an education in kingdom-studies to hear the ordination message for Christ's apostles (Matthew 10), His stories describing the kingdom (Matthew 13), His object lesson on little things that matter (Matthew 18) and His exciting prophetic message about the end of two worlds — the Jewish and ours (Matthew 24). But, most of all, in analysis of sermon structure the most widely known Sermon on the Mount (Matthew 5-7) will meet our needs.

THE SERMON ON THE MOUNT: PROPOSITION

As a sample of Jesus addressing those who believe in and follow Him, consider the first of the five Matthew has saved for future generations. At the end of each discourse, Matthew, reflecting his literary plan, writes the recurring phrase, "When Jesus had finished saying these things" (Matthew 7:28 cp. 11:1; 13:53; 19:1; 26:1).

The words of Christ from Matthew 5:3 through 7:27 constitute what we have come to call the Sermon on the Mount. These one hundred ten verses can be read in fifteen minutes. We will consider them here as a unified sermon and not as a compilation of religious remarks made by Christ on a variety of occasions and to different listening groups. The way the message reads now from the opening beatitudes to the concluding illustration it follows its proposition and develops its theme in well-structured progression.

In the sermon Jesus states His proposition at the end of His introduction and just before He moves into the main body of His message. Wanting His disciples (5:1) to understand what was expected of His followers, the Teacher stated, "I tell you that unless your righteousness surpasses that of the Pharisees and the teachers of the law, you will certainly not enter the kingdom of heaven" (5:20).

THE SERMON ON THE MOUNT: MAJOR DIVISIONS

No one tried harder than the Pharisees to live up to the Law given at Mount Sinai through Moses. Now in Galilee on another mount than Mount Sinai (5:1), the nucleus of Christ's New Israel hear of the even higher ground to which they are being called. They are to have a "righteousness (that) surpasses" the former. To establish that proposition the sermon outline falls into three parts; and, conveniently for the reader, each part is the burden of a different chapter. The first point (5:21-47) is that there are higher demands. The second (6:1-34) calls for higher devotion and the third (7:1-27) for higher demonstration.

In the first division of the sermon we find six contrasts between the devotional practices Christ expects of His disciples over those being done by the religionists among whom He lived. The sub-points, that develop the idea that in the kingdom or church of Christ the moral demands exceed those given by Moses, begin, "You have heard that it was said to the people long ago" (5:21,27,31,33,38,43). Some of these come straight out of the Ten Commandments: "Do not murder" (5:21), "Do not commit adultery" (5:27). All of them come from the writings of Moses: "Anyone who divorces his wife must give her a certificate of divorce" (5:31), "Do not break your oath, but keep the oaths you have made to the Lord" (5:33), "Eye for eye, and tooth for tooth" (5:38), "Love your neighbor and hate your enemy" (5:43).

Immediately after each Old Testament quotation comes Christ's pivotal words, "But I tell you" (5:22,28,32,34,39,44). No one can miss the intended contrasts between the way things were and the way Christ wants them to be. In no case does Jesus lower a standard. In every instance He points to higher ground. If Mosaic Law forbade evil acts, the Messiah will forbid the evil thoughts that led to those evil acts. There would be no murder, if anger and name-calling were nipped in the bud (5:22,25-26) and reconciliation between brothers preceded even worship acts at the temple (5:23-24). There would be no acts of adultery, if lustful thoughts were stopped at their first entrance into the mind and lustful glances were shut out at the eye gate (5:27-30). From divorce (5:31-32) and oath swearing (5:33-37) to revenge (5:38-42) and hate (5:43-48), Jesus prescribes that antidote of faithfulness and love. The traits of "pagans" can never be acceptable to children made in the image of a "heavenly Father." Since God is "perfect," no goal short of godlikeness will suffice (5:47-48).

Every major division of Jesus' sermon is aimed at getting people ready for His gospel of grace. If the most ardent of the Pharisees fell short of total obedience to the law that came through Moses, how can Jesus' disciples ever climb the higher mountain trails He is mapping out? The strong absolute standards spoken of by Christ aid the hearer to see his failure and his need for a Savior. Chapter five is a call to total righteousness, a fatal blow to worldliness, a prick to every conscience and the stimulus to hope that this man who speaks is ready, willing and able to help His disciples make it by His power.

The sixth chapter moves us from seeing the higher demands of Christ's law to the higher acts of devotion expected from a disciple of the Nazarene. The topic turns to "acts of righteousness" (6:1). In most religions, pagan or revealed, there will be times of almsgiving, prayer and fasting. Jesus wants His disciples to give to the needy, motivated by a concern for the poor and not for the ego-concern of the donor. The eyes of God will see. The eyes of men need not be aware (6:2-4). The desire "to be seen" (6:1) in doing acts of righteousness is poor motivation. Giving is to be "in secret," (6:4) as far as intention is concerned; yet, a life-style of helpfulness "cannot be hidden" (5:14). Men will "see your good deeds and praise your Father in heaven" (5:16). The church will be no Secret Society. Everything it believes and teaches will be open for all eyes to see and hear. But, the reason for benevolent acts will be the needs of our brothers, not the applause of our neighbors.

Prayer is, likewise, a religious act between a man and God and is perverted when it becomes a hypocritical show for the public eye (6:5-15). The pagan practices of prayer beads, prayer wheels, prayer gongs, etc. go with the mistaken notion that to "keep on babbling" or using "many words" (6:6) is what God wants. The simple model prayer Jesus gives (6:9-13) holds up the better way to commune with the Father.

If fasting (6:16-18) is intended to impress one's neighbors as to the depth of sacrifice to which one has gone, that is all that will be accomplished. But to go without food for oneself, so a hungry child can eat or a missionary be supported, can be pleasing to God with no one but Him to know about it. In such a case there could be no mixed motives.

The lengthiest sub-division of chapter six grapples with the giving issue every disciple must face. Will his "acts of righteousness" include support of the kingdom? Some feel insecure without large bank balances on which to rely (6:19-34). Without stored up "treasures on earth," life is filled with "worry" about food, clothes and housing. But, the one who does "seek first his kingdom and his righteousness," evidences real trust in the loving care of his "heavenly Father."

The third division of the Sermon on the Mount (7:1-23) shows a third way in which the righteousness of Jesus' followers "surpasses that of the Pharisees and the teachers of the law" (5:20). For the sake of alliteration, I have used the phrases higher demands, higher devotion and now use higher demonstration for chapter seven. What evidence would convince the world that a certain individual was a true follower of Christ? Is being legalistic and judgmental a mark? How about using religious phrases like "Lord, Lord" or reporting the performance of miracles?

Jesus can spot one who walks in His steps by the way he uses his eyes and lips. A disciple is not for ever out to "judge" others or look for a "speck" in some brother's eye. A disciple's mouth will not be heard criticizing fellow men before the world, but lifting them in prayer before God, asking, seeking, knocking and walking the road that leads to life (7:1-13). The evidence of being an apple tree is bearing apples. He who bears Christ-like fruit is one who belongs to Christ. It is not how loud we sing, "Lord, Lord," or how much we claim to be charismatic with successes in demon exorcisms. It is not the performing of modern miracles in Christ's name that are both many and mighty. The one demonstration, for which Christ looks, is higher than those mentioned. In a sentence, Jesus called it the doing of "the will of my Father who is in heaven" (7:21).

THE SERMON ON THE MOUNT: INTRODUCTION AND CONCLUSION

How did Jesus begin and close this message on the need for a "righteousness that surpasses" (5:20)? The conclusion (7:24-27) was a dramatic story drawn from the imagination of one who had been a careful carpenter, building not only with good materials and superstructure but with concern for a firm foundation. The solid rock foundation of life was under everyone who heard and put into practice Christ's teaching. The shifting sand base, for a life that will not stand in rough times, is disobedience. That strong conclusion to His reasoned sermon left the "crowds . . . amazed at his teaching" (7:28).

No less amazing were His opening words and His sermon's introduction. The introduction clarified both the joy and the job of being a disciple of the Master. The task was to serve as "the salt of the earth," adding flavor to life and leading to its preservation (5:13). It was to be "the light of the world," dispelling the darkness of ignorance and sin (5:14-16). The nine "blessed" statements, we call the beatitudes (5:3-12), reflect the attitudes of a disciples and the source of his joy. In the gospel, righteousness is the unmerited gift given freely to Christ's followers. They claim no righteousness of their own, as did some of the Pharisees who were proud of their attainments. Those who felt no need were self-righteous men. They sensed no need of a savior, for they considered themselves rich in spirit, never mourning over sins committed or hungering and thirsting for righteousness. Looking in a mirror they see a person stuffed with goodness and in no need of mercy. Those, however, who will become followers of Jesus, feel "poor" in spiritual attainment, broken hearted over sins committed, hungering for a righteousness never tasted and seeking a mercy undeserved. Rather than proud, they are meek. What they want more than life itself is to be pure in heart, so they can see God.

The introduction moves toward the body of the message with Christ's claim to have come "to fulfill' the Old Testament by meeting its every demand. Here He states the proposition to be developed. The opening word, "Blessed" fits the good-news being proclaimed. The cross on the hill called Calvary makes possible the righteousness taught from this mount in Galilee called the Horns of Hattin. It is Christ who lived the sinless life and then died the atoning death. It is His righteousness in which we stand and not our own. No wonder people "listened to him with delight" (Mark 12:37). No wonder He became the "friend of . . . 'sinners' " (Matthew 11:19). No wonder the apostle, who considered himself "the worst of sinners" (I Timothy 1:16), could preach such a Christ to sinners such as himself.

31

FROM THE ACTS: A SERMON BY PETER

While the Gospels deal with "all that Jesus began to . . . teach" (Acts 1:1), the book of Acts in sermon after sermon goes on with Christ continuing to speak through His body the church. Some sermons in *precis* form will be spoken by deacons like Stephen (Acts 7) and Philip (Acts 8), but more will be proclaimed by apostles such as Peter (Acts 2,3,10) and Paul (Acts 13,17,20).

Peter did make other speeches to guide elections (Acts 1:16-23), settle theological questions (Acts 15:7-11) and relate experiences (Acts 11:4-18), but sermons of sufficient size to reflect structure are three. There is the earliest sermon preached this side of Calvary on the inauguration day of the church (Acts 2:14-37). Acts 3:12-26 and 10:34-44 carry the same material in some length, as 4:10-12 and 5:29-32 do in a sentence or two. Pooled together they show that Peter preached the age of fulfillment had arrived in the ministry, death and resurrection of Jesus and that, as presently head of the New Israel and giver of the Holy Spirit, He will one day return and consummate all things. The human response was to be faith and repentance culminating in baptism, with assurance of the divine outpouring of forgiveness and His Spirit.

Paul's sermons, distinguished from conversations (Acts 14:15-18) or defenses (Acts 22:1-22; 23:1-7; 26:2-23), are basically three also. The first is a sample of what he would say to Jews (3:16-41), the second an idea of what he would say to Gentiles (17:22-32) and the last a taste of what a message to believers would sound like (20:17-36). In Antioch Paul began with the deliverance of Israel from Egyptian bondage and ended with the potential deliverance from sin through the crucified and risen Jesus (13:17,37-38). In Athens he led the hearers' minds from the power evident in creation to the power that raised Christ from the dead (17:24,31). Always he preached Jesus Christ and called it more than "the gospel" or the "church's gospel." He termed it "my gospel" (II Timothy 2:8), for he had personalized it, internalized it and made it his own.

Again, for our homiletical purposes, out of all those sermons in Acts by several men, let us review one sermon by Peter, as we have from the Gospels highlighted but one sermon by Jesus.

PETER'S PENTECOST SERMON: ITS PROPOSITION

When Peter finished his message of Acts 2, no one was left in a quandary as to what he was aiming at; His point was clear. His instructions, step by step, were evident. What he believed and why he believed it was certain. What his gospel promised and what the conditions were for enjoying those promises was unveiled with no points left draped in mystery. What Jesus had asked His followers to proclaim and command in the great commission, Peter was heralding and asking in the full gospel sermon. Each fact, each promise and each command was spelled out, so all future missionary sermons could be compared or contrasted to this standard of genuine gospel proclamation. In that sermon on the first day of the church (Acts 2:14-40), attention was captured (2:14-15), interest sustained (2:16) and Scripture explained (2:17-21). The intellects of the hearers were challenged with facts (2:22-39) and their wills were moved by appeals (2:40).

The proposition of this great message, while in the mind of the spokesman from the beginning, is not expressed until the end. The sermon in one sentence is, "Let all Israel be assured of this: God has made this Jesus, whom you crucified, both Lord and Christ" (2:36). How is such a grand affirmation to be supported? By what well-grounded facts can this confidence be sustained?

PETER'S PENTECOST SERMON: ITS OUTLINE

It is evident to all that these words recorded by Luke, which we can read aloud in a minute or two, must carry the tone, truth and movement of Simon Peter's message, but not every word of it. Yet, what is preserved, is enough to suggest three evidences the big fisherman pointed to in order that he might convince others of Jesus' Lordship. After the introduction (2:14-21), the first major proof of Jesus' divine Sonship was His life already known to the Jerusalem listeners. This man of Nazareth was "accredited by God . . . by miracles, wonders and signs" (2:22). The second indisputable evidence was His resurrection. After the people of Israel had done their worst, "nailing him to the cross" (2:23), God did His best, having "raised him from the dead" (2:24). The validity of that claim is supported by prophets, who witnessed before the fact, like David in Psalm 16 and 110 (2:25-31) and the apostles, who stood then and there as witnesses after the fact (2:32). The third and final point to nail down the conclusion of Jesus' Lordship was the out-pouring of the Holy Spirit from His throne. How could anyone present on Pentecost deny the audio-visual that was there as a display for all to "see and hear" (2:33)?

PETER'S PENTECOST SERMON: ITS CONCLUSION

One wishes he could have been present to hear "the many other words (through which) he warned them and pleaded with them, 'Save yourselves from this corrupt generation' " (2:40). But we have heard enough already to learn that after making the case for Jesus' death, resurrection and exaltation, the desired response was made clear and a strong invitation was issued. It was considered apporopriate to appeal to the will, having given information to the mind.

Once the listeners "were cut to the heart" and open to the answer for their question, "Brothers, what shall we do?" 2:37), no mystical answer was given. The invitation had not yet deteriorated into coming to an altar to pray through or repeating after the evangelist the sinner's prayer. The apostles did not go through the present-day routine of down-playing baptism and church-membership by labeling them works and denying them any status in God's plan of salvation. Quite the contrary. The apostles of Christ under the Holy Spirit's guidance, and in harmony with Jesus' great commission, told the believers with neither equivocation nor hesitation, "Repent and be baptized" (2:38). There were to be no excuses or exceptions, for the instruction was to "everyone of you." There was to be no question as to the authority behind such a command. That order was not a human decision, congregational decree or brotherhood rule. It was given "in the name of Jesus Christ."

The conclusion to Peter's sermon tied wonderful promises to these simple commands: "Sins . . . forgiven" and "the Holy Spirit . . . received." What a bottom line for a gospel sermon. It was good news from introduction, through development to conclusion.

PETER'S PENTECOST SERMON: ITS INTRODUCTION

For a message to end so well, with "about three thousand . . . added to their number that day" (2:41), how did it get launched? We will find it began in much the same way as many other apostolic messages or the sermons of Christ. Several of Jesus' lessons sprang out of something He just had done or a question someone just had raised. Likewise miracles by the hands of the apostles drew the crowds and sparked the interest of the audience. It was never a sermon followed by a healing line. It rather was a single miracle drawing the crowd to hear the message that explained it. So it was on Pentecost. The phenomena of Pentecost left crowds bewildered by a loud "sound like the blowing of a violent wind" (2:2) and the appearance of "what seemed to be tongues of fire . . . on each of them (apostles)" (2:3). This was followed by the twelve from Galilee being enabled to declare the wonders of God in the native language of persons from across the Roman world. The introduction to the sermon following such divine manifestations needed only to be an explanation of what was happening.

Peter began, "Let me explain this to you, listen carefully to what I say" (2:14). Since the audience was Jewish, the occasion was religious and the locale was the temple area, the prophecy of Joel became the text that not only explained what was being experienced, but introduced the new day when "everyone who calls on the name of the Lord will be saved" (2:16-21). Here was an introduction that was brief, convincing and helpful. It did what an introduction was supposed to do. It introduced the theme of Jesus as savior.

Halford E. Luccock, the master of preaching, made these observations concerning Peter's sermon:

> It was aimed at a definite mark. Peter did not sail gracefully around in the upper air like a sea gull. His talk went to its mark like a bullet. . . . No one went away wondering what Peter had been talking about. What he said about Jesus was a jolt to most of his

> hearers, but it was not a blur. . . . The audience realized the preacher was not indulging in vocal gymnastics or taking breathing exercises in public. He wanted them to do something. The conclusion was specific. He did not end up in a verbal sunset, or with the first-century equivalent of "Well it was nice to have seen you." He said, "Repent and be baptized." Many of them did so.[1]

The preaching of Peter, like that of his Master, was clear. "Go and do likewise" (Luke 10:37).

---

1. *Communicating the Gospel* (New York: Harper and Brothers, 1954), p. 128.

32

FROM THE EPISTLES: A SERMON BY APPOLLOS (?)

If Paul were ever put on trial for having a pastor's heart, he would have been found guilty in very short time. The overwhelming evidence in the New Testament could not be refuted by the best defense lawyer available. Paul, because of his love, not only had gone with the gospel where Christ was not known, he then would return, again and again, to strengthen and encourage them. In addition, he would write letters to hold them to Christ and build them up in their new-found faith. Each epistle was but a "love letter" from the preacher who had brought that particular congregation into existence. When that letter was read to the gathered congregation, it was as if they were hearing another helpful sermon from their now absent preacher.

That is the way it also was for James, who had been a leading elder of the Jerusalem church in the early days. When persecution arose in that city at the time of Stephen's martyrdom, the flock scattered. Still caring for those people, Jesus' half brother writes to them a message, as he had previously and often preached to them before they had become "the twelve tribes scattered among the nations" (James 1:1).

Paul's letter to Galatians or Peter's first epistle to "God's elect . . . scattered throughout Pontus, Galatia, Cappadocia, Asia and Bithynia" (1:1) are sermonic words in epistle form. Many scholars speak of I Peter as a "baptismal homily" and most call I John also a "homily." John's letter lacks the opening and closing marks of most epistles. It begins like a sermon with its strong opening affirmation (1:1-4) and concludes with a powerful closing sentence that bears an unmistaken punch at the Gnostic heresy that threatened the Ephesian church where John had preached so long. John's three-point sermon is not arranged in the usual style but a cyclical style that covers his points more than once and each time on a higher level. Though the approach of John is different from that of Paul, you know when you are through hearing the message, that the way to be assured you are right with God and in His family is threefold. You pass the creedal test, the social test and the ethical test. Faith in Christ, love of the church and holiness of life are indelible marks, all followers of the Ephesian heretic Cerinthus to the contrary.

The best sermonic sample from the epistles is the book of Hebrews. Its length and structure allow for a fuller homiletical review. In addition, its own self-designation is a "word of exhortation" (Hebrews 13:22). This is the common idiom for sermon in any Jewish synagogue (cp. Acts 13:13 KJV). Hours could be spent in futile argument as to who wrote this sermon. I lean toward Apollos, but do not let authorship keep you from seeing sermonic structure.

HEBREWS: ITS PROPOSITION

The key word running throughout this message is "better" (KJV) or "superior." Over a dozen times the listeners hear the affirmation that the way of Christ in the church is greater than the option offered in Judaism.

The message to Hebrew Christians was pertinent, because while persecution at that time was aimed at the followers of Christ, no similar hardships were targeted against the synagogues. The very real temptation to the Jews, who had accepted Jesus as their Messiah, was to play down that decision and to become again what they had earlier been. Why not stay with Jehovah, Torah and Haftorah? Why enter a new covenant with new revelation and a new name, if with it comes tribulation, hardship and government opposition?

The time is likely 68 A.D. The place the recipients live is apt to be Rome. The synagogues involved possibly may be those whose leaders were turned toward Jesus during Paul's days of Roman house arrest. It was of this situation that Luke wrote: "They arranged to meet Paul on a certain day, and came in even larger numbers (and he) . . . tried to convince them about Jesus from the Law of Moses and from the Prophets (with the result that) some were convinced" (Acts 28:23-24). To keep that gain for Christ's kingdom from being turned into a loss, this written sermon of Hebrews pleads for staying with their decision for Christ. The recurring plea is "hold firmly to the faith" (4:14), "hold unswervingly to the hope we profess, for he who promised is faithful" (10:23). The proposition on which such an appeal can be based is that Christianity is superior to Judaism — the saving gospel is better than the demanding law.

HEBREWS: ITS OUTLINE

No Bible book has an outline easier to recall than Hebrews. The superiority of Christ is established in five areas. Chapters one and two prove that the revelation from God through His Son far exceeds the information from Him in Old Covenant days. The two subpoints are "prophets" (1:1) and "angels." It was through angels that the Old Covenant of the Ten Commandments was delivered to Moses (Acts 7:53; Galatians 3:19). It was through inspired humans that Israel was encouraged to stay in covenant with the Lord. "But in these last days (God) has spoken to us by his Son" (1:2). No one should retain doubts that Jesus is "much superior to the angels" (1:4). When the "great salvation" of the gospel is "first announced by the Lord" and then is "testified to" by God Himself through miracles, would it not be foolishness to turn from the higher to the lower — from the greater to the lesser?

The second major argument (Chapters 3-4) contrasts the deliverance God provided from Egyptian bondage through Moses and Joshua in olden days and the rescue from sin now being offered through Christ. It would not be true to the Old Testament hero, Moses, who "was faithful in all God's house" to renounce Jesus whom they had confessed (3:1-2). Let them remember that "Christ is faithful" (3:6) and we are to "hold firmly till the end the confidence we had at first" (3:14). The old deliverance that began with Moses was completed by Joshua, who brought them into the Promised Land. But, antitype always excels the type. The heaven that awaits believers in Christ, when they cross the Jordan of death, is a superior rest than Israel enjoyed, when nomadic days were over and they could settle down in Palestine (4:8).

As the new revelation is better than the old (Chapters 1-2) and the deliverance in the gospel is superior to that in the Jew's exodus story (Chapters 3-4), so is the new priestly intercession of Christ high above that offered through the priesthood of Levites or Melchizedek (Chapters 5-7). The contrast again is not between the evil and the good, but between the wonderful and the even more wonderful. "Because Jesus lives forever, he has a permanent priesthood . . . able to save completely those who come to God through him, because he always lives to intercede for them" (7:24-25).

The final argument used to establish the proposition is that the New Covenant exceeds the Old (Chapters 8-10). Even in the Old

Covenant period, the prophets were pointing the people to the coming New Covenant. The preacher reasons that by God "calling this covenant 'new,' he . . . made the first one obsolete" (8:13). The supportive subpoints move from the better covenant (Chapter 8) to the better tabernacle (Chapter 9) and the better sacrifice (Chapter 10). The distinction in covenants makes a difference in eternity. To "shrink back" is to be "destroyed." To continue as "those who believe" is to be "saved" (10:39).

HEBREWS: ITS INTRODUCTION AND CONCLUSION

All readers of Hebrews find their attention caught up in the sermon's opening words. They are a captivating affirmation of faith:

> In the past God spoke to our forefathers through the prophets at many times and in various ways, but in these last days he has spoken to us by his Son, whom he appointed heir of all things, and through whom he made the universe. The Son is the radiance of God's glory and the exact representation of his being, sustaining all things by his powerful word. After he had provided purification for sins, he sat down at the right hand of the Majesty in heaven (1:1-3).

If the sermon had ended here you still would feel you had been to church. No vacillating in getting started. No wavering in conviction. Rather a strong confession of Christ, who "became as much superior to the angels as the name he has inherited is superior to theirs" (1:4).

The conclusion (Chapters 11-13) is an equally strong plea for remaining true to Christ. The five points that logically establish the reason Christianity is superior to what was available in Judaism without Christ, must move from intellectual persuasion to decisive action. With eternity in the balance for every reader, the preacher pleads with all his heart. Scattered throughout his message there has been the stirring of conscience and the clear call to the will. Now, at the end of ten chapters of reasoning, come three chapters of appeal. The plea is to keep their faith in Christ (Chapter 11), their hope for tomorrow (Chapter 12) and their love for each brother (Chapter 13).

No sermon has ever made clearer the distinction in covenants, basic to rightly dividing the word. To mix law and gospel is to "pour new wine into old wineskins" (Matthew 9:17). No message has ever called more urgently for loyalty to Christ. No model for preaching shows more grasp of Biblical content and fire for people's souls. When you preach your next sermon, may it be said of you as Luke wrote of Apollos: "He was a learned man, with a thorough knowledge of the Scriptures . . . instructed in the way of the Lord . . . (one who) spoke with great fervor and taught about Jesus accurately" (Acts 18:24-25).

CONCLUSION: THE MASTERY

Preaching is love in action. Because of love, man's Creator communicated with His creatures. Because of love, Jesus gathered round Him disciples and taught them. Because of love, God has given us His Spirit and His Scripture to enable His messengers to have both the story and the strength to tell it.

We have listened to the Bible respond to our questions regarding preaching: "Who?", "What?", "Why?", How?", "When?" and "Where?" At each response we have become further convinced that preaching is, indeed, love in action.

Who goes forth to preach, but one who loves the world and with God's help hungers to get heaven's saving message to the perishing earth? What is the loving truth delivered, but that revelation regarding Jesus, that is so carefully recorded and preserved in the Holy Scriptures? Love demands that only the message be preached that guides men to glory and never the false gospels that mislead men down roads that dead-end in destruction. Why, with so many other things one could do in life's short span, do some persons give all their years to preaching Christ? Again, the only answer is love, for it is only preaching that saves. Even the question that seeks to know how to improve one's skills in forming and delivering the message of the gospel, underscores that preaching is love in action. How else explain the many hard years of learning the art, plus the tireless hours of preparing each message, were it not for the love of people kindled by the love of God. Ask the missionary far away or the evangelist nearby about his choice in where and when to preach. "Christ's love compels us" (II Corinthians 5:14) is the only answer. It was for Peter, Paul and John. Preaching was, is and will be love in action.

This glorious privilege and serious responsibility is love motivated. In no other world religion but Christianity does preaching have such a central role. The religion of Christ is the world's greatest love story. Sometimes the telling of God's love gets acceptance (Acts 17:11) and at other times rejection (Acts 28:24), even active opposition (Acts 13:50; 18:6). But always the message keeps being preached for love is a fire that cannot be quenched. Preaching that is Christ-centered, people-concerned and love-compelled cannot be stopped. Love "always perserveres" (I Corinthians 13:7). Resist every discouragement. Turn from every side road. Press on toward the goal. Until Jesus returns and ends "the time of God's favor . . . the day of salvation" (II Corinthians 6:2), "Preach the Word" (II Timothy 4:2)! That is *What the Bible Says About Preaching*.

Index of Names

Index of Topics

Index of Scriptures

(Psalms)

(Psalms)

Proverbs

(Proverbs)

Ecclesiastes

(Ecclesiastes)

Song of Solomon

Isaiah

Malachi

New Testament
Matthew

(Matthew)

(Matthew)

Mark

(Mark)

(Romans)

I Corinthians

(I Corinthians)

(I Corinthians)

II Corinthians

(II Corinthians)

Galatians

(Galatians)

Ephesians

Philippians

(Philippians)

Colossians

I Thessalonians

(Revelation)